The Morris 'Mini-Minor': 1959

The Light Car

by

C. F. CAUNTER

*A Technical History of Cars
with Engines of Less than
1600 c.c. Capacity*

1971
ROBERT BENTLEY, INC.
872 Massachusetts Avenue
Cambridge, Massachusetts 02139

First published in the United States of America 1971

(The first edition of this work was originally
published in the United Kingdom in 1958. The present
book is a reprint of the second revised edition
published in the United Kingdom in 1970.)

Library of Congress Catalog Card Number 75-183607
ISBN 0-8376-0053-7

Manufactured in the United States of America

Contents

ILLUSTRATIONS   page vii

INTRODUCTION   xv

CHRONOLOGY   xvi

HISTORICAL SURVEY

Chapter 1. The first small Motor Cars: to 1900   1

Chapter 2. Tricars and Quadricars: 1898–1908   8

Chapter 3. Voiturettes: 1898–1910   18

Chapter 4. Cyclecars: 1910–1918   34

Chapter 5. Light Cars: 1912–1918   49

Chapter 6. Cyclecars: 1919–1939   60

Chapter 7. Light Cars: 1919–1929   72

Chapter 8. Light Cars: 1930–1940   89

Chapter 9. Minicars: 1945–1955   101

Chapter 10. Light Cars: 1945–1955   109

Chapter 11. Minicars: from 1956   120

Chapter 12. Light Cars: from 1956   132

Chapter 13. Accessories and Ancillaries: from 1956   146

Chapter 14. Future Trends   166

BIBLIOGRAPHY   177

ACKNOWLEDGMENTS   179

INDEX   181

Illustrations

Frontispiece: The Morris 'Mini-Minor': 1959

PLATE

1 Ford: 1896
  Wolseley tricar: 1896
  Bollée-Darracq: 1898

Plates 1 to 8 between
pages 14 – 5

2 De Dion-Bouton tricycle: 1899
  Ariel quadricycle: 1900
  Riley tricar: 1903

3 Peugeot engine: 1896
  Benz engine: 1900
  De Dion-Bouton engine: 1899
  De Dion-Bouton engine: 1903

4 De Dion-Bouton voiturette: 1898

5 De Dion-Bouton voiturette chassis: 1899
  Renault voiturette: 1898
  Peugeot voiturette: 1902

6 Vauxhall voiturette: 1905
  Austin voiturette: 1909
  Sizaire-Naudin voiturette: 1910

7 Morgan cyclecar: 1910
  Autocarrier cyclecar: 1913
  Scott cyclecar chassis: 1916

8 Bedelia cyclecar: 1912
  G.N. cyclecar: 1911
  G.W.K. cyclecar: 1914

9 Autocarrier engine: 1910
  G.W.K. engine: 1913
  J.A.P. engine: 1914
  Jowett engine: 1916

Plates 9 to 16 between
pages 46 – 7

vii

PLATE

10 Jowett: 1906
   Humberette cyclecar: 1914
   Perry: 1914

cont: Plates 9 to 16 between
pages 46 – 7

11 Morris Oxford: 1914
   Austin: 1922

12 Saxon: 1914
   Bugatti Type 13: 1914
   A.C.: 1914

13 White and Poppe engine: 1912
   Bugatti Type 13 engine: 1914
   Stellite engine: 1914
   Wanderer engine: 1914

14 G.N. cyclecar: 1920
   Rover cyclecar: 1922
   Morgan Aero cyclecar: 1923

15 Peugeot: 1915
   Morris Cowley: 1923
   Wolseley: 1924

16 Morris Cowley engine: 1925
   Austin engine: 1926
   Riley engine: 1927
   Bugatti engine: 1928

17 Ford chassis: 1937
   Austin chassis: 1935
   Fiat chassis: 1937

Plates 17 to 24 between
pages 78 – 9

18 Citroën: 1934
   M.G. Midget: 1937
   Vauxhall: 1938

19 Trojan engine: 1927
   Wolseley Hornet engine: 1930
   Morris engine: 1935
   Citroën engine: 1938

viii

PLATE

20 Bond minicar: 1950
Messerschmitt minicar: 1956

21 Villiers engine: 1950
Villiers engine: 1954
Anzani engine: 1955
Goliath engine: 1956

22 Citroën minicar chassis: 1954
D.K.W.: 1955
Dyna-Panhard: 1956

23 Renault: 1954
Morris Minor: 1952
Fiat: 1957

24 Renault: 1956

25 Gutbrod engine: 1951   Plates 25 to 32 between
D.K.W. engine: 1953   pages 126 – 7
Renault engine: 1954
Fiat engine: 1956

26 Volkswagen: 1954
Ford Prefect: 1955

27 Porsche engine: 1955
Ford Consul engine: 1955
Trojan engine: 1955
Lancia engine: 1954

28 H.R.G.: 1956
Porsche: 1956

29 Reliant minicar chassis: 1955
B.M.W. Isetta minicar chassis: 1956
Goggomobil minicar: 1956

30 Hillman: 1956

PLATE

31 Scootacar: 1958   *cont:* Plates 25 to 32 between
    Fiat 500: 1961   pages 126 – 7
    Honda 500: 1962

32 Citroën 2 c.v.: 1957
    Fiat 600D: 1961
    N.S.U. Prinz: 1962

33 N.S.U. Spider with Wankel engine; 1965   Plates 33 to 40 between
    Simca 1000: 1963   pages 158 – 9

34 Renault 4L: 1963
    Reliant Rebel: 1964

35 Austin Seven Mini: 1959

36 Saab: 1956
    Volkswagen 1600: 1965
    Honda racing car: 1964

37 N.S.U. Prinz two-cylinder engine: 1962
    Fiat 500D engine: 1966

38 ⎧ Skoda 1000 MB engine: 1965
    ⎨
    ⎩ Coventry Climax racing car engine: 1965

39 ⎧ Peugeot 204 transverse engine: 1965
    ⎨
    ⎩ Rover gas turbine racing car engine: 1963

40 ⎧ Wankel rotary engine: 1965
    ⎨
    ⎩ Lotus Elan chassis: 1966

The following are obtainable from the Science Museum:

			Neg. No.
Frontispiece:	The Morris 'Mini-Minor': 1959		521/62
PLATE 1	Bollée-Darracq: 1898		7864
PLATE 2	De Dion-Bouton tricycle: 1899		776/52
	Ariel quadricycle: 1900		612/51
PLATE 3	Peugeot engine: 1896		135/56
	Benz engine: 1900		435
	De Dion-Bouton engine: 1899		128/56
PLATE 5	Peugeot voiturette: 1902		792/55
PLATE 10	Humberette cyclecar: 1914		597/54
	Perry: 1914		657/55
PLATE 15	Peugeot: 1915		7863
	Wolseley: 1924		668/38
PLATE 16	Morris Cowley engine: 1925		7865
	Austin engine: 1926		129/56
	Riley engine: 1927		130/56
PLATE 17	Ford chassis: 1937		27/39
	Austin chassis: 1935		26/39
PLATE 19	Trojan engine: 1927		245/56
PLATE 20	Bond minicar: 1950		132/56
PLATE 21	Villiers engine: 1950		133/56
PLATE 33	N.S.U. Spider with Wankel engine: 1965		431/68
PLATE 40	Wankel rotary engine: 1965		398/68
PLATE 40	Lotus Elan chassis: 1966		397/68

Diagrams

FIGURE

1 Léon Bollée tricar: 1896   Figures 1 to 8 between
2 Benz: 1897   pages 30 – 1
3 G.N. Vitesse engine: 1922
4 Bugatti Type 37 engine: 1925
5 Riley engine: 1927
6 Austin engine: 1928
7 Morris Cowley chassis: 1929
8 M.G. Magna: 1931

9 Wolseley Hornet: 1931   Figures 9 to 16 between
10 Morris: 1931   pages 62 – 3
11 Riley: 1932
12 B.S.A.: 1932
13 Crossley: 1933
14 Austin chassis: 1934
15 Mercedes chassis: 1934
16 Jowett engine: 1935

17 Jowett chassis: 1949   Figures 17 to 24 between
18 Austin engine: 1952   pages 110 – 1
19 Ford engine: 1953
20 Dyna-Panhard: 1953
21 Citroën engine: 1953
22 B.M.W. Isetta engine: 1956
23 B.M.W. Isetta minicar: 1956:
24 Zündapp Janus minicar: 1956

25 Ford Cortina engine: 1966   Figures 25 to 28 between
26 Porsche Super 90 engine: 1960   pages 142 – 3
27 B.R.M. racing car engine: 1965
28 Wankel rotary engine: 1959

xiii

Introduction

Some thousands of individual designs of widely varying sizes, forms and technical details have contributed during the first half of the twentieth century to the evolution and development of the light, simple and economical motor car as it exists today. The full story of this development is therefore both long and complex. The text which follows, which is perhaps the first to deal comprehensively with this subject, presents the more important phases of the evolution of the light car during the first eighty years of its commercial production and general use. Although the story is necessarily curtailed in a book of this size, the endeavour has been to present a broad and connected survey of the whole period.

The light car movement resulted not only from the general development of the motor car, but also from the evolution of the social order which, by 1910, had begun to extend the advantages of the industrial revolution to other levels of society than the well-to-do. It was therefore essentially a popular movement which from that period has helped to change for the better the mental outlook and physical well-being of a large number of people all over the world. It has endowed the individual with a high degree of personal mobility and has helped to place, conveniently and economically, the country within the reach of townsfolk and the town within reach of country folk, as well as meeting a great variety of needs from occasional shopping journeys to Continental touring.

The popularity of the light car, particularly in its minicar form, had the effect in the 1960's of reducing the average size of motor cars in general and demonstrating the redundancy of the large expensive car whose function, except for special occasions, could be adequately and with greater economy performed by the modern medium sized car.

In the historical survey which follows, separate chapters are devoted to the main categories of light car, so that the specialised forms of development may be followed more clearly from their inception, through their technical evolution and commercial production, to their decline and replacement by other more advanced forms. A bibliography of some of the more important reference sources relating to the light car is included.

Chronology

1884 Medium-speed engine of Gottlieb Daimler
1888 Invention of the pneumatic tyre by John Boyd Dunlop
1893 Spray carburettor of Wilhelm Maybach
1895 High-speed engine of Count Albert de Dion and Georges Bouton
1895 De Dion-Bouton motor tricycle
1895 Simms-Bosch low-tension magneto
1896 Development of the pneumatic tyre for motor cars by André and Edouard Michelin
1896 Léon Bollée tricar
1898 De Dion-Bouton voiturette with divided rear axle
1898 Renault voiturette with differential rear axle
1900 Daimler P.D. voiturette
1900 Motor tricars and quadricars
1902 Honold-Bosch high-tension magneto
1903 Pressure-lubrication systems in use
1904 Twin-cylinder voiturettes
1909 Four-cylinder voiturettes
1910 Bedelia, Morgan and G.N. cyclecars
1912/14 Development of the cyclecar
1912 First use of light-alloy pistons
1912 Morris Oxford light car
1912 Peugeot-Bugatti ultra-light car
1913 Bugatti Type 13 sports light car
1913 Adoption of detachable wheels
1914 Electric-lighting and engine-starting systems for light cars
1915 Morris Cowley light car
1919 Mass production applied to light car construction by William R. Morris and André Citroën
1920 Vigorous development of the light car
1922 Austin Seven and Citroën 5 c.v. ultra-light cars
1923 Adoption of four-wheel brakes and shock absorbers
1926 Large-section, low-pressure tyres adopted
1928 Development of the high-efficiency high-speed light car engine
1929 Schnuerle loop-scavenge two-stroke engine
1929 Development of the light sports car
1930 Vigorous development of four- and six-cylinder light car engines
1932 Hydraulic brakes adopted

1935	Adoption of independent front suspension and body-chassis construction
1935	Synchro-mesh gearbox in use
1946	Development of the ultra-light car, with body-chassis construction, small high-efficiency engine located adjacent to driving wheels, and independent suspension on all four wheels
1950	Development of the minicar with both two and four-stroke engines
1955	Two-pedal control (automatic clutch) adopted for light cars
1956	Tubeless tyres in use
1956	Fibre glass bodies in use
1958	Fuel-injection systems introduced in production
1959	B.M.C. Mini transverse-engine design in production
1959	Transistor-ignition systems introduced
1959	Wankel rotary engine prototype
1960	Disc brakes in production
1961	Michelin radial-ply tyre
1962	Small high-speed Diesel engines in production
1962	Alternator generators introduced in production
1963	Rover-B.R.M. gas-turbine car at Le Mans
1963	N.S.U. Wankel rotary engine in production
1964	Automatic transmission systems for light cars in production
1964	Spencer Moulton Hydrolastic compensated suspension system in production
1965	Anti-gas-pollution devices introduced
1966	Inherent safety features studied in car design

The First Small Motor Cars: to 1900

In considering the history and development of the light car, it is necessary to appreciate that, when motor cars appeared in the 1890's, they were for the most part small, light and simple for reasons of technical necessity rather than economic desirability. Moreover, since motoring in its early years was virtually a prerogative of the well-to-do class, the demand for economy as such hardly existed. It was not until after 1910, when increasing numbers of the middle class began to adopt the motor car, that economy, both in first cost and operation, became one of the chief reasons for the existence of the light car.

These early forms not only initiated the concept of the light car, but also materially assisted in its subsequent development by providing the essential roots from which was evolved the light and economical motor car adapted to the particular needs of a wide variety of users. In the process of this evolution many hundreds of different designs, having engines of cubic capacities from 100 c.c. to 1600 c.c., have since 1900 gone to the making of the modern light car in its various forms. The countries which contributed most to this development are Great Britain, France, Germany, Italy and Austria; the United States of America was also concerned with the light car up to 1916, but later abandoned it to concentrate on the large motor car which the continental distances of this country necessitate. In the smaller, war-impoverished European countries, however, the light car has proved to be the practical solution to the problem of economical and convenient personal travel, and the large specialised industry which is now devoted to its production has already assumed a world-wide importance.

This chapter contains brief descriptions of a selection of the first small motor cars which were produced commercially. These vehicles were generally uncertain in conception, crude in design, limited in performance and unreliable in operation. Yet they were the forerunners of a new and potentially important means of road transport from which the modern motor car, in all its forms and with all its potentialities, has been evolved and which, in particular, foreshadowed the light car.

THE DAIMLER ENGINE

The most important single invention which made possible the early commercial production of light mechanical road-transport vehicles was the medium-speed internal-combustion engine invented by Gottlieb Daimler (1834–1900) in 1884. The few previous experimenters in this field had available only the heavy slow-speed gas and oil engines of the period, which developed about 1 h.p. for every 300 lb. of engine weight at crankshaft speeds up to 250 r.p.m.

The Daimler engine was capable of running at 800 r.p.m. and was much lighter in construction and smaller in size; it developed about 1 h.p. for every 90 lb. of engine weight. This comparatively light petrol engine provided one of the prime requirements of the motor car: namely, a comparatively

1

high power-weight ratio, and it gave a great impetus to the development of the motor car after 1890. The majority of the first commercially-produced motor cars, with the chief exception of the initial designs produced by Carl Benz (1844–1929), adopted it and thrived upon the fundamental advantages which it provided. Consequently, the engines used by the primitive small motor cars which appeared before 1900 were generally of the Daimler medium-speed variety. Cylinder capacities were about 1 litre, and crankshaft speeds varied from 400 r.p.m. to 900 r.p.m. The average specific output was about 3 to 4 h.p. per litre capacity per 1000 r.p.m.

THE PRIMITIVES: *circa* 1895

One of the first examples of a small car to be made, as distinct from the larger, more cumbersome prototype vehicles of the earliest period of development, was the motor vehicle built by Henry Ford (1863–1947) in 1896 at Detroit, Michigan, U.S.A. This vehicle (Plate 1) had a simple open chassis frame supported on four tangent-spoked wire wheels, fitted with thin-section pneumatic tyres; the front axle was supported on fully elliptical leaf-springs and incorporated tiller-controlled Ackermann steering; the rear axle was unsprung. The engine, consisting of two horizontal cylinders of 65 mm. bore and 152·5 mm. stroke, open crankshaft and connecting rods and a large central flywheel, was located in the rear. About 3 h.p. was developed by this engine at a speed of 600 r.p.m. The drive was taken from the crankshaft by a jockey-pulley-tensioned flat belt to a countershaft, and thence to a solid rear axle by means of a second belt which could be transferred from one pair of pulleys to another pair for the purpose of changing the gear ratio. The vehicle was capable of speeds up to 25 m.p.h.

This first Ford design[1], called by its maker a 'quadricycle', was both light and simple; it was a good example of the early motor car from which were eventually developed better and more elaborate designs, ranging from the lightest and most economical to the most powerful and expensive types. In particular, this prototype was the ancestor of the famous Model T Ford, as well as later examples of the light car.

Another early example was the English Roots and Venables 'Petrocar' of 1895. This vehicle was driven by a 2½ h.p. single-cylinder (133 mm. bore by 152·5 mm. stroke) four-stroke engine, which ran at about 500 r.p.m., and was adapted to use the heavier petroleums such as paraffin. It was a simple three-wheeled vehicle, weighing 8 cwt., with side-by-side seats for two persons. The paraffin fuel was vaporised by drawing air during the suction stroke through a circuitous heating chamber, and was ignited by means of a hot tube. The drive was transmitted from the crankshaft through a disc friction clutch, a 2-speed epicyclic gear and a double chain drive to a differential rear axle. The single front wheel was steered by means of a tiller. It is recorded that some 2000 miles were covered successfully with this car. A heavier, four-wheeled design was built in the following year.

---

[1] This vehicle is preserved in running condition at the Edison Institute, Dearborn, Michigan, U.S.A.

It may be claimed that the Benz 'Velo' model, first produced in 1893 and continuing in production until almost the end of the century, was the prototype of the light car. This model, fitted with a 1½ h.p. engine followed the general lines of the conservative and primitive, yet nevertheless practical, Benz formula of a slow speed single-cylinder open crankshaft form of stationary engine, driving by a flat belt over fast and loose pulleys which also served as a clutch, through a counter-shaft form of two-speed gear to a layshaft, and thence by chains to the rear wheels. A third Crypto or epicyclic gear was later added to provide a specially low gear for hill climbing.

A larger version (Fig. 2) of the 'Velo' model was the Benz 'Comfortable' model, which cost £125 and of which some 4000 were made between 1895 and 1900. The single-cylinder (110 mm. bore and 110 mm. stroke) horizontal engine (Plate 3) developed 3 h.p. at 600 r.p.m., and drove the rear wheels through a system of primary belts and a gear, which provided three gear ratios. The final drive to the rear wheels was by a pair of chains. This car was fitted with light radial spoked wheels and solid rubber tyres and weighed 8 cwt.

Two other pioneer designs of great importance during the 1890's were produced by the Panhard and Levassor and the Peugeot firms. The former concern was the first to exploit the Daimler engine in the motor car field and, from 1891, the production of Panhard and Levassor cars fitted with the 1060 c.c. (75 mm. by 120 mm.) and the later 1235 c.c. (75 mm. by 140 mm.) capacity 15° vee twin-cylinder Daimler engines proceeded vigorously. The larger of these two engines developed about 3½ h.p. at 750 r.p.m. This initial Panhard and Levassor motor car was of fundamental importance because it originated the formula upon which the majority of subsequent designs were generally based. The chief features of the design included the engine being mounted in front under a bonnet, and a transmission consisting of a flywheel cone clutch, a 3- or 4-speed layshaft gearbox and a differential cross-shaft, from which the drive was taken to the rear wheels through two primary chains. In 1895, the improved Daimler 'Phénix' twin-cylinder vertical engine replaced the earlier vee-type engines. This 1235 c.c. (80 mm. by 120 mm.) capacity unit developed 4 h.p. at 800 r.p.m.; it had a compression ratio of about 3 to 1 and weighed 180 lb., which was considerably lighter than the vee-type engines.

The Peugeot cars before 1895 had the same Daimler vee-type engines as the Panhard and Levassor cars, but they were mounted in the rear and the drive to the rear wheels was by shafts to a change-speed gear and differential cross-shaft and thence by chains to the rear wheels. Although this transmission of the Peugeot cars was less advanced than that used on the Panhard and Levassor cars, the chassis and body of the former were lower and lighter than the latter. In the following year, the Peugeot concern produced their 980 c.c. (76 mm. by 108 mm.) twin-cylinder horizontal engine. (Plate 3.)

An early commercially-produced design that may perhaps be defined specifically as a light car was the Léon Bollée tricar of 1896 (Fig. 1), three examples of which took part with success in the historic Emancipation Run of that year. This design was remarkable for its originality and effectiveness. It carried two persons in tandem, and its unladen weight was only 3¼ cwt. The 2 h.p. single air-cooled cylinder of 650 c.c. capacity (76 mm. by 145 mm.), with a Maybach type of spray carburettor and hot-tube ignition, was mounted horizontally on the left side of the rear-wheel frame stays. The cylinder head was detachable and contained an automatic inlet valve, a mechanically operated exhaust valve and a hot tube. The crankshaft ran in plain bearings supported on the main frame, and carried an overhung balanced crank at one end and a flywheel at the other end. A centrifugal governor regulated the speed of the engine to about 700 r.p.m. by cutting out the action of the exhaust valve. The crankshaft had three spur-gear wheels of different diameters integral with it, which meshed with three other gears on a layshaft to provide a 3-speed drive. The final drive was taken from the layshaft through a broad flat belt to a rim on the single rear wheel. A lever moved the rear wheel backwards or forwards to achieve respectively the tightening of the belt to serve as a clutch, and the loosening of the belt to disengage the drive and also bring the belt rim into contact with a stationary brake-block fixed to the frame. A spade grip on the same lever was rotated for the purpose of changing the gears by means of a rack-and-pinion striker mechanism. The two front wheels were steered by means of a handwheel, and a foot-applied brake acted on the flywheel. Although the Bollée tricar was primitive in various features, its simplicity and straightforward ingenuity of design provided one of the most successful small cars of its time. Moreover, it foreshadowed what became known some fifteen years later as the cyclecar.

A modified version of this design, known as the Bollée-Coventry 'Motette' (a diminutive which even at this early period revealed the appreciation of the small car as such) was made by C. McRobie Turrell about 1897. One of the improvements used was the extension of the fins over the cylinder head to improve cooling. The earlier Bollée cylinder heads were unfinned and tended to overheat in the vicinity of the exhaust-valve housing.

A three-wheeled Humber 'Sociable', generally on the same lines as the 'Motette', and using the improved single-cylinder Turrell engine, was produced in 1898. In partnership with J. C. Accles, Turrell also gave much thought at this time to the design of a light quadricycle, having a large vertical single-cylinder engine which drove the rear wheels by a long flat belt and stepped pulley, and also a 7 h.p. light car with chain drive. C. McRobie Turrell has strong claims to have been the pioneer of the light car in its most primitive form in this country.

The American Duryea car of 1898 was in the form of a light buggy. It was driven by a 4 h.p. twin-cylinder horizontal four-stroke engine having a bore of 4 in. and a stroke of 4½ in. The maximim crankshaft speed was 900 r.p.m., and the engine was throttled by controlling the opening of the inlet valves. This vehicle was capable of a maximum speed of 30 m.p.h. Various other simple American small cars were on the market before 1900.

The Pennington tricar and quadricar designs of 1896, also of American origin, appeared only as prototypes; they were fitted with two- and four-

4

cylinder horizontal engines of unusual design, one of the chief features of which was the very long stroke. These vehicles were of exceptionally light construction, and were fitted with low-pressure large-section tyres which Pennington is credited with having pioneered at this early date.

LATER DESIGNS: before 1900

From the earlier Humber 'Sociable' was developed in 1899 the Humber 'Phaeton' which had a 3 h.p. Bollée single-cylinder form of engine mounted horizontally in front, belt transmission and a 3-speed gear. An earlier development on the same lines was the four-wheeled car which Léon Bollée designed for A. Darracq in 1898 (Plate 1). It had the same form of large air-cooled single-cylinder engine mounted horizontally in front, which drove the rear wheels through a belt-and-pulley change-speed gear, clutch, spur-gearing and differential gear. The engine was somewhat more powerful, developing 5 h.p. at 800 r.p.m., and the spray carburettor and hot-tube ignition system were retained. The engine shaft had mounted on it a five-step pulley. A flat belt connected this pulley with a similar multiple pulley on a countershaft mounted beside the rear axle on a sub-frame which was adjustable by means of a screw. The belt-striker for gear-changing purposes was actuated by means of a wheel on the steering pillar. A cone clutch, operated by a pedal, connected the second pulley with a pinion meshing with a bevel wheel on the differential rear axle. Reversing was effected by a clutch and countershaft gear. Brake bands on the rear wheels were controlled by a lever, and a pedal controlled another band on the clutch casing. Ackermann-type steering was used, which was operated by a hand wheel on the vertical pillar. The front axle was pivoted in the centre to compensate for the absence of springs.

One of the most important English developments in connection with small cars at this time was due to Herbert Austin (1866–1941), who, on behalf of the Wolseley Sheep-Shearing Machine Company of Birmingham, produced the first Wolseley car in 1895. This three-wheeled design (Plate 1) is perhaps important more as the earliest work of Herbert Austin, rather than as a forerunner of the light car. It had a 2 h.p. air-cooled horizontally-opposed engine mounted at the side of the frame. Two years later, an improved three-wheeled design appeared, fitted with a 3 h.p. twin-cylinder engine, with the side-by-side valve water-cooled cylinders arranged horizontally. The light open frame was of tubular construction, having a compartment in rear which housed the engine and drive and also provided support for two back-to-back seats for the passengers. The single front wheel was steered by a tiller.

The Simms three-wheeled tandem car of 1899 was driven by a 2¾ h.p. single-cylinder air-cooled engine incorporated in the front wheel, which it drove through epicyclic reduction gearing. The vehicle was of the simple open type with two seats in tandem, and the unladen weight was 3 cwt. Examples of this design were used in the Thousand Miles Trial of 1900.

A self-contained propulsion unit, known as a 'Motorwheel', was produced in 1899 by H. J. Lawson, as an easily-applied and self-contained unit for various purposes, such as substitution for a pony in the shafts of a trap.

5

The single-cylinder air-cooled engine was mounted on a light open frame which also contained the single road wheel, which was driven by the engine through reduction gearing.

By about 1900 there were also a few light cars which were powered by other means than the internal-combustion engine. These included such vehicles as the electric carriage, which had a certain pupularity as a town vehicle because of its silence and smoothness of operation, the Liquid Air Company's compressed-air-driven carriage, and the Dunkley governess-cart which operated on coal gas.

In this matter of unorthodox power units, it is of interest to recall the initial list of entries for the Paris-Rouen Trials of 1894. Among these were motor cars reputed to operate on such unorthodox and improbable means as gravity, hydraulic mechanisms, multiple system of levers, weight of passengers, system of pendulums and even self-acting mechanisms, whatever these may have been. None of these actually materialised and the Paris-Rouen Trials were fought out between orthodox steam and petrol-engined vehicles. In the next year, during the Paris-Bordeaux-Paris Trials, the petrol engine effectively demonstrated its superiority over steam in particular and all other types in general as a power unit for the motor car.

By 1895, therefore, the variety of primitive designs already described had provided the basis for future development, and the motor car in what may be called its orthodox form began to appear and be developed to the rapid exclusion of unsound and even, in some cases, fantastic formulae.

ACCESSORIES AND ANCILLARIES

In this earliest period of motor car design and construction, the accessories and ancillaries of the small motor car were generally of the simplest and most primitive forms. These were at first largely adaptations from existing equipment and methods appertaining to related items such as gas engines and horse-drawn vehicles, but under the influence of the commercial development of the motor car in the 1890's, specialisation of design for motor car needs began and provided a basis for fuller development after 1900.

The combustible mixture was supplied at first by surface vaporisers, which had been used by E. Lenoir as long ago as 1862 and were adopted in more advanced form by Daimler and Benz in 1884. The invention of the much more compact and positive spray carburettor by Wilhelm Maybach (1846–1929) in 1893 provided a satisfactory solution to the problem of the efficient and controlled supply of ignitable petrol mixture to the internal-combustion engine. The spray carburettor was generally adopted by 1900.

Although electrical ignition systems consisting of a Ruhmkorff coil, battery and contact-maker had been used for gas engines since 1860, these were generally too heavy and cumbersome to be wholly suitable for use with the motor-car engine. Consequently, the primitive but simple hot tube form of ignition was fitted to a number of the earliest engines. The appearance of the improved and compact De Dion-Bouton coil and battery system and the low-tension magneto of F. A. Simms (1863–1949), both in 1895, provided a sound basis for the later development of reliable and efficient high-tension ignition systems of both the coil and magneto types.

Arrangements of flat belts or combinations of belts and chains were initially used on various motor car designs, but the Panhard and Levassor layout of a front-mounted engine driving through a clutch, a change-speed gearbox and a differential gear to the rear wheels established in 1891 the best general arrangement for future development. The differential incorporated in a cross-shaft carried on the chassis frame minimised the amount of unsprung weight which the alternative system of incorporating the differential in the rear axle entailed.

The earliest motor car wheels were of the carriage type, constructed of wood with iron tyres and, later, with solid rubber tyres. The smaller and lighter motor cars after 1895 were fitted with light wire-spoked wheels. Within ten years of the invention of the pneumatic tyre by J. B. Dunlop (1840–1921) in 1888, the solid rubber tyre had been almost entirely superseded for most forms of light mechanical road transport by the motor car size of pneumatic tyre which, from 1895, was energetically developed by André and Edouard Michelin.

The bodies of the earliest cars were largely adaptations of the horse-drawn form of coachwork and spring suspension. After 1895, specialisation began to be apparent and lightness and a lower centre of gravity were given more consideration. The chassis frame was largely of steel tube construction, and the springing was of the semi- or fully-elliptic varieties. Ackermann-type steering was early adopted and was, at first, controlled by a tiller, a pair of handlebars or a small wheel. After 1895, the steering wheel mounted on a column positioned conveniently in front of the driver became generally established.

Brakes were usually of two kinds: the carriage form of lever-operated shoe type which acted directly on the tyre treads, and the pedal-operated external-band type which acted on drums incorporated with the rear wheel chain sprockets.

Night travel with these primitive motor cars was seldom normally undertaken, and the simple candle or oil lamps provided for horse-drawn vehicles and cycles generally served when necessary for this purpose. The Lucas Company, as the pioneers of cycle lamps, was among the earliest providers of these lamps and was presently engaged in developing designs of lamps specialised for motor car use.

Tricars and Quadricars: 1898-1908

Soon after the appearance of the first practical solo motorcycles, there arose a demand for light and economical passenger-carrying vehicles of the same general form. The first and simplest method to be adopted of supplying this need was the separate trailer, mounted on two wheels, which was attached behind the motorcycle. Then followed the development of the motor bicycle and tricycle respectively into three- and four-wheeled vehicles having provision for an extra seat for the passenger. Later still, the sidecar was invented, which preserved the normal form of the motor bicycle, and became the standard means for converting it readily into a comparatively comfortable passenger-carrying machine. From the early three- and four-wheeled conversions already mentioned were evolved a variety of forms and sizes of more specialised tricars and quadricars. These had a certain popularity in the first decade of the twentieth century among users who required simpler and less expensive motoring than was possible with the motor car proper. But the technical and commercial development of these new forms of light motor vehicle and, indeed, of motor cars and motorcycles in general, would not have been possible but for a new and important technical advance in the form of the high-speed internal-combustion engine which occurred at this time.

The motor tricar and quadricar were, like the later cyclecar, essentially adaptations from the motorcycle and were therefore limited in scope and potential development. Since, however, these vehicles could be purchased for about £75, compared with the £130 or more required for a small motor car at this time, and could convey two persons over long distances at average speeds up to 20 m.p.h., they provided pleasurable and useful motoring at about half the cost entailed by the more elaborate voiturette of the same period.

THE DE DION-BOUTON ENGINE

Ten years after Gottlieb Daimler's invention of the medium-speed internal-combustion engine, there occurred another advance of like fundamental importance upon which subsequent petrol-engine development was based. This was the invention in 1895 by two Frenchmen, Count Albert de Dion (1856–1946) and Georges Bouton (1847–1938) of the light, high-speed petrol engine, which was a logical development of Daimler's medium-speed principles. This much improved and versatile form of engine contributed greatly to the rapid evolution and development of motorcycles and motor cars which now took place because of the important advantages of lightness, compactness and relatively high specific output which it made generally available.

De Dion and Bouton had, since 1883, built various steam-driven road vehicles which established them among the pioneers of mechanical road transport. In 1895 they turned their attention to the petrol engine, and produced a small single cylinder, air-cooled four-stroke unit of 50 mm. bore and 70 mm. stroke, which weighed 40 lb. and developed $\frac{1}{2}$ h.p. at 1500 r.p.m.

Extensive tests with this engine showed that no undue wear resulted from running at this unprecedentedly high speed. The double flywheels were enclosed in an aluminium-alloy crankcase, which considerably reduced the overall weight of the unit. Hot-tube ignition was used initially, but was soon replaced by a coil, battery and contact-maker system; a surface vaporiser of compact design supplied the combustible mixture. This form of De Dion-Bouton engine (Plate 3) was produced with little modification in powers from $\frac{1}{2}$ h.p. (1895) to 8 h.p. (1902) with an average weight of about 25 lb. for every horse power developed. It was used to equip a great variety of De Dion-Bouton motor bicycles, tricycles, quadricycles and small motor cars or voiturettes. It was also manufactured under licence in its various forms and sizes in several countries, and it served in 1898 as the power units for Louis Renault's first automobile and Alberto Santos-Dumont's first airship. A large number of De Dion-Bouton engines were also supplied over several years as proprietary units for installation in many different types of vehicles produced by other manufacturers.

The De Dion-Bouton Motor Tricycle

The prototype De Dion-Bouton engine was installed in a pedal-tricycle immediately behind a differential rear axle, which it drove through an open 6 to 1 ratio spur gear and pinion. (Plate 2). The surface vaporiser was placed in the frame under the saddle, and the ignition battery was supported from the top tube. A separate tank held fuel and oil. The weight of this first De Dion-Bouton motor tricycle was about 200 lb. The tests of the prototype were encouraging, and in the following year improved models fitted with $\frac{3}{4}$, 1 and $1\frac{1}{4}$ h.p. versions of the engine were produced. Three $1\frac{1}{4}$ h.p. motor tricycles were entered in the Paris-Marseilles-Paris trial of 1896, one of which gained first place in its class at an average speed of more than 14 miles an hour. Later, these motor tricycles became popular since they provided a novel form of practical and reliable personal transport that was a great advance on the generally unsatisfactory performance of previous motorcycle designs. Although they were at first to some extent a fashion in Paris, even for ladies, they were soon to be seen on country roads demonstrating their capabilities as reliable touring machines. They were produced in increasing numbers at the De Dion-Bouton works at Puteaux, and also under licence in England, Belgium, Germany and America. Larger engines of $1\frac{3}{4}$ h.p. (Plate 3), $2\frac{1}{4}$ h.p. and $2\frac{3}{4}$ h.p. followed in quick succession. The impetus which this highly practical power unit gave to the young motor industry in general was of the greatest importance.

EARLY MOTOR TRICYCLES AND QUADRICYCLES

Soon after these practical motor tricycles had proved themselves by their reliable performance, the possibilities of evolving passenger-carrying vehicles from them were considered. The attachment of an open two-wheeled trailer to the motor tricycle had a certain popularity, although additional assistance by means of the pedals was required at times from the rider, and the passenger was subjected to exhaust fumes and road dust.

9

The tendency of the early motor bicycle to side-slip on wet or greasy roads, because of its high centre of gravity, had created a preference for the tricycle for winter use. A simple method was evolved for converting the motor bicycle easily and quickly to a motor tricycle. This was to replace the single front steering wheel by a pair of wheels mounted on a light axle, equipped with Ackermann steering and a central vertical support tube. This arrangement, which was used soon after 1900 to convert motor bicycles and tricycles into passenger-carrying motor tricycles and quadricycles respectively, permitted the addition of a passenger-carrying forecar mounted between the two front wheels and immediately in front of the rider. Handlebars were used to operate the steering mechanism and, in some cases, additional horizontal or diagonal stiffening members were added to connect the bicycle frame and front axle.

This quadricycle form, in particular, was used not only with De Dion-Bouton machines, but also with the several other makes of the same type then being produced in various countries, such as the Phébus-Aster, Marot-Gardon, Déchamps, Ariel, Humber, Swift, Enfield, M.M.C. and Clarke. A typical example of the early quadricycle was the 2¼ h.p. Ariel of 1900 (Plate 2), which had a 344 c.c. air-cooled single-cylinder engine, with the addition of a water-cooled head to deal with the higher continuous output required by the passenger-carrying machine. The engine was placed in front of the rear axle, thus providing an improved weight distribution compared with the original De Dion-Bouton arrangement, and drove the axle through enclosed gears which ran submerged in lubricant. The usual pedalling gear was provided for assistance on hills and in traffic. All the engine controls were located on the top tube in front of the driver. Band brakes were fitted to the rear driving wheels and were operated by means of a handlebar control lever.

A variation of this general arrangement was the Beeston quadricycle of 1898, which had the normal form of De Dion-Bouton rear axle incorporating the engine and drive, but whose front part was designed specifically to have two steerable wheels and a forecar for the passenger. Although not so flexible as the orignal arrangement, this form of quadricycle was perhaps stiffer in construction, and foreshadowed the later and larger tricars which were of necessity individual designs and not adaptations.

In similar manner, a tricar could readily be formed from a motor bicycle. Perhaps the earliest example of this form of adaptation was the Humber 'Olympia Tandem' tricar of 1898. This machine was based upon the pedal tricycle of the same name, and had two steerable wheels in front and a single driving wheel behind. The passenger sat in an open seat between the front wheels, and the single-cylinder air-cooled engine was mounted behind the rear wheel on an outrigger support and drove the rear wheel by a chain. In 1899, the Rover Company produced a motorised bath-chair, which included strengthened rear wheels, a power unit which drove the rear axle in the De Dion-Bouton manner, and a seat behind for the driver. More advanced designs of this kind consisted of the conversion of the normal form of motor bicycle, having its engine incorporated in the frame between the wheels.

The engines of these early tricars were fitted with coil-and-battery ignition and surface vaporisers, the latter of which were later replaced by spray carburettors, such as the Longuemare. The engine was usually started by direct hand-cranking at either the engine crankshaft or the gearbox layshaft. Carburettor and ignition controls were of the current motorcycle type, namely, by means of levers situated on the petrol tank or top frame tube immediately in front of the driver, and thence by rods to the various control centres. Brakes were usually of the external-contracting band type acting on the two front wheels and operated through cables by means of foot-pedals located on the foot-boards.

EARLY DEVELOPMENT OF TRICARS AND QUADRICARS

From these early forms of tricycles and quadricycles there began by 1902 to be developed larger, heavier and more elaborate forms of the same general kind of passenger-carrying motor vehicle, which for a few years provided the most economical form of motoring then available. A few of these more advanced designs were of the quadricar form, which became associated with the more elaborate small car or voiturette, as outlined in the next chapter. The majority, however, were of the tricar form which soon became accepted practice for this type of motor vehicle. By 1904, tricars were being produced by a larger number of firms both in this country and on the Continent.

Among the pioneers of this development was J. Van Hooydonk who had, since 1900, been building the Phoenix motor bicycle, which was a design on conventional lines with a small air-cooled engine clipped to the down tube of the diamond frame. A belt-driven motor tricycle was developed from this design, which was somewhat more complicated and robust than the simpler conversion already described; it incorporated a horizontal sub-frame to the front end of which were attached the pair of steering wheels, and the rear ends of which were clamped to the rear chain stays of the frame. In addition, the steering head was supported from the sub-frame by two stiff diagonal stays. This structure, although it was heavier than the earlier and simpler forms, provided a more satisfactory and efficient support for the addition of a passenger-carrying forecar.

This Phoenix design of 1902 which became popular for some years as the 'Trimo' forecar, was the forerunner of a series of larger, heavier and more powerful vehicles which, by about 1908, began to approach the initial cyclecar form of 1910.

The improved Phoenix 'Trimo' tricar of 1904 was a typical example of this form of motor vehicle. The tricycle main frame and the forecar sub-frame were substantially as already described. The earlier clip-on type of 2 h.p. engine was replaced by a 3½ h.p. air-cooled engine with mechanically-operated valves, mounted vertically in the diamond frame and equipped with a spray carburettor and coil-and-battery ignition system. The engine was cooled by an engine-driven fan, working in conjunction with ducts; efficient cooling was necessary since the tricar engine often had to operate for long periods at large throttle settings and on low gear, since the power-weight ratio of the tricar was generally low. The engine was started by means of a handle engaging with the countershaft spindle, through which the drive from the engine was taken to the single rear wheel by primary and secondary chains. A 2-speed epicyclic gear, which incorporated a clutch, was also fitted, thus adding to the flexibility and convenience of operation essential in a passenger-carrying machine. The performance of this typical vehicle of this period may be judged by its performance in the first London–Edinburgh Run in 1904, when it covered the 400 miles in twenty-two hours. It was a good, if slow, hill climber. It cost £80.

Another early form of tricar conversion was the Humber 'Olympia', which was based upon the 3½ h.p. Humber motor bicycle, with chain and countershaft 2-speed drive of the Phelon and Moore type, and a single-cylinder water-cooled engine. A smaller and simpler variety of tricar was produced by the Triumph Cycle Co. Ltd. of Coventry, based upon their 3 h.p. motorcycle of 1904 in water-cooled form. The drive to the rear wheel was by a single belt, with no clutch or gears. Other examples of this medium-powered form of tricar included the Alldays and Onions, Ariel, Hobart Bird, Bradbury, Riley, Rover, Quadrant, Lagonda, F.N., Singer, Raleigh, Phelon and Moore, Hubbard, Bat, Chase, Clyde and Matchless. These designs were fitted with either air or water-cooled single-cylinder engines, chain or belt drive to the rear wheel and, in the majority of cases, clutches and gears. As the passenger-carrying tricar developed and was used for long-distance touring, it tended to become heavier, and the necessity for clutch and gears became imperative.

The form of seating accommodation for the passenger in the forecar was at first of the same general type of a simple open seat, with arms, back rest and footrest, which was constructed either of coach work or light wicker-work and upholstery. Greater comfort was provided by such improvements as padded upholstery, more spacious body work, a padded bucket seat in place of a saddle for the driver and even, at a later date, a folding hood and an apron on the forecar for better weather protection.

Improved riding comfort was also sought by developments in frame design, such as the mounting of the forecar on coil or cee leaf-springs, as in the Phoenix 'Trimo' and Humber 'Olympia' designs, and the still more elaborate method of mounting all three wheels on semi-elliptic leaf springs as was used with the 'Suspended' Rexette. The Bat spring seat-pillar was used on the machine of that name, and the shaft-driven Garrard had rear-wheel springing of the swinging-arm type. The Sharpe tricar was mounted on pneumatic buffers.

A certain number of other forms of forecar arrangement was also tried and used to some extent, such as Young's Bentinck design which had an open dog cart form of body capable of seating more than one passenger, and the Goodchild Rear Carriage which provided for the attachment to a motor bicycle of a close-coupled rear carriage seating two passengers side-by-side.

The side-by-side form of seating was also adopted in the original Wellan design, which had a rear carriage supported on two wheels and carrying an open side-by-side seat, and a single tiller-steered front wheel; a single-cylinder air-cooled engine, mounted on the steering head, drove the front wheel by means of a belt. This latter arrangement was not adopted to any extent in this country, but was used with success in Germany for several years in the forms of the later Phänomobil and Cyklonette designs, the former of which was originated in 1906.

As early as 1904, the tricar began to be used for commercial purposes, such as trade and postal deliveries. The forecar was replaced for this work by an enclosed rectangular container, which was usually made of wicker-work to reduce weight.

LATER TRICARS

By about 1904, the quadricar had been abandoned in favour of the tricar which, with a stiffer and more complex frame, was adequate for the larger and more powerful vehicles of this type which were now being developed. In this heavier form, the tricar was getting further away from its motorcycle origin and was beginning, although still crudely and without individuality, to adopt some of the characteristics of the early motor car.

Some of the first of these later designs, such as the 5 h.p. Lagonda, the 4 h.p. Wallace, 4 h.p. Revolette and the 4½ h.p. Mars 'Carette', were substantially on the same general lines as the earlier models, except that they used larger engines, and additional aids to comfort such as weather proofing, sprung and padded bucket seats, and long footboards for the driver. Pedalling gear was now abandoned because tricars were becoming too heavy to pedal, and engines had become powerful and reliable enough to make this operation unnecessary. Handlebar-steering was retained for a while in some of the medium-weight machines, but the larger types had by the end of 1904 adopted wheel-steering.

The 5 h.p. 'Suspended' Rexette of 1905, while it retained the general form of the tricar, adopted some of the features of contemporary motor car design, such as a braced tubular chassis, large semi-elliptic leaf-springs for both front and rear wheels, wheel steering and a braced steering column. The 5 h.p. (615 c.c.) single-cylinder water-cooled engine was mounted in the chassis frame under the driver's seat, and drove the rear wheel through a short chain and a 2-speed epicyclic and clutch gear mounted on the engine shaft. Pedal-operated external-contracting band brakes operated on all three wheels. The Rexette had a good performance, in spite of its unladen weight of 5 cwt.; it could, for instance, climb the then difficult test hill, Sunrising, in Warwickshire, which has a maximum gradient of 1 in 5, with two passengers as well as the driver. Other examples of this advanced construction were the 5 h.p. King, the 5 h.p. Scarsdale and the 4½ h.p. Riley (Plate 2) which employed a robust form of 2-speed layshaft countershaft gearbox in conjunction with a leather-lined cone clutch.

Still further improvements appeared, such as the adoption of twin-cylinder engines to provide increased power and smoother torque, and still more

13

elaborate and heavier bodies to improve comfort. The Singer tricar of 1905 was fitted with a 5 h.p. 90° vee twin-cylinder fan-cooled engine, a countershaft 2-speed epicyclic gear and chain drive. A special model of a Quadrant tricar was fitted with two single-cylinder water-cooled engines, mounted vertically in the frame. The 1904 Garrard tricar was one of the most progressive of this early period; it had either a 4 h.p. or a 6½ h.p. single-cylinder water-cooled engine, a leaf-spring suspended forecar, articulated spring-mounted rear wheel stays, and a shaft and worm-gear drive to the rear wheel. Moreover, the engine, clutch and 3-speed layshaft type of gearbox unit was installed in the frame in motor-car fashion, with the crankshaft axis set in line with the frame. The unladen weight of the Garrard tricar was 3½ cwt. The Sharpe tricar was fitted with a vee twin-cylinder engine, and the unorthodox triangulated frame was mounted at front and rear on Sharpe pneumatic spring buffers.

The Premier and Rexette designs of 1907 were actually four-wheeled vehicles in three-wheel form, since the rear driving wheel of each was constructed as a double wheel with two tyres for the purpose of increasing road grip and reducing the possibility of tyre failure. The sociable arrangement of tricar was also tried; this form departed radically from the tandem arrangement of the forecar, since it had two forecar seats arranged side-by-side over a wide rear axle and two wheels, and the steering was effected by means of a single wheel carried in the front fork.

Some of the later sociables of 1907–1908 became still more powerful, elaborate and heavy. Although the large single-cylinder engine was retained for some designs, the majority used more complicated and powerful forms of engine. Examples of these later and larger types using twin-cylinder vee-type designs were the 6 h.p. Riley, the 6 h.p. Raleighette, the 6 h.p. Zenette and the 8 h.p. Rexette, the 9 h.p. Advance and the 10 h.p. Lagonda. Even more complex engines were eventually provided and adopted, such as the three-cylinder 9 h.p. air-cooled J.A.P. vertical engine unit, which included an integral 3-speed gear, and a 12 h.p. four-cylinder water-cooled car-type engine which was used in both the Barnes and Fafnir tricars of 1908. French examples included the 4 h.p. Mototric-Contal and the 9 h.p. Lurquin-Coudert.

THE LAST TRICARS

The final form of the tricar began to foreshadow the cyclecar of a few years later and to discard many of the features of its motorcycle ancestry. As far back as the end of 1904, the Jackson and Kimmys tricar design possessed many such advanced features. This machine had a tubular chassis frame and raked wheel steering; the block-type radiator was mounted in front in car fashion, and the 8 h.p. M.M.C. single-cylinder water-cooled engine was mounted immediately behind the radiator, from where it drove the rear wheel through chains and a gearbox. The single driving seat, moreover, was enclosed in a form of abbreviated car body.

Another design of this period which must be given special consideration was the A.C. Sociable, originated by J. Weller in 1906. This design generally had the features of the tricar in its centrally-positioned 631 c.c. (89 mm. by

14

Plate 1

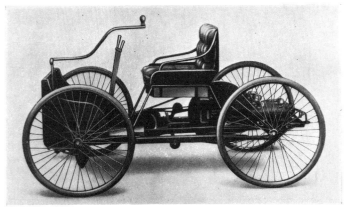

Ford: 1896

Wolseley tricar: 1896

Bollée-Darracq: 1898

Plate 2

De Dion-Bouton tricycle: 1899

Ariel quadricycle: 1900

Riley tricar: 1903

Plate 3

Peugeot engine: 1896

Benz engine: 1900

De Dion-Bouton engine:
1899

De Dion-Bouton engine:
1903

Plate 4

De Dion-Bouton voiturette: 1898

Plate 5

De Dion-Bouton voiturette chassis: 1899

Renault voiturette: 1898

Peugeot voiturette: 1902

Plate 6

Vauxhall voiturette: 1905

Austin voiturette: 1909

Sizaire-Naudin voiturette: 1910

Plate 7

Morgan cyclecar: 1910

Autocarrier cyclecar: 1913

Scott cyclecar chassis: 1916

Plate 8

Bedelia cyclecar: 1912

G.N. cyclecar: 1911

G.W.K. cyclecar: 1914

103 mm.) engine and chain drive to the single rear wheel, in the hub of which was incorporated a Roc 2-speed epicyclic gear and clutch. Both driver and passenger were, however, accommodated side-by-side in the forecar and the steering of the two front wheels was controlled by means of a tiller. The A.C. Sociable was a link between the tricar and the cyclecar; its simple and practical design ensured its continuance in production in substantially its original form until 1915, and it continued in general use until the middle 1920's.

The Howard sociable tricar of 1906–1907, although it offered little weather protection, used several of the standard characteristics of designs of some six years later. It had side-by-side padded bucket seats, a Fafnir twin-cylinder water-cooled engine enclosed in a front bonnet, a tubular chassis, semi-elliptical front and rear leaf springing, and wheel steering. The drive to the rear wheel was through primary and secondary chains in conjunction with a 3-speed countershaft gearbox of Chater-Lea manufacture.

The cyclecar, which appeared in 1910, owed much to the development of the tricar. Some of the pioneers of the cyclecar, such as H. F. S. Morgan, H. R. Godfrey, A. Frazer Nash, R. Bourbeau and others were engaged during this period in trial essays of ultra-light and ultra-economical car design and construction, which served them in their later and more progressive work.

The year 1908 saw a number of these designs which partially anticipated the true cyclecar form of two years later. The $5\frac{1}{2}$ h.p. O.T.A.V. four-wheeled design had a single-cylinder (100 mm. by 110 mm.) fan-cooled and ducted engine, mounted in the front end of its chassis, which drove by chain to a 2-speed epicyclic cross-shaft gear, and thence by double belt drive to the rear wheels. The broad features of later cyclecar layouts may be seen in this design. The successful 7 h.p. Jowett car, with horizontally-opposed water-cooled engine and unit gearbox, was originated as early as 1906. The 7–9 h.p. Vindec design had a vee twin-cylinder engine which drove by chain and single belt to the near side rear wheel. The 6–8 h.p. Piccolo and 7–8 h.p. Colibri were more ambitious designs, with 3-speed gears, cardan shafts and live axles. The 8 h.p. Pilgrim was equipped with a twin-cylinder horizontally-opposed air-cooled engine which drove the front wheels through a worm and differential gear. It was fitted with detachable wire wheels, and weighed 6 cwt. This very advanced Pilgrim design of 1908 foreshadowed not so much the cyclecar of 1912, but rather the ultra-light car of the 1920's.

Simple speed-gears providing two ratios were soon standardised as a necessity and, by 1905, 3-speed gearboxes were beginning to be used; some of these even included a reverse gear, thus giving the more elaborate tricar the flexibility and handiness of the normal four-wheeled car. The later form of the light car began to emerge with such refinements as the location of the radiator in front of the side-by-side seats, and the addition of engine bonnets and windscreens. Finally, by 1908–1909, there were produced a few individual three-and even four-wheeled cars which, with their relatively orthodox chassis and body layouts, were the immediate predecessors of the real cyclecar-light car era which began in 1910.

15

ACCESSORIES AND ANCILLARIES

The tricars and quadricars made after 1900 became increasingly reliable and serviceable vehicles, which could be used for long journeys by night as well as by day. Consequently, the need grew for a variety of accessories and ancillaries to assist mechanical reliability, road safety and travel comfort.

As has already been indicated, the most important engine type of this period was the De Dion-Bouton upon which most others, whether specialised for different manufacturers or made as proprietary units, were based. These units intended for tricar propulsion were made in sizes from 2 h.p. to 8 h.p. (200 c.c. to 900 c.c. capacities) in the single-cylinder form. After 1905, the vee twin-cylinder type of engine began to be adopted in the interests of greater power and smoother torque. Many of the established manufacturers designed and manufactured their own engines, but a few concerns, in particular J. A. Prestwich and Company, produced a range of proprietary designs.

Except for the earliest forms, the spray type of carburettor was at first generally used, such as the Viet, which was standardised for De Dion-Bouton engines; and the Longuemare was used for several other makes. After 1905, other designs such as the Brown and Barlow and the A.M.A.C. were also used in this country. They were generally of the single jet, semi-automatic type with separate throttle and air controls, and a float chamber for maintaining the petrol level in the jet.

An improved and compact coil-and-battery ignition system was early adopted for De Dion-Bouton engines and was used consistently for them and most other makes up to about 1904. The success of the self-contained and reliable high-tension magneto, soon after its introduction by G. Honold and Robert Bosch in 1903, ensured its general adoption and within three years it had virtually superseded other forms of ignition.

Although some of the lighter and earlier tricars used direct single-gear belt drive, in conjunction with pedalling gear, the increasing weight and power of tricars after 1904 necessitated the adoption of change-speed gears and clutches to provide flexibility and convenience of operation. These were in general of: (i) the epicyclic type mounted either on the engine shaft (N.S.U.) or in the rear wheel hub (A.C. Sociable); (ii) the sliding-gear layshaft type of gearbox (Rex and Riley) mounted as a countershaft; and (iii) the sliding-dog (Anglian) and expanding clutch (Phelon and Moore) type of counter-shaft, which had two primary chains running on pairs of sprockets of different diameters. After 1905, 3-speed countershaft gearboxes of the Chater-Lea type began to be used for still greater flexibility. The drive to the rear wheel was normally by chain; chain-cum-belt and even shaft drives were also used to some extent. Reverse gears were used in a few of the last and largest tricars.

Chassis frames were generally of tubular construction, although some channel forms were used. After 1904, fairly efficient springing of all three wheels was provided. Bodies were either of coach or wicker-work construction, and the rider sat on an ordinary motorcycle saddle or in a padded and sprung bucket seat. The saddle tube as well as the rear wheel fork stays were sometimes sprung to provide additional riding comfort.

Wheels were of the motorcycle tangent-spoke variety of either 28 in. or 26 in. diameter, and were designed to take beaded-edge pneumatic tyres. Tyre sections were at first $2\frac{1}{4}$ in., but later were increased to $2\frac{1}{2}$ in.

External-contracting band brakes, operated by foot pedals, were generally fitted to all three wheels of tricars. Occasionally, the simple motorcycle type of block brake acting on the wheel rim or belt rim was also used for the lighter and simpler machines.

The forms of oil and acetylene lamps then being developed for use with motorcycles were generally used for tricars. The smaller varieties of car headlamps were used on some of the heavier machines.

Voiturettes: 1898-1910

The light and comparatively powerful high-speed De Dion-Bouton engine which, since 1895, had revolutionised the motor cycle, and later had materially helped in the evolution of passenger-carrying tricars and quadricars, was at the same time developed for use with small motor cars.

In 1899, the De Dion-Bouton engine (Plate 3) was produced as a $3\frac{1}{2}$ h.p. (80 mm. by 80 mm.) 402 c.c. water-cooled unit for installation in a new and advanced design of 'small car' produced by the De Dion-Bouton firm. Thus was initiated the voiturette form of motor car which, with single-cylinder engines developing from $3\frac{1}{2}$ to 8 h.p. and later with twin-cylinder engines developing from 7 to 12 h.p., had a considerable popularity until about 1910, when it was replaced by more advanced twin- and four-cylinder forms of light car.

The voiturette provided motoring at something less than twice the cost of tricaring and half the cost of full-size motoring, and so introduced the conception of motoring economy in first cost, operation and maintenance. This awareness of the benefits of economy was a legacy of primary importance which the designers of the voiturette bequeathed to the light car proper when it eventually appeared about a decade later.

THE WATER-COOLED DE DION-BOUTON ENGINE

Some of the larger air-cooled De Dion-Bouton engines were used at first for the propulsion of small cars, such as, in particular, the first Renault car of 1898, as well as for the various tricars and quadricars which were in general use just before and just after 1900. The water-cooled versions of the single-cylinder De Dion-Bouton engine in powers of $3\frac{1}{2}$, $4\frac{1}{2}$, 6 and 8 h.p. (402 c.c. to 942 c.c. capacities), which were produced between 1899 and 1902, provided excellent units for the new voiturette form of motor car. Other makes of engine, based upon De Dion-Bouton principles, such as the Aster, Fafnir and others, also appeared in various capacities and in both air and water-cooled forms. These units were supplied in very large numbers from the Puteaux factory, either in motor cars or as proprietary units; they were by far the best and most popular design, and were for a time the main source of supply to the motor car industry in various parts of the world, particularly in England, Belgium, Germany and America.

The De Dion-Bouton voiturette engines were made to the same general pattern. The cast-iron cylinder was formed in a single casting with integral head, water jacket, and valve pocket which contained a mechanically-operated exhaust valve, and an automatically-operated inlet valve positioned immediately above. The sparking plug was located in the valve pocket of the combustion chamber, and was energised by a high-tension coil in conjunction with a contact maker driven from the half-time pinion shaft. Mixture was supplied by a Viet spray carburettor. The split aluminium-alloy crankcase enclosed two heavy flywheels, which also served as crank webs. Oil was

18

introduced into the crankcase by a hand pump and distributed to the moving parts by splash.

The immediate success of the prototype De Dion-Bouton voiturette ensured the rapid adoption of the design in production. Prior to 1909, the engine unit of a succession of improved models remained substantially the same, namely, in single-cylinder form and in ratings up to 12 h.p. (1020 c.c. capacity), with the logical additions of mechanically-operated valves, magneto ignition, and a more efficient spray carburettor of De Dion-Bouton design.

After 1905, the chassis arrangement of voiturettes in general was standardised upon the original Renault layout, which consisted of a front-mounted engine, clutch, gearbox, cardan shaft with universal joints, and a differential and bevel-gear rear axle. Before that standardisation was achieved, however, the chassis and drive arrangements of voiturettes were quite varied, as will be seen from the descriptions of the main types which follow.

TYPES OF VOITURETTE DESIGN

The availability of the light high-speed petrol engine in particular, and the example of the De Dion-Bouton 'small car' in general, quickly caused a considerable number of new designs to appear which were based upon the same general principles, but which at first differed considerably in details of chassis layout, transmission arrangement, and engine and gearbox location. The chief types of these voiturette chassis and drive arrangements, which were in use between 1900 and 1905, were as follows:

(i) A rear-mounted engine, with gears, clutch and differential gear all contained in a compact unit, driving the rear wheels through universally-jointed half-shafts, as used by De Dion-Bouton and Decauville.[1]

(ii) A front-mounted engine, with clutch, primary shaft drive to a differential cross shaft, and final drive by chains, as used by Mors.

(iii) A front-mounted engine, with primary belt drive to a gearbox incorporated in the rear axle, as used by Vivinus-Orleans.

(iv) A front or centre-mounted engine, with clutch, primary chain drive to differential cross shaft, and final drive by chains to the rear wheels, as used by Wolseley and Brouhot.

(v) A front or centre-mounted engine, directly geared to the gearbox, clutch and differential cross-shaft unit, and final drive by chains to the rear wheels, as used by Peugeot and Antoine.

(vi) A front-mounted engine, clutch, gearbox, universally-jointed cardan shaft to a differential and bevel-gear rear axle, as used by Renault in 1898 and, after 1905, generally adopted for the great majority of light motor cars.

---

[1] It is of interest to note here that, although the De Dion-Bouton drive system was abandoned by 1911, it was nevertheless again adopted after 1945 as a progressive arrangement which, besides permitting independent wheel suspension, also had the advantages of simplicity, compactness, lightness and reduced unsprung weight. Similarly, the principle of locating the engine adjacent to the pair of wheels to be driven, employed by some of these early voiturette designs, has been adopted in many of the present day minicar designs.

The Light Car

There was also a vigorous development of generally similar forms of light motor car in America. The single-cylinder horizontal engines used in American light cars at this time were inclined to be heavier and of slower speed than the De Dion-Bouton type of engine; they were also of a greater variety, and included examples of the crankcase-compression type of two-stroke engine, which was then popular in America for motorboat propulsion.

Voiturettes weighed from between 4 and 10 cwt., and were capable of carrying up to four people at average speeds of from 16 to 25 m.p.h. Just before 1910, when the real light car development began with economy as a first consideration, these small cars were ceasing to be voiturettes in the original sense, and were merging into the early light car form proper, with multi-cylinder engines beginning to replace the characteristic single-cylinder engines which hitherto had been generally used.

EARLY VOITURETTES: to 1900

A considerable number and variety of voiturette designs appeared before 1900 as has been indicated. Of them all, however, two of the first, the De Dion-Bouton and the Renault, were the most important and had the greatest influence on the eventual evolution of the light car. All voiturettes were fitted with the high-speed De Dion-Bouton form of engine.

The Dion-Bouton Voiturette

The original form of voiturette, the De Dion-Bouton (Plates 4 & 5), was introduced by this company in 1897, but it took some half a dozen experimental models and about two years before the first model was announced as a practical vehicle. This prototype was a small four-wheeled car with an open body providing two side-by-side seats facing forward and a third seat in front facing to the rear. The body was mounted on a tubular frame, supported in front on semi-elliptical leaf springs and was at first unsprung in the rear, but was later supported on three-quarter elliptical leaf springs. A $3\frac{1}{2}$ h.p. single-cylinder water-cooled De Dion-Bouton engine (Plate 3) of 402 c.c. capacity (80 mm. by 80 mm.) was mounted vertically at the rear end of the chassis frame and immediately under the rear seat. The drive was taken through a 2-speed expanding-clutch-layshaft form of gearbox, to a differential gear unit, mounted on the chassis midway between the two rear wheels. The drive to the rear wheels was transmitted from the differential unit by means of two universally-joined half-shafts. The rack-and-pinion front wheel steering was of the Ackermann type, controlled by a two-handed lever on a vertical column. Below this steering lever was a wheel by means of which the clutches for the individual gears were selected and operated; the central position between the two gears provided a neutral position. Two contracting-band brakes were fitted: one on the differential gear, and one on the engine shaft, and each brake was operated by a separate pedal. The car weighed $7\frac{1}{4}$ cwt. and was capable of a maximum speed of 20 m.p.h. on the level. The price in this country was £175.

The De Dion-Bouton voiturette quickly proved successful, and, as the De Dion-Bouton tricycle had revolutionised the motorcycle, so did this voiturette establish the practical 'small car'. It could transport two or three persons in comparative comfort on quite long journeys with a high degree of reliability, and the method of control was simple and foolproof. The demand for it from countries other than France was great, and large numbers were rapidly produced which initiated a new and advanced form of motoring. In addition, this successful form was quickly copied by various other manufacturers, including Beeston, Progress and Déchamps. The Alldays and Onions 'Traveller' voiturette was generally similar and was developed from an earlier quadricycle form with a 3 h.p. air-cooled engine, a layshaft type of gearbox, and wheel and column steering.

The Renault Voiturette

At about the same time, Louis Renault (1877–1944) was also producing a prototype voiturette (Plate 5) on original lines, the general features of which soon became standardised for the majority of cars. He fitted a 1¾ h.p. air-cooled De Dion-Bouton motorcycle engine at the front end of a simple tubular chassis frame, and provided it with an external flywheel in which was incorporated a leather-lined cone clutch. A 3-speed and reverse layshaft type gearbox was mounted separately in the frame immediately behind the flywheel, and the drive was taken thence by means of a central universally-jointed cardan-shaft to a bevel and differential-gear rear axle, in the manner patented by F. Lamplough in 1896. All four wheels were mounted on three-quarter elliptic leaf-springs, and Ackermann-type steering was directly operated by means of handlebars mounted on a column. The engine was enclosed in an embryo bonnet, and a simple open body provided side-by-side seating for two passengers. Two band brakes on the rear wheels were operated by a hand lever, and a third band brake on the transmission shaft, immediately behind the gearbox, was foot operated. The Baby Renault, as it was called, had a top speed of less than 20 m.p.h., but it at once proved to be a practical vehicle and considerable numbers were made during 1899, among which was the first totally-enclosed saloon car.

These important De Dion-Bouton and Renault prototypes not only initiated the voiturette and so made possible the first form of motoring that was both economical and reliable, but also established the basic forms upon which the motor industry has largely been founded. There were also a variety of other chassis and transmission arrangements, as already outlined, which had a short life before they were eventually superseded by the Renault arrangement.

Other Early Voiturettes

The Decauville design was originated in 1898 and, superficially, had much the same external appearance as the De Dion-Bouton voiturette, with a light open two-three seat body mounted on a light tubular frame. The rear-mounted engine, however, had two vertical cylinders, each of which was generally similar to the 1¼ h.p. air-cooled De Dion-Bouton design. The drive from the engine shaft was taken through a simple open 2-speed layshaft-type gear assembly; a pinion mounted on the end of the layshaft engaged with a bevel wheel incorporated with a differential gear, from which the two rear

21

wheels were driven by means of half shafts. Two band brakes acted directly upon the differential gear casing and were pedal operated. The engine was started by means of a hand wheel, projecting from the side of the car and operated from the driver's seat, which turned the crankshaft by means of bevel gears.

A number of other designs employed the arrangement, used by the larger cars of that period, of the front or centrally-mounted engine which drove, by means of a primary chain, shaft or direct gearing, a separate differential cross shaft. The final drive from the cross shaft was by secondary chains to the rear wheels.

The Panhard and Levassor design of 1899 had the usual light open two-seat body, with simple pivot-steering front wheels, operated directly by means of a steering wheel. The 4 h.p. single-cylinder air-cooled engine was mounted horizontally in rear. An extension of the engine shaft carried a cone clutch and three freely mounted spur gears, which meshed constantly with three other gears fixed to a differential cross shaft, from which the drive was taken to the rear wheels by means of two chains. Individual gears were engaged by means of a selector key which locked the required gear wheel to the engine shaft. The Clément voiturette was manufactured under Panhard and Levassor licence. The 3½ h.p. Peugeot single-cylinder water-cooled car was of the same general arrangement, except that the more efficient Ackermann type of steering was used.

The Gladiator design had a 3¼ h.p. Aster single-cylinder air-cooled engine set along the front of the chassis frame. It had a chain-driven countershaft, which incorporated a 2-speed epicyclic gear, and thence the drive was taken to the differential-gear rear axle by means of a secondary chain. This layout was used by a number of the cyclecars of 1910–1914, since it provided one of the simplest and cheapest drive arrangements.

A more advanced design, which incorporated a differential cross shaft and final chain drive, was the Mors 'Petit Duc' car of 1899. This vehicle was very well made, with a somewhat more substantial body than was usual with this kind of car, so that it provided a greater degree of riding comfort. The 4 h.p. twin-cylinder horizontally-opposed engine, which was set across the frame, had air-cooled barrels and water-cooled cylinder heads. A primary shaft and cone clutch transmitted the drive to the differential cross shaft. The weight was 7 cwt.

An example of a voiturette of this early period using the simple form of belt drive was the Belgian Vivinus. The 3½ h.p. single-cylinder air-cooled engine was mounted in front, and two pulleys of different diameter were mounted on the engine shaft. A flat belt connected these pulleys to a second set of pulleys mounted on a cross shaft, which was geared to the rear axle. The belt was shifted from one pair of pulleys to another to change the gear ratio, and a jockey pulley controlled to tension of the belt for the purpose of taking up or releasing the drive. This design was one of the simplest of the voiturettes, and the total unladen weight was only 3½ cwt. A heavier, more elaborate version with a two-cylinder engine was later produced in England and known as the New Orleans. The Belgian Antoine design was equipped with a native-built Kelecom engine.

The De Dion-Bouton voiturette also found considerable favour in America, and numbers were sold as the Pierce 'Motorette'; some American designs also appeared which were based closely upon the original. American development of light cars, however, was also proceeding upon characteristically national lines, which involved the horse-drawn vehicle forms of the 'buggy' and the 'buckboard'. One of the most typical of the former was the Oldsmobile, which had a 5 h.p. single-cylinder water-cooled engine arranged horizontally in the centre of the chassis, which consisted of a small rectangular frame, supported by two semi-elliptical leaf-springs extending the whole length of the wheel base, and secured at their extremities to the front and rear axles. The open type of buggy body was secured to a rectangular frame, and the steering was of the Ackermann type controlled by means of a tiller. A 2-speed and reverse epicyclic gear unit was mounted on an extension of the engine shaft, and the final drive to a differential rear axle was by means of a single chain, in the manner of the Stanley steam cars. The Orient buckboard was a yet simpler vehicle which consisted of a platform and seat mounted on four wheels; a 4 h.p. single-cylinder air-cooled engine was located in rear and drove the rear axle through a 2-speed epicyclic gear and chain. It weighed only 4 cwt. The 3½ h.p. air-cooled Crestmobile was another example of the simplest and cheapest form of voiturette.

A small car of considerable importance, to both light and heavy car development in general, was the P.D. of 1900. This design was due to Paul Daimler, Gottleib Daimler's eldest son. It had a 4 h.p., 1230 c.c. twin-cylinder engine, of 86 mm. bore and 116 mm. stroke, with automatic inlet valves and low-tension ignition. The crankshaft speed was 850 r.p.m., which gave the car a speed of 40 k.p.h. The gearbox was integral with the crank case. The change-speed lever was on the handlebar type steering column. The clutch was of the contracting spring type, and transmission to the rear axle was by a single chain. Engine control was by foot accelerator and the radiator was of the honeycomb type.

The P.D. design of 1900 can be considered in its own right as a true forerunner of the light car, but it has also perhaps the greater merit of providing Wilhelm Maybach with his inspiration for the famous Mercédès prototype of 1901 which established the form of the motor car in general.

Another transient, yet nevertheless interesting design from this same source appeared in 1902. This was a 6/8 h.p. Mercédès car having a two-cylinder water-cooled engine, with the crankshaft set transversely across the frame; it had four gears and handlebar steering, and appears to have been derived from the earlier P.D. design. But the Mercédès range, which began with 35 h.p., continually increased in power and the Mercédès light car prototype was not put into production. It is, however, of interest to note that there was a Mercédès light car.

Later Voiturettes: 1901-1905

Before the Renault system of chassis and drive layout began to render obsolete the original De Dion-Bouton and other early systems, some of the more important of these developed along their own lines during the first three or four years of the twentieth century. In general, these designs, although retaining their essential characteristics, tended to become somewhat larger, heavier and more powerful.

The model G De Dion-Bouton voiturette of 1901 appeared in a variety of body styles, including a four-seat tonneau, an open vis-à-vis, a phaeton, and a closed delivery van. This model was fitted with a 4½ h.p. engine of 500 c.c. capacity (84 mm. by 90 mm.), and a reverse gear was added to the 2-speed expanding-clutch epicyclic gear. By April, 1901, some 1500 of these voiturettes had been made at the Puteaux works, and production proceeded at the rate of two hundred cars a month. One of the De Dion-Bouton engined vehicles produced at this time was the small four-wheel car of Henry Sturmey, which was fitted with a 2¾ h.p. air-cooled engine and a light wicker-work two-seat body. This vehicle was later claimed as the first cyclecar, although the term was not coined and defined until some eleven years later.

In the meantime, both on the Continent and to a lesser extent in this country, a considerable variety of voiturettes were appearing, some of which were prototypes for larger models which later became famous. Among these were such designs as the F. N., Brouhot, Eole, Métallurgique, Decauville and Antoine, on the Continent; and the Argyll, Alldays and Onions, Star, Marshall, Vauxhall and Wolseley, in this country.

The Wolseley voiturette of 1901, fitted with a 5 h.p. (4½ in. by 5 in.) single-cylinder engine was an English example of the final phase of the development of what may be called the non-Renault designs. This original Wolseley layout, evolved by Herbert Austin, was successfully used in powers up to 20 h.p. for touring, and up to 70 h.p. for racing before the type disappeared by the end of 1906. The 1260 c.c. single-cylinder, water-cooled engine, which ran at a normal speed of 700 r.p.m., was mounted in a horizontal position towards the front end of the chassis frame. The drive was taken through a large cone clutch in the flywheel and a silent primary chain to a sliding-gear layshaft type of 3-speed and reverse gearbox incorporated in the differential cross shaft, which was mounted on adjustable trunnions in the middle of the chassis. Two chains transmitted the drive to the rear wheels. The final version of this car, which appeared in 1904, was on generally similar lines but was simplified and lightened. The same single-cylinder engine was used, but the speed was increased to a maximum of 1000 r.p.m.; the drive was transmitted by means of a single primary chain to a 3-speed and reverse gearbox, attached to the engine crankcase, and a single centrally-placed secondary chain to a differential rear axle. This design may be regarded as the culmination of the old-style voiturettes, before they were replaced by the Renault arrangement. Another late example of this type of voiturette was the Chambers, which was fitted with a 7 h.p. two-cylinder horizontal engine.

THE IMPROVED VOITURETTE

By the end of 1901, the De Dion-Bouton Company produced a new and more powerful model. The single-cylinder 8 h.p. engine of 942 c.c. capacity (100 mm. by 120 mm.) was mounted in front of the chassis frame and enclosed within a removable bonnet, which was now becoming conventional. A cardan shaft transmitted the drive to a 2-speed and reverse epicyclic gearbox, which was supported in the chassis frame, and which was formed in a neat integral assembly with the pinion and bevel-gear differential unit. The universally-jointed half shafts used on the older models were retained. Other improvements were introduced such as a steering wheel mounted on an inclined column, and the steering mechanism was also made irreversible; the levers for change speed, spark advance and mixture adjustment were retained on the steering column for ease and convenience of control.

At the end of the following year, a smaller and lighter version of this design, called the 'Populaire', was produced. It was fitted with a new 6 h.p. single-cylinder engine of 700 c.c. capacity (90 mm. by 110 mm.) which ran at a speed of 1500 r.p.m.; the total unladen weight of the car was only 6 cwt., and the maximum speed was 28 m.p.h. After 1902, the De Dion-Bouton designs began to evolve towards the larger form of car; the 10 h.p. 1400 c.c. capacity (90 mm. by 110 mm.) two-cylinder model of 1903 (Plate 3) had the advanced features of pressure lubrication by means of an engine-driven pump, and a 3-speed expanding clutch epicyclic gear, which was later replaced by what was now becoming the more normal layshaft sliding-pinion type of gearbox, used in conjunction with a plate clutch. This twin-cylinder vertical engine, however, retained the simple automatically-operated inlet-valve. De Dion-Bouton cars were sometimes entered in the great European road races of this period for the purpose of testing them under severe conditions of operation. Three of the larger 9 h.p. cars of this type ran in the voiturette class of the Paris–Madrid race in 1903.

In the meantime, the Renault voiturette, apart from influencing progressive current design generally and setting the standard of future practice, was also developed on the same lines, using the larger single-cylinder De Dion-Bouton engines as they became available. Like the De Dion-Bouton models of this time, the later Renaults were entered in the Continental road races, and quite soon larger four-cylinder Renault racers were built. The next most important voiturette design produced by this company was the famous twin-cylinder light car of 1906, which in 8 h.p. and 9 h.p. forms was produced in large quantities for a number of years and used extensively for private, commercial and taxi-cab duties. Other early examples of the small twin-cylinder voiturette were the Peugeot, Grégoire and Star. The 1905 9 h.p. Vauxhall (Plate 6) had the unusual feature of a three-cylinder vertical engine.

The Renault system had, in the meantime, considerable influence on several other designers of voiturettes and, between 1901 and 1905, a whole series of different models appeared, both on the Continent and in this country, which were based upon the arrangement of the 5 to 6 h.p. single-cylinder water-cooled engine mounted in the front of the chassis and driving a live axle through a gearbox and cardan shaft. Among these were the 5 h.p. Baby Peugeot (Plate 5), 4½ h.p. M.M.C., 5 h.p. Humberette, 6 h.p. Argyll, 6 h.p. Simms and the 5 and 6 h.p. Vauxhall designs. One of the first German voiturettes was the Dixi of 1905. These proved to be practical and reliable vehicles, within their limitations, and they did much to establish the motor car generally in these first years of the motor car industry.

The simple American motor buggy and buckboard type of small car were similarly emerging soon after 1900 from their primitive forms, and the designs became larger, more powerful and more complex. The larger 9 h.p. single-cylinder Oldsmobile of 1904 was substantially the same as the original run-about of 1901, and the 4½ h.p. Duryea with a horizontally-opposed twin-cylinder water-cooled engine was a development of the earlier model. The 6½ h.p. Cadillac of 1903 had a single-cylinder engine of 5 inches bore and stroke which ran at 1100 r.p.m. The power was taken through a 2-speed and reverse gear and a final chain to the rear axle. The Model A 9 h.p. Ford car of 1903, with its twin-cylinder horizontally-opposed engine (4 inch bore and stroke) and chain transmission, gave place to a new four-cylinder design, introduced in the following year, from which was eventually evolved the famous Model T of five years later. The Elmore car was fitted with either a single-or twin-cylinder two-stroke engine of the crankcase-compression type. Several American manufacturers, including Studebaker, Overland, Maxwell, Chalmers, Chrysler, Dodge, Packard, Buick, Pierce and others were about now beginning their industrial careers with light and simple designs. These examples were the forerunners of much larger and more complex vehicles which, within a few years, became standard American practice. The Knox, which was advertised as 'waterless', and the Franklin were early examples of air-cooling technique. The latter design was, by about 1906, developed sufficiently to make use of fan, duct and cowl cooling systems.

FORERUNNERS OF THE LIGHT CAR: 1905–1909

After 1904, the original voiturette form of car began to develop naturally from the small simple car produced in the first years of the motor industry into the larger more elaborate cars evoked by the vigorous development and evolution which was now in full progress. The simple single-cylinder voiturette of the original Renault formula, however, continued to develop along its own lines as a light runabout which, towards 1910, was beginning to be appreciated primarily for its inherent characteristic of economy. These latter forms of voiturettes were the immediate forerunners of the light car proper which appeared soon after 1910.

Although the voiturette for the most part retained its simple single-cylinder form, other progressive features which were being used in the larger forms of cars were also gradually adopted. The engine became more efficient through the use of mechanically-operated inlet and exhaust valves, coil or magneto high-tension ignition and improved spray carburettors. The radiator was now of the honeycomb type, instead of the earlier finned-tube type; moreover, besides being more thermally efficient, it began to be given individual and characteristic form and was placed in front of the chassis. A hinged bonnet was used to enclose the engine, and also incidentally to continue smoothly the line of the body. Windscreens and folding hoods began to be adopted for weather protection.

Among the first designs to represent this final phase of voiturette-development was the novel 8 h.p. single-cylinder 1300 c.c. capacity (114 mm. by 127 mm.) Rover car of 1905, which was produced continuously in various sizes for seven years. Engine, gearbox, transmission and live rear axle were all designed to form one assembly, which also served in part as the chassis supporting the body and to which the front and rear wheels were attached. The engine had the advanced features of mechanically-operated valves, high-tension magneto ignition and an efficient spray carburettor of Rover design. The engine crankcase, flywheel and clutch case, and gearbox with two large supporting arms for the body, were of aluminium alloy. The 3-speed and reverse gearbox was of the sliding-pinion layshaft type, with direct drive on top gear. The metal-to-metal plate clutch ran in oil, and was kept in contact by a large central spring, the mechanical effort of which was multiplied through levers. This form of clutch was smoother and easier to use than the leather-lined cone type and could be slipped with impunity. This Rover light car design was a considerable improvement on the earlier voiturettes, and it was an important link between them and the later light car. It was made in 6 h.p. and 8 h.p. single-cylinder sizes up to 1912, and one of the last models, priced at £250, incorporated a 1060 c.c. capacity (102 mm. by 130 mm.) single-cylinder Knight double sleeve-valve engine. The weight was 11 cwt.

The 1120 c.c. capacity (105 mm. by 127 mm.) 7 h.p. Swift was another soundly designed and well built single-cylinder light car of this period, which was arranged upon the now standardised chassis layout of a channel-section frame, supported on semi-elliptic leaf-springs at front and rear. The first 7 h.p. Austin design (Plate 6) also appeared at this time, having the same chassis and engine as the 7 h.p. Swift. The weight of this car was under 10 cwt. and it was sold for £150. Other examples of this formula included the 8 h.p. Thames, the 6 h.p. Elburn-Ruby, the 6 h.p. Jackson, the 5 h.p. friction-driven Pilot and the 6 h.p. Zebra. The average capacity of the engines fitted to these cars was about 750 c.c. Certain single-cylinder proprietary engines for light cars were now also being produced, such as the 5 h.p. 710 c.c. capacity (89 mm. by 114 mm.) Coventry-Simplex side-valve engine, with Simms high-tension magneto and pressure lubrication by means of an engine-driven pump. The latter feature was unusual for such a simple engine at this time.

A design which was originated in 1906 and which was produced continuously for nearly half a century with the same basic specification was the Jowett. The prototype weighed 6 cwt. It had an 826 c.c. capacity (72 mm. by 101·5 mm.) forward-mounted horizontally-opposed two-cylinder water-cooled engine, an integral 3-speed and reverse gearbox with central-gate gear change, and a worm-driven differential rear axle. A light open two-seat body with tiller steering was used. Although this design was not produced commercially until 1910, its origin in the voiturette period constitutes an important evolutionary link between this early period and the more advanced light car and cyclecar period which followed.

By 1910, the more advanced conception of the light car, as distinct from the voiturette, was being considered and the advantages of multi-cylinder engines were beginning to be utilised. Apart from the larger and more powerful single-cylinder voiturettes, whose engine capacities were about 1 litre for touring models and as high as 2 litres for special racing models, there were now a variety of twin-cylinder designs with engine capacities of about 1 litre, which weighed unladen from 9 to 12 cwt., and which cost from £150 to £250.

The vertical side-by-side valve form of engine was the most generally used since it conformed more nearly to large car practice, to which the bigger and more complicated category of voiturette was now tending. Among examples of this form were the Darracq, Renault, Grégoire, Mass, Phoenix, Alldays and Onions, Singer, Peugeot, Morgan-Adler, N.S.U., Argyll, Charron and Napier. The Riley of 1909 employed a 90° vee twin-cylinder water-cooled engine set across the frame. The French Côte twin-cylinder two-stroke engine, which used trunk pistons working in cylinder bores of different diameters, was sufficiently reliable to be used for racing purposes. A few examples of forced-induction air-cooling, employing engine-driven fans and efficient ducting and cylinder shrouding, were being used in France by 1908. The Lion-Peugeot design, whose unusual narrow-angle vee twin-cylinder engine had a bore of 80 mm., and a stroke of 280 mm. performed with distinction in the Coupe des Voiturettes of 1910.

HIGH-PERFORMANCE VOITURETTES

For some years after its inception, the voiturette was regarded as a vehicle of essentially moderate performance, although engine power and efficiency were improved in due course by the adoption of mechanically-operated valves, magneto ignition, larger engine capacities and higher crankshaft speeds. By 1907, however, Continental manufacturers in particular began to realise that the light car had a considerable potential market and that the type was now worth developing technically on the lines of the larger cars. Racing as a means of technical development had been appreciated by motor manufacturers for the past thirteen years, and this technique was now applied to the voiturette.

The Coupe des Voiturettes was organised by the French sporting paper *L'Auto* and was first run in October 1905 over a short triangular course near Paris. In the 1907 event, the cars had to cover 147 miles on six consecutive days at an average speed of 25 m.p.h. as a preliminary endurance test and to qualify for the actual race on the seventh day, which was over a distance of about 190 miles. Some 60 voiturettes, mostly fitted with single-cylinder engines, started; among them were such designs as the Sizaire-Naudin, Lion-Peugeot, Alcyon, Delage, Werner, Grégoire, Sinpar and Corre-la Licorne. Forty-one cars survived for the actual race, which was won by a single-cylinder 942 c.c. capacity (100 mm. by 120 mm.) Sizaire-Naudin car (Plate 6) at an average speed of over 40 m.p.h. This car, which incorporated one

28

of the earliest forms of independent front suspension, had a maximum speed of about 50 m.p.h. and a maximum crankshaft speed of 2400 r.p.m.

The results obtained from the racing of voiturettes were unexpectedly favourable, and the possibilities of higher compression ratios and crankshaft speeds and more complex multi-cylinder engines were investigated in the following year. The regulations for the 1908 Grand Prix des Voiturettes limited the vehicle weight to between 500 and 650 kilos. depending on the number of cylinders used, and the cylinder bore to 100 mm. for single-cylinder engines, 78 mm. for twin-cylinder engines, and 62 mm. for four-cylinder engines. The general result of these regulations was that exceptionally long strokes were used—such as 180 mm. (1420 c.c. capacity) in the case of the Aries voiturette—for the purpose of increasing the cylinder capacity as much as possible. The race was run over 6 laps of a 47·8 miles triangular course near Dieppe, and was won by a 1180 c.c. (100 mm. by 150 mm.) Delage car, fitted with a single-cylinder De Dion-Bouton engine at an average speed of nearly 50 m.p.h. This advanced performance was achieved with the aid of such means as four separate sparking plugs to assist efficient combustion in the larger cylinder, and a high compression ratio.

The high performance and reliability of these early voiturette engines are of particular significance, and perhaps the real development of the light car engine can be dated from the first few of the Coupe des Voiturettes and the Grand Prix des Voiturettes races. A contemporary comment[1] emphasised the increasing importance that the small car was now assuming: 'There is no longer the same demand for powerful and costly touring cars, for these have given way to the lighter class of vehicle, which fully satisfies requirements in speed and comfort and is, besides, much more economical'. By 1910, therefore, the inherent quality of economy combined with adequate and reliable performance, which the voiturette could now provide, was recognised as of the first importance, and the advent of the light car proper was imminent.

The limitation of the cylinder bore in the Coupe des Voiturettes races, however, now began to produce some grotesque designs which had excessively long strokes for the purpose of increasing power outputs as much as possible. This policy produced engines with capacities of up to $3\frac{1}{2}$ litres, and power outputs of up to 45 h.p., which put them quite outside the reasonable definition of a light car. These abnormal designs included a Corre-la Licorne with a 2300 c.c. single-cylinder (100 mm. by 300 mm.) De Dion-Bouton engine; a 2920 c.c. narrow-angle vee twin-cylinder engined (80 mm. by 280 mm.) Lion-Peugeot; and a 3450 c.c. narrow-angle vee four-cylinder (65 mm. by 260 mm.) engined Lion-Peugeot. The more normal designs included the 2660 c.c. four-cylinder in-line Hispano-Suiza, which won the $282\frac{1}{2}$ miles race in 1910 at an average speed of $55\frac{1}{2}$ m.p.h., and the 2260 c.c. four-cylinder in-line Calthorpe.

DEVELOPMENT OF THE VOITURETTE ENGINE

The development of voiturette engines during the first decade of the twentieth century was of the greatest importance because, during this period,

---

[1] *The Autocar*, p. 652, 14 May, 1910.

there were evolved the basic types and techniques upon which subsequent progress was founded. This development comprised, on the one hand, the refinement and elaboration of the simple De Dion-Bouton type of single-cylinder unit with automatic inlet valve, to the considerably larger units with mechanically-operated poppet valves and even Knight double sleeve valves; and on the other hand, to more advanced and complex two- and four-cylinder vertical units. This general development was assisted and hastened, not only by the increasing use of the voiturette as a practicable means of personal travel which was now taking place, but also through the similar development that was being given to, and the practical use that was being made of, the motor car proper.

The cubic capacity of the largest designs of the normal category of voiturette engine was about 1800 c.c., crankshaft speeds approached a maximum of 2000 r.p.m. for multi-cylinder units, and specific outputs averaged about 6 h.p. per litre capacity per 1000 r.p.m.

By 1907, mechanically-operated valves of the side-by-side variety were standardised. Main and big-end and small-end bearings were usually of phosphor bronze, but white-metal lined bearings began to be used as specific power outputs, and consequently rubbing speeds and loads of bearings increased. Multi-cylinder blocks were cast together with integral heads and water jackets. Detachable valve caps permitted the insertion and removal of the valves. Pistons were of cast iron with two to four compression rings. Cam-shafts were driven by half-time spur gears from the front end of the crankshaft, and valve tappets were adjustable. Magneto and distributor drives were also taken from the gear drive in front of the engine. The crank-case was of light-alloy castings with integral flanges for the attachment of the gearbox in the case of unit-contruction engines. The base of the crankcase constituted an oil sump for use with either drip and splash or pressure lubrication systems.

With a few notable exceptions, such as the Rover, two and four-cylinder engines had been firmly established by 1910 as the most suitable units for efficient, quiet and flexible operation with light cars. The single-cylinder engine was in general used after this period solely for the essentially simple and economical cyclecar.

ACCESSORIES AND ANCILLARIES

The design of accessories and ancillaries which were used up to 1910 with the voiturette was improved and elaborated considerably, not only through the increasing use to which this form of motor car was put during this period, but also as a result of the parallel development of similar equipment for use with large motor cars which was now vigorously proceeding. It was during this first decade of the twentieth century that motor car design, both particularly and generally, finally broke away from the horse-drawn vehicles tradition, and began to evolve types and forms specialised to the motor car. Later development of accessories and ancillaries was based upon this initial specialisation.

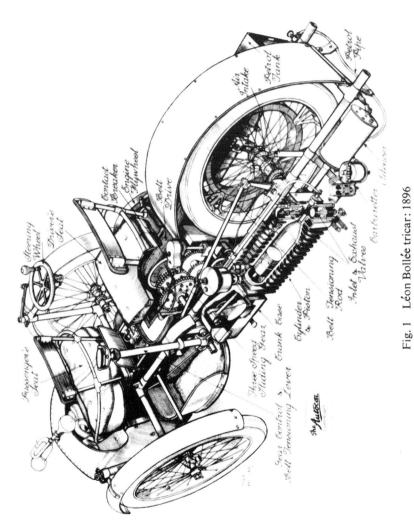

Fig. 1 Léon Bollée tricar: 1896

Steering Wheel

Driver's Seat

Passenger's Seat

Contact Breaker

Engine Flywheel

Belt Drive

Air Intake

Petrol Tank

Petrol Pipe

Carburetter (Mixer)

Inlet & Exhaust Valves

Belt Tensioning Rod

Cylinder & Piston

Crank Case

Three Speed Sliding Gear

Gear Control & Belt Tensioning Lever

The Autocar

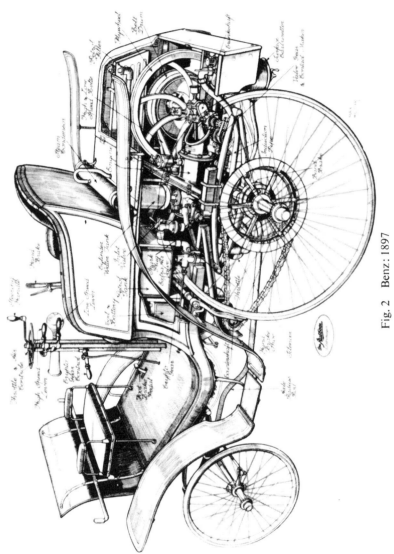

Fig. 2   Benz: 1897

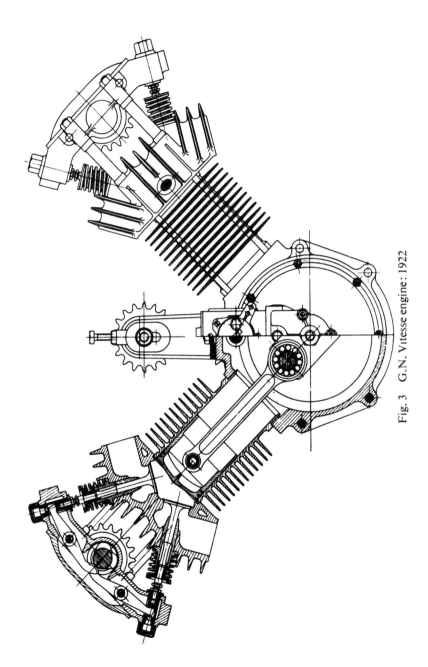

Fig. 3   G.N. Vitesse engine: 1922

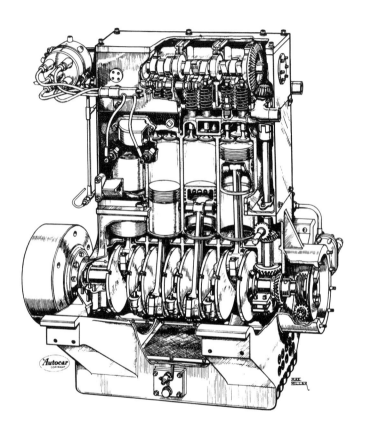

Fig. 4   Bugatti Type 37 engine: 1925

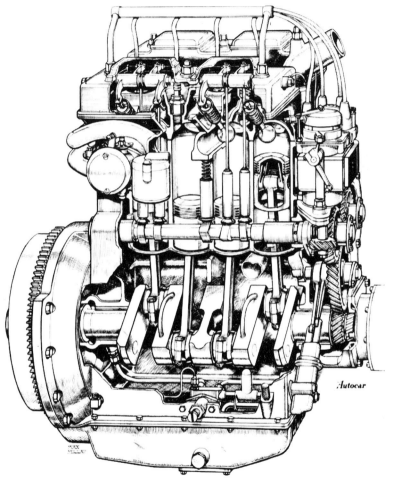

Fig. 5　Riley engine: 1927

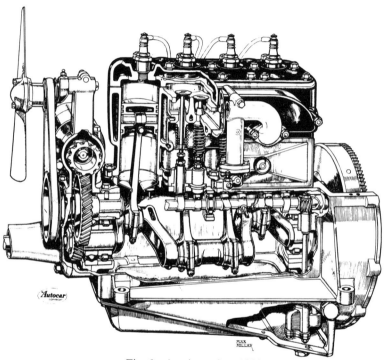

Fig. 6   Austin engine: 1928

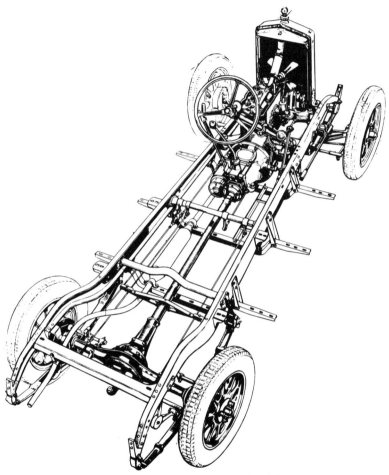

Fig. 7   Morris Cowley chassis: 1929

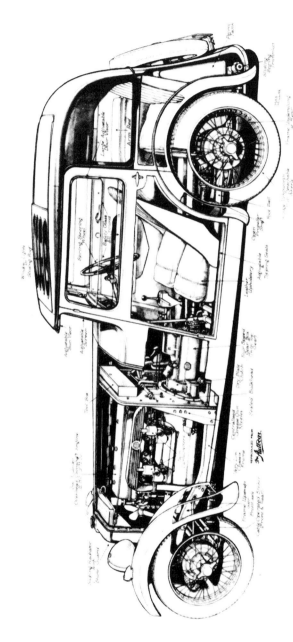

Fig. 8   M.G. Magna: 1931

Soon after the turn of the century, the surface vaporiser ceased to be used and the spray carburettor was generally adopted. Development of the simple single-jet type began to produce a reliable automatic instrument of both the single compensated-jet and multi-jet types. Of the former category the Zenith, Claudel, Solex and Longuemare designs employed a main and compensating-jet systems, and the S.U. design incorporated a main jet which was varied in aperture by a tapered needle operated by a manifold pressure-controlled diaphragm. Automatic or manually-controlled extra-air valves, which admitted additional air proportioned to the manifold pressure, were also employed to give greater flexibility and economy to some of the simpler semi-automatic designs. Multi-jet carburettors, such as the Smith four-jet and the Binks three-jet instruments, were designed to give a more accurate mixture strength at all operational loads than was deemed possible with the simpler single-jet instruments.

After 1905, coil-and-battery ignition systems began to be superseded during the following five years by the now reliable high-tension magneto. These compact instruments could conveniently be driven by means of suitable couplings, some of which were of the vernier type for achieving exactness of timing, from the crankshaft by gear or chain. The Bosch design soon began to predominate in many European countries, but designs such as the Simms, E.I.C., Eisemann and others were also developed and used to some extent. Considerable advance was also made in the design and construction of sparking plugs.

The majority of light car engines during this period were lubricated by means of the simple drip-feed and splash method and, in view of the low specific outputs of these units, the method was adequate. As early as 1903 however, some of the more elaborate engine designs were fitted with engine-driven oil pumps which fed oil under pressure from the crankcase sump to the main and big-end bearings, and thence to the remaining parts by splash. This positive system of lubrication became the more essential as engine outputs, crankshafts speeds and general design complexity increased.

The simple and robust leather-lined cone clutch continued to be largely used during this period, but some designs of the metal-to-metal plate or cone clutch running in oil varieties were also used with success.

The epicyclic form of change-speed gear used with a number of the early voiturettes was eventually superseded by the straightforward sliding-pinion spur-gear type of gearbox. This unit was at first generally mounted in the chassis frame as a separate unit, but later the trend to combine engine and gearbox in one unit in the interests of compactness and stiffness began to be manifest. Both quadrant and gate forms of change-speed mechanism were used. These later gearboxes generally included three forward speeds and a reverse gear.

As has been indicated, both chain and belt transmission for voiturettes were almost wholly replaced after 1905 by the universally-jointed cardan shaft and differential rear axle form of drive. Examples of chain drive survived on the cheapest and simplest forms of voiturette. The possibilities of friction drive and gearing were also considered before 1910.

Two main forms of brakes became standardised before 1910: a pedal-controlled contracting band-brake acting on the transmission shaft behind the gearbox, and a pair of hand-lever controlled band brakes acting on the rear wheels. The latter were usually of the external-contracting type, but examples of the enclosed internal-expanding type began to appear before the end of this period.

The direct reversible form of steering used with the earliest voiturettes was soon replaced by improved rack-and-pinion or worm-wheel forms which were irreversible and which, by virtue of the reduction gearing, provided an improved driving 'feel'. Track-rods and steering-arm rods were provided with spring-loaded spherical joints. The Ackermann form of steering was now universally used. King-pin and similar bushes were lubricated by means of pressure grease cups.

The earliest steel-strip reinforced wood and other primitive forms of chassis frame were developed into a standard arrangement of stiffened tubular or channel-section pressed steel frame, which could provide secure attachment for engine, gearbox and body, and be conveniently supported on front and rear axles through the medium of leaf springs. Frames tended to be hung lower, and the car as a whole began to assume a lower centre of gravity. One or two examples of independent wheel suspension existed, but solid front and rear axles were generally used.

The wheels were for the most part of the wooden non-detachable artillery type, with steel rims designed to take high-pressure beaded-edge tyres, which were generally of the 650×65, 700×80, 710×90 and 760×90 millimetre sizes. The wire and pressed-steel forms of detachable wheel, although they were beginning to be used on larger cars by 1910, were not adopted for the light car until somewhat later. Tyres were by no means wholly reliable by 1910, but they had advanced far beyond the primitive stages of a few years earlier.

A marked improvement in the design of bodies, chiefly as a result of the advances made in this field for large cars, was seen in well made coach-built bodies, which were usually of the two-seat variety. Travel comfort and weather protection were given increasing consideration. Hoods and wind-screens were introduced by 1903. They were not much used until later, however, when the higher performance and lower, sleeker build of the later designs could offset the high wind resistance involved and their greater touring capability made such adjuncts more and more a necessity. The all-enclosed coupé type of body began to be popular by 1910, particularly as a doctor's or professional man's car.

The increasing performance and touring potentialities of the voiturette necessitated a degree of adequate lighting. By 1910, this was usually provided by a pair of oil side lamps, an oil rear lamp and either one or a pair of large oil or acetylene head lamps, sometimes fitted with magnifying front lenses and reflectors.

32

Bulb horns as warning of approach devices were usually fitted, although carriage bells were used with some of the earliest voiturettes.

Instruments for measuring road speeds, usually of the centrifugal type such as those made by Watford, Jones and Cowey, and sometimes of the magnetic type, such as the Cooper-Stewart, were mounted on the dashboard. They were driven through flexible cables, either from gearing on a front wheel, or from a countershaft, itself driven by belt from the cardan shaft.

Cyclecars: 1910-1918

By 1910, motor cars and motorcycles in general had evolved from their primitive stages of development into vehicles which embodied the basic essentials necessary for convenient and dependable operation. These vehicles could now embark upon long journeys and even continental tours without undue mechanical failure or tyre trouble. Their engines were robust and, although still somewhat crude, were designed and made upon sound and ever improving specialised engineering principles. Ignition systems were reliable and efficient, practical spray carburettors were in production, and gearboxes and clutches, although still crude, were effective and were, moreover, already beginning to improve in detail design. Such refinements as electric-lighting, mechanical and electric engine-starting systems, and shock absorber devices were now becoming available.

This general technical progress in motor car engineering now revealed the motor tricar as an archaic and inadequate compromise between the motorcycle and the motor car, which had served an initial period of development and had now come to the end of its useful life. Moreover, the quickening trend in social progress created a need for passenger-carrying motor vehicles which were more economical than the voiturette and more technically advanced and more physically comfortable than the motor tricar or the motorcycle and sidecar. With the general experience in motor car and motorcycle design and production which was now available, a vigorous development ensued in consequence of the emergence of two new and advanced forms of light motor vehicle, namely, the cyclecar and the lightcar proper.

The simpler of these was a light three- or four-wheeled vehicle, which seated one or at most two people, and was constructed on light, simple and economical lines of motorcycle-type components and assemblies rather than the more complicated and heavier motor-car type components. At a joint Committee of the Royal Automobile Club and the Auto-Cycle Union, which was convened in the spring of 1912 to consider this new form of light motor car, it was decided that it should be called a cyclecar.

On 14th December, 1912, at a meeting of the Fédération Internationale des Clubs Moto Cycliste, it was formally decided that there should be an international classification of cyclecars to be accepted by England, Canada, United States, France, Holland, Belgium, Italy, Austria and Germany. In addition, it was also decided to establish two classes of cyclecars, as follows:

    (i) *Large class*
        Maximum weight 772 lb.
        Maximum engine capacity 1100 c.c.
        Minimum tyre section 60 mm.

    (ii) *Small class*
        Minimum weight 330 lb.
        Maximum weight 660 lb.
        Maximum engine capacity 750 c.c.
        Minimum tyre section 55 mm.

All cyclecars were to have clutches and change-speed gears. This requirement could be fulfilled even by the simplest devices, such as provision for slipping the belt on the pulley to act as a clutch, and the varying of the pulley diameter to change the gear ratio. The cyclecar, with economy as its chief feature, was optimistically hailed as 'the new motoring', a claim which was not fully substantiated until after 1922, and then by the miniature car rather than by the more limited cyclecar.

ORIGIN OF THE CYCLECAR

After having accorded due recognition to the few near cyclecars of 1908 mentioned in the previous chapter, the origin of the vigorous initial development of the four-wheeled cyclecar as it finally materialised in 1910 was due, in particular, to the inventors of two separate but concurrent designs: the Bedelia and G.N. Both designs were a progressive breakaway from the obsolescent motor tricar formula, which constituted the prototypes from which a large number of other makes were evolved during the next few years not only in this country, but also on the Continent and in the U.S.A. The three-wheeled cyclecar, which retained some affinity with the tricar, was originated by the inventors of the A.C. and the Morgan designs.

This new form of light and economical motor car which could, at a cost of about a penny a mile, transport one or two people in moderate comfort and at fairly high average speeds over long distances, quickly found favour among a now rapidly growing motoring and motorcycling public. In 1911, there were less than a dozen different makers of cyclecars in this country, and the same number in France, while there were as yet none in the United States. By 1914, there were well over a hundred different makers of cyclecars in each of these countries, as well as others in Germany, Austria and some other European countries. These designs, a considerable proportion of which were produced in small quantities only, employed varying arrangements of wheels, seating accommodation, and engine and transmission systems; they ranged in general form from the simplest open construction with a single-cylinder engine to a multi-cylinder car in miniature. Their prices varied from £60 to £200.

It is only possible to mention a few of these many designs which appeared during this prolific period of cyclecar evolution, such as the pioneer designs already mentioned and a selection of those which, by 1914, had reached a certain degree of evolution and reliability and were being produced in comparatively substantial numbers. The majority of these designs can be classified under the following broad headings.

BELT-DRIVEN FOUR-WHEELED CYCLECARS

The credit of producing the first true cyclecar has been accorded to Robert Bourbeau of Paris who, early in 1910, produced a light, long-wheel-based cyclecar, called the Bedelia (Plate 8), with two seats arranged in tandem; the driver's seat was located over the rear axle. An 8 h.p. twin-cylinder air-cooled motorcycle engine was situated in front and drove a countershaft by chain; the final drive to the rear wheels was effected by two long V-section belts running over pulleys. A clutch action was obtained by arranging for the rear axle to be moved slightly backwards or forwards by means of a hand control, thus tightening or slackening the belt tension; in addition, moving the rear axle forward still further brought the belt pulleys on the wheels against fixed shoes for braking purposes, in the manner used by Léon Bollée in his tricar design of 1896. The addition of two-diameter driving pulleys, in conjunction with the forward movement of the rear wheel, provided a variation in gear ratio. The track was only 3 ft. wide, thus avoiding the necessity of a differential gear, and the steering was by means of wire cables and pulleys which controlled a centrally-pivoted front axle. The weight of the vehicle was less than 400 lb.

In spite of the crude and unhandy appearance of the Bedelia cyclecar, it had a considerable success for some years, both on the Continent and in England for touring, commercial and racing purposes. The first public appearance of the car was over a course of 138 miles, which it covered at an average speed of 38 m.p.h.; its maximum speed on the track was 55 m.p.h. Its practicability and comparatively high speed created a demand for this early Bedelia, and also inspired other manufacturers to enter this new field of production. This design continued in production for some years, and the firm of Bourbeau et Devaux survived until 1925.

A number of other designs soon appeared in France which followed the general form of the Bedelia, such as the Automobilette and the Super. The former was a more compact version of the prototype, with side-by-side seating, and a streamlined body; the latter was arranged with tandem seats, the driver's seat being located in front. Both of these designs employed similar forms of control to the Bedelia. The long body space of these vehicles provided a large carrying capacity, and some single-seat forms were arranged as commercial delivery vans. The weight of these designs was about 400 to 500 lb.

Almost contemporary but with independent of the Bedelia, a cyclecar was produced in England by H. R. Godfrey and A. Frazer Nash, both of whom had from about 1905 experimented tentatively with primitive forms of runabouts fitted with motorcycle engines. In the autumn of 1910, they designed and built a simple four-wheeled runabout (Plate 8), which consisted essentially of a wooden frame chassis mounted on leaf springs at the front and rear. An 8 h.p. air-cooled vee twin-cylinder J.A.P. engine was mounted in front and drove through duplicated vee belts to a countershaft, on which a single-plate clutch was mounted. A second countershaft was driven by two chains from the first; either of these chains could be engaged by means of sliding dog clutches to provide two forward speeds. The second countershaft had pulleys on its extremities which drove the rear wheels by vee belts. The Ackermann type of steering was controlled through a wheel and cable and pulleys. The weight of the vehicle with a simple two-seat body was about 500 lb.

The commercial production of the car was begun, and by the summer of 1911, the firm was established as G.N. Ltd. and located at Hendon. One of the first improvements was the production of a suitable cyclecar-type of engine to replace the light motorcycle engines that had, of necessity, been originally installed, and at the same time a chain was used for the primary drive instead of the duplicated belts. This prototype G.N. engine was the first to be designed especially for cyclecar requirements. It was a 90 degree vee twin-cylinder air-cooled unit having a capacity of 984 c.c. (80 mm. by 98 mm.), with automatic inlet valves located over mechanically-operated exhaust valves; production engines, however, had the inlet valves mechanically-operated by means of push rods and rockers. A single-throw crankshaft was carried in a long plain bearing, and a heavy external flywheel was used. A fan assisted cooling. With this improved engine, which made possible a top speed of about 45 m.p.h., the G.N. cyclecar became a practical vehicle.

The decision about this time to fix a maximum engine size of 1100 c.c. capacity for the cyclecar engine made advisable the increase of the G.N. engine capacity to 1087 c.c. (84 mm. by 98 mm.). In addition, the engine was set across the frame, with the exhaust valves facing forward to assist cooling, the dry single-plate clutch was incorporated in the external flywheel, and the primary drive was taken through a shaft and bevel gearing to a cross shaft. Twin chains, running on different diameter sprockets to provide two gear ratios, imparted the drive to a second cross shaft, which carried the pulleys for the final double belt drive to the rear wheels. This model was the type used in the 1913 Cyclecar Grand Prix at Amiens and was capable of 60 m.p.h. Some of the 1913–14 models had four chains providing three forward speeds and reverse or four forward speeds.

Apart from the standard production models, considerable attention was given in 1914 to the building of two special high-performance models, known as 'Kim' and 'Bluebottle', which had various advanced features such as bronze cylinder heads with inclined overhead valves of large diameter, a hemispherical combustion chamber, and ball bearings for the support of the main shaft. This type of engine developed 30 h.p. at 3400 r.p.m., and gave the G.N. cyclecar a maximum speed of 80 m.p.h. The model which was designed for the 1914 Cyclecar Grand Prix had a developed standard engine with deep cylinder fins, and was capable of 55 m.p.h.

A new factory was built at Hendon in 1913, and the following year production started with two cars a week. The improved 'Grand Prix' model, and a simple touring model, to sell at 88 guineas, were scheduled for 1915. Production then stopped during the war, and the only car work carried out during that time was the design and building of the chain-driven prototype which was to become the post-war model.

The chain-cum-belt driven cyclecars produced by J. F. Buckingham from 1912 were of the same general layout. They were fitted with efficient overhead-valve air-cooled (746 c.c.) single and (1095 c.c.) vee-twin cylinder engines; two primary chain drives running on different ratio sprockets provided high and low gears, and individual cone clutches coupled the selected chain to a cross shaft, which ran in bearing secured to the chassis members. The final drive to the rear wheels was taken through two external vee belts running on pulleys on the cross shaft. The vee-twin cylinder engines had their cylinders set at 90° to each other, and were therefore better balanced than the majority of other vee-twin cylinder engines of this period which were of 50° to 60° dispositions.

Most of the simpler cyclecars, of the kind now under consideration, were not fitted with reverse gears in the interests of simplicity and lower manufacturing costs since they were light enough to be pushed backwards. The later Buckingham cyclecars, however, had incoporated in their transmission a reverse gear which was operated through a separate primary vee belt.

The Premier cyclecar, which employed a 7–9 h.p. Precision air-cooled engine, embodied various motorcycle assemblies besides the engine unit. In particular, it used an Armstrong-Triplex 3-speed motorcycle epicyclic hub gear, with which was incorporated a multi-plate clutch. This unit was arranged in the chassis as a countershaft gear, to which the engine drove through a primary vee belt and a secondary chain to the rear axle. The Cumbria, fitted with an 8–10 J.A.P. engine, employed a 3-speed Sturmey-Archer motor cycle hub-gear in the same manner. Another example of the cyclecar epicyclic gear was the American Spacke 2-speed, clutch and reverse unit incorporated in the cross shaft. This unit contained two epicyclic-gear trains operated by individual contracting-brake bands; in top gear the whole unit was locked solid, and the operation of either gear train provided respectively low gear or reverse gear. Another form of American 2-speed epicyclic gear for cyclecars was designed for incorporation in the main shaft drive to the rear axle.

This form of chain-cum-belt or all-chain driven cyclecar was the most favoured for the cheaper designs at this period. Among the many others of this type which appeared before 1914 may be mentioned the Globe, which used a flat primary belt, Adamson, Victor, Duo, Gilyard, Gordon, J.A.R., L.M., Winter, Warne and Ranger in this country; the Sabella, Hurlin, Rollo and C.I.D. in France; and the Pioneer, Falcon, Malcolm, Imp, Scripps-Booth and Ranger in the U.S.A. A number of these designs used the long double vee-belt secondary drive, as in the Bedelia design, to minimise abnormal belt wear and improve belt grip on the small-diameter driving pulleys.

CHAIN-DRIVEN THREE-WHEELED CYCLECARS

In 1910, there appeared the prototype of a cyclecar which, while deriving to some extent from the earlier tricar type, also combined certain progressive features which made it a unique and highly successful design. This was the three-wheeled cyclecar produced by H. F. S. Morgan, who, in 1906, had opened a garage at Malvern Link, and soon after began to experiment with light motor vehicles. His first experience with three-wheeled motor vehicles was with the Eagle and Century tricars. He then built a motorcycle and fitted it with a 7 h.p. vee twin-cylinder Peugeot engine but, being dissatisfied with the motor bicycle, he again turned his attention to the three-wheeler as being much more safe and stable. In conjunction with Stephenson Peach, an engineering master at Malvern College, he evolved a three-wheeled design which consisted essentially of a single central propeller tube, with the Peugeot engine mounted at the front end. A bevel gear and cross shaft and two secondary chain drives, providing two forward gear ratios which were selected by dog clutches, transmitted the power to the sprung rear wheel. A simple fixed axle held the two steerable front wheels through the medium of independent coil springs. This prototype Morgan (Plate 7) cyclecar embodied the essential features upon which all Morgan three-wheelers produced during the following forty years were based. Fitted with a single bucket seat, footboards and tiller-steering, it made its first appearance under the designation of a 'runabout' at the Olympia Show of 1910. In addition, two improved versions of this prototype were exhibited, fitted respectively with $3\frac{1}{2}$ h.p. single and 6 h.p. twin-cylinder air-cooled J.A.P. engines. The Morgan demonstrated its qualities of economy, compactness and good performance, and quickly developed into a complete cyclecar, with a side-by-side body, and a more powerful vee twin-cylinder engine. Still later models had an enclosed two-seat side-by-side body, the engine was enclosed in a bonnet, a steering wheel was substituted for the original tiller steering and a windscreen and a hood could be fitted as extras.

A variety of body styles were available by 1913, including the two-seat tourer, 'Grand Prix', 'Aero' and also the four-seat tourer. Vee-twin cylinder air and water-cooled J.A.P. engines of 996 c.c. capacity (Plate 9), were initially fitted, but soon other units of the same general type were also used, including the M.A.G., Precision and Green designs. In addition to proving itself to be an excellent touring cyclecar, as was shown by its successes in long distance trials such as the London–Edinburgh and London–Exeter, it was also very successful in sprint races, hill climbs and track and road racing. In December, 1912, H. F. S. Morgan established a cyclecar record by covering nearly 60 miles in an hour at Brooklands, for which he gained the Cyclecar Trophy. The three-wheeled class of the first Cyclecar Grand Prix race at Amiens in June, 1913, was won by W. G. MacMinnes on a Morgan at an average speed of 42 m.p.h. against a strong field of Continental competitors. Although essentially simple, particularly when compared with the later light cars of the 1920's, the Morgan continued in favour for some forty years, during which about 20,000 were built.

In 1910, the Autocarrier design, known as the A.C. (Plate 7), mentioned in the previous chapter, was produced in improved form with side-by-side or 'sociable' seating, as well as in tandem form with two passenger seats in front. Another three-seater form was produced in 1910 to serve as a machine-gun carrier for military purposes. The price of the A.C. Sociable varied from £85 to £95, and additional optional items such as a hood, side and front aprons, windscreen and luggage carrier added to convenience and comfort. The Warrick design was virtually a copy of the A.C. Sociable.

The rapid progress of the light car generally up to 1914 caused the tricar arrangement to be outmoded to some extent, and production of the A.C. Sociable three-wheeler was discontinued. An A.C. four-wheeled design of orthodox light car form was produced as a prototype in 1913, fitted with a 1500 c.c. water-cooled four-cylinder engine. Intermediate between the old and the new types, there appeared a light A.C. four-wheeled cyclecar on small car lines, which used the large 725 c.c. (95 mm. by 103 mm.) single-cylinder air-cooled engine (Plate 9) of the Sociable model. Few of this type were made, however, and the firm concentrated upon the more elaborate four-cylinder car which was put into production after 1918.

The 6 h.p. Girling was somewhat similar to the A.C. Sociable, but incorporated a third seat over the single rear wheel. It carried a spare detachable wheel, and was thus one of the first of the cyclecars to adopt this refinement. The Jackson was provided with a channel-steel chassis and a layshaft-type gearbox and final chain drive. The Eric was another example of the Morgan type. The unusual German Phänomobil, originated about 1906, continued to be produced in various versions fitted with both two-and four-cylinder fan-cooled engines, and served a useful purpose for several years on the Continent. It was also copied in America. An open tubular frame, providing side-by-side seats, was carried on a rear axle which was fitted with band brakes. The front of the frame was supported by a steering head and was carried on a single steerable wheel. Incorporated with the steering head was an 8 h.p. two-cylinder vertical air-cooled engine with a large outside flywheel, and the drive was taken to the front wheel by means of a chain and sprockets. Steering was through a tiller, with which were incorporated the controls for the clutch and the 2-speed gear. A larger, more elaborate version of this design was produced in 1913 fitted with a 12 h.p. four-cylinder fan-cooled engine. This model had considerable popularity in Germany because of its reliable, if unspectacular, performance, but it found little favour elsewhere, where it was considered, in a contemporary phrase, as 'a successful freak car'. It was used for a variety of purposes including private touring, commercial delivery and light taxi work. Another design of this type was the German Cyklonette.

The Wall three-wheel design was rather an elaborated motorcycle and sidecar outfit than a cyclecar in the accepted sense. A tubular framework, with a single steerable wheel in front and two driven wheels behind, supported an open sidecar type of two-seat body on leaf springs. A 4 h.p. single-cylinder or 6 h.p. twin-cylinder air-cooled engine was located in front, just behind the front wheel, and drove through a clutch, gearbox and shaft to a live rear axle.

FRICTION-DRIVEN CYCLECARS

An alternative system of transmission which recommended itself for use with the cyclecar because of its simplicity was friction drive. The most successful and popular of the friction-driven cyclecars which were produced during this period was the G.W.K. (Plate 8), which was produced initially by Messrs. Grice, Wood and Keiller in 1911. This form of cyclecar provided the maximum flexibility of operation with the minimum complexity of construction, and so long as it was driven intelligently it was a reliable and practical vehicle. The G.W.K. design survived in improved form until the early 1920's.

As far as the general layout was concerned, the design of the G.W.K. was normal, having a strong girder-sectioned chassis mounted on four wheels with leaf springing, wheel and rack-and-pinion type steering, and a live rear axle with bevel drive and differential gear. The engine location and form of drive were, however, both unusual. The 1069 c.c. (86 mm. by 92 mm.) two-cylinder vertical water-cooled Coventry-Climax engine (Plate 9) was mounted across the frame on the near side, immediately behind the side-by-side seats. The face of the external flywheel served as a friction-driving disc, across which the periphery of a driven fabric disc could be moved along splines on the shaft upon which it was mounted. This shaft was flexibly supported so that the fabric disc could be pressed against or released from the face of the flywheel for the purpose of increasing or decreasing the friction between the two members. The moving of the driven disc across one side of the flywheel face varied the forward gear ratio, while moving it across the centre to the other side of the face provided a reverse rotation. The driven shaft was extended to couple with the live rear axle.

This simple transmission arrangement was effective, although a certain amount of care and skill in operating it was necessary, particularly in the application of the drive through the friction surfaces. Any harshness which caused the flywheel face to revolve for an undue length of time against the stationary periphery of the driven wheel tended to wear flats in the fabric of the latter, which resulted in a rough and unreliable drive. With careful use, the friction rim would cover some 5000 miles without trouble before renewal was required as a normal maintenance procedure. The gear ratio could be varied in four steps from 4 to 1 on top gear, to 14 to 1 on the lowest gear. Many G.W.K. cars were made before 1914, and were used for touring, competition and even racing purposes. After 1919, they were produced for a few years in larger and improved form. The car weighed 9½ cwts., and was sold for 150 guineas.

The Crescent design was of more orthodox external appearance, having its 1094 c.c. (88 mm. by 90 mm.) twin-cylinder water-cooled engine mounted in front under a bonnet. The drive was taken by shaft to a friction disc carried on a cross shaft, and thence by a final chain drive to the rear axle. The Pyramid, fitted with an 8–10 h.p. J.A.P. air-cooled engine, also employed a final chain drive.

The French Tweenie appeared in 1913, and was of the light four-wheeled type, having a 6–8 h.p. (90 mm. by 120 mm.) single-cylinder water-cooled engine and final chain drive from a countershaft, which incorporated friction drive. Settings were provided for seven forward speeds and a reverse.

The successful Violet-Bogey design was produced in 1913 by M. Violet of Paris, who continued to produce cyclecars of original designs for the next decade. This car was especially notable for the efficient form of friction drive used, and the unusually high output of its engine. The engine and chassis layout was of normal four-wheeled type with a primary-transmission shaft and a friction disc and secondary-chain drive to a solid rear axle.

The compact 1088 c.c. (73 mm. by 130 mm.) twin-cylinder water-cooled vertical engine was reputed to be capable of developing some 22 h.p. at a speed of 2400 r.p.m. in the special racing form in which it was used with distinction in the Cyclecar Grand Prix held at Amiens on 13th July, 1913. Each inlet valve was arranged over its exhaust valve, and both valves were operated by a push-pull rod from a single camshaft, thus avoiding the necessity for external rocker arms; this arrangement permitted the use of large valves of 40 mm. diameter, with a consequent beneficial effect on volumetric efficiency and high power output, and simple valve-operating gear. Moreover, the Grand Prix engine was reported to have been fitted with aluminium-alloy pistons, possibly of the French Corbin type which had first appeared in 1910. The single-throw crankshaft, which caused both pistons to move together, was carried on large-diameter ball bearings. Lubrication was provided by a low-pressure circulating system; a Gobbi carburettor and a Bosch magneto were used.

There were also some interesting features in the Violet-Bogey transmission. The long shaft from the flywheel had just sufficient fore and aft movement to allow for declutching, which was effected by means of a pedal, with a catch to keep the two friction surfaces apart to provide a neutral position. The driving disc was faced with a surface made of compressed paper, across which moved the driven disc which was mounted on a splined cross shaft. The bearing housings of this cross shaft were interconnected with the radius rods securing the rear axle, and had a slight oscillatory movement, so that the pressure between the driving and driven surfaces increased proportionately with the thrust of the rear wheels. The final drive was by chain.

Other examples of friction-driven cyclecars of this period included the English D-Ultra, Pyramid, Lord, Ajax and Winter, all of which were of simple design. The American Metz design was substantially on the same simple lines, with a vee-twin cylinder air-cooled engine driving a friction-disc, across the face of which was moved the periphery of a driven wheel mounted on a splined countershaft set across the chassis; the final drive was by means of two vee belts running on pulleys. A considerably more complicated friction-driven car which was also made in the United States at this time was a water-cooled four-cylinder 3 litre Trumbull, produced by the American Cyclecar Co. This was on the same broad lines as the lighter types, but it had final chain-drive and was of heavier construction and greater output. Higher powers than 8 h.p. were not usually suitable for friction drive, although the French Charles Fournier design of 1914 and the G.W.K. design of 1921 successfully employed four-cylinder engines of 1500 c.c. capacity. Friction drive for both cyclecars and light cars was little used after 1914.

MONOCARS

Although cyclecars of this period were essentially simple, attempts were made in a few designs to achieve the greatest degree of simplicity by employing the lightest and simplest forms of body and suspension, and mounting a single or twin-cylinder air-cooled engine in a manner calculated to provide the least complicated method of drive. Of these few designs, the monocar produced in 1913 by J. V. Carden was one of the first and most successful.

The simple shell body, consisting of a wooden framework and thin metal sheeting, was supported in front on a single coil spring and steering pivot. Steering was effected through a wheel and flexible cables and bobbins. Either a single or twin-cylinder air-cooled J.A.P. engine was mounted in the tail of the body, immediately behind the driver, which drove the rear axle through a clutch and chains. Its low weight, 3 cwt., and low centre of gravity made it capable of speeds in excess of 80 m.p.h., and it was used for track racing as well as other sporting events. In its simplest form it cost under £60, and was later produced in two-seat form. It continued in small production until the 1920's.

The Dew monocar was a simple open vehicle, with a $3\frac{1}{2}$ h.p. single-cylinder engine located in front. The drive was by a primary chain to a cross shaft, and the final drive was by two belts. The body provided a single bucket seat and the steering was of the Ackermann type, controlled by a wheel. The 4 h.p. Aviette and the 5 h.p. Crompton were other examples of this simple type.

TWIN-CYLINDER, SHAFT-DRIVEN CYCLECARS

The most elaborate form in the cyclecar class which appeared before the end of 1914 was the shaft-driven type with a 2- or 3-speed gearbox, a live rear axle, and a twin-cylinder engine of not more than 1100 c.c. capacity. This form derived more from motor car than motorcycle design and manufacturing technique. In the medium-priced field, namely between £100 and £150, this type was undoubtedly the most practical and popular at this time, since it offered reliability combined with the convenience, comfort and weather protection of a true car. The several designs which appeared had two or, at most, three-seat bodies equipped with windscreens, folding cape-cart type hoods, and boots for conveying equipment or luggage. They were capable of speeds up to 40 m.p.h., of averaging 25 m.p.h., and of covering some 40 to 50 miles on a gallon of fuel. This class of cyclecar included a few examples from some of the established manufacturers such as Humber, Swift, Alldays and Onions, Enfield, Douglas, Peugeot, Charron and Adler. The remainder were mostly produced by small new concerns which had neither the experience nor the facilities of the established companies but which, nevertheless, contributed to the cyclecar development of this period. The types of engines employed included units having the vee, the vertical and the horizontally-opposed arrangements of cylinders.

The single-cylinder Humberette voiturette, first produced by the Humber Company of Coventry in 1903, was succeeded in 1912 by a well-designed model equipped with an 8 h.p. vee-twin cylinder air-cooled engine of 998 c.c. capacity, a leather-lined cone clutch, a 3-speed and reverse gearbox attached as a unit to the crankcase, and shaft drive to a differential rear axle (Plate 10). Lubrication was by sight drip-feed. Although the car only weighed 7 cwt., the neat two-seat body, with windscreen and hood and tapering bonnet with front gills, gave it the appearance of a scaled-down car. A foot-operated band brake was incorporated behind the gearbox in the transmission shaft, and the hand brake operated two external-contracting brakes on drums on the rear wheel hubs. Steering was by rack-and-pinion gearing. The front axle was mounted on a transverse semi-elliptical leaf spring; the rear of the tubular chassis was suspended on the rear axle by means of two quarter elliptic leaf springs. Two spring-loaded torque rods transmitted the thrust of the rear wheels to the chassis. A Bosch or Eisemann high-tension magneto supplied ignition, and a flexible Smith four-jet carburettor supplied the mixture. Hand-controlling levers for both throttle and ignition settings were mounted on the steering column. The wheels were fitted with 650 mm. by 65 mm. beaded-edge tyres. The price was £125.

The 1914 model was improved in detail but remained substantially the same in general layout, although a water-cooled version with a front radiator was added. Production ceased in 1915 and the design was not revived after the war.

Other examples of the vee-twin cylinder, shaft-driven cyclecar included the Chater-Lea, Crouch, Warren-Lambert and Omnium. Their details varied, but generally conformed to the specification of the Humberette.

Like the Humber Company, the Swift Company of Coventry had also produced a single-cylinder voiturette. In 1912, this company produced a well-designed cyclecar equipped with a twin-cylinder vertical water-cooled engine. The chassis of the improved 1914 model was of channel steel, and was carried on four semi-elliptical leaf springs; the general layout closely followed car practice. Worm-and-sector steering was used. The two-seat body had the seats slightly staggered for comfort, and the specification included a cape-cart hood, an adjustable windscreen, a boot, mudguards and running boards, and an acetylene-lighting set. The wire wheels were fitted with 700 mm. by 80 mm. beaded-edge tyres. A transmission brake and two rear-wheel external-contracting brakes were operated respectively by a pedal and a hand lever.

The 972 c.c. capacity (75 mm. by 110 mm.) two-cylinder water-cooled vertical engine was a well designed unit mounted in normal manner on the front chassis members. An Eisemann magneto and a Claudel carburettor were fitted, together with a leather-lined cone clutch which was incorporated in the external flywheel. The drive was taken through a primary shaft to a separate 3-speed and reverse gearbox, located in the centre of the chassis, and from the gearbox to the live axle through a cardan shaft fitted with fabric flexible couplings. The petrol tank was carried behind the dash-board, and fed the carburettor by gravity. Lubrication was by splash. The Swift cyclecar cost £140 fully equipped.

The Alldays Midget, built by the old established firm of Alldays and Onions Ltd., was on generally similar lines to the Swift, differing in particular in the width of body, which was exceptionally large and therefore provided greater comfort than was usual with the small cyclecar bodies of this period. The 1069 (86 mm. by 92 mm.) water-cooled vertical twin-cylinder engine drove through a 3-speed and reverse gearbox and cone clutch to a worm-type differential axle. A Bosch magneto and a Zenith carburettor were fitted. The price was £130. The Perry (Plate 10) was a good example of sound design and solid construction. The specification included an 879 c.c. (72 mm. by 108 mm.) two-cylinder water-cooled vertical engine, unit 3-speed and reverse gearbox, and a metal cone clutch running in oil. Sankey detachable pressed-steel wheels equipped with 700 mm. by 80 mm. beaded-edge tyres were fitted.

Another example of this type was the Enfield Autolette produced by the Enfield Autocar Co. of Birmingham, which was fitted with a 1069 c.c. (86 mm. by 92 mm.) engine, and was mounted on four quarter-elliptic leaf springs, the rear two of which had torque rods incorporated with them. A worm-driven differential axle and a separate 3-speed and reverse gearbox was used.

Other examples of the vertical, twin-cylinder engined and shaft-driven cyclecars of this period included the Melen.

The good balance characteristics and even firing periods of the horizontally-opposed form of four-stroke engine recommended its use in motorcycles and cars, although comparatively few designers actually adopted it for production purposes, chiefly because it was not an easy unit to install on account of its width. One of the earliest cyclecar concerns to adopt this form of engine was the Jowett Company of Bradford, whose basic design of a simple twin-cylinder water-cooled engined car of low weight and economical characteristics, combined with an exceptional capacity for hard work, continued in production over several decades. The Jowett design, as already mentioned in Chapter 3, was originated in 1906; it was one of the very few to survive successfully this first development period of the cyclecar.

The total weight of the first production 7 h.p. Jowett of 1910 was only 6½ cwt., yet it comprised a full specification of a steel chassis mounted on leaf springs, an 826 c.c. (72 mm. by 101·5 mm.) water-cooled engine mounted transversely in the chassis (Plates 9 and 10), a cone clutch, a 3-speed gearbox, shaft drive, and a bevel-gear differential rear axle.

Another firm which had early adopted the horizontally-opposed engine was the Douglas Company of Bristol, which since 1907 had been producing successful motorcycles fitted with this form of engine. In 1912, a larger version was produced in both air and water-cooled forms, having a capacity of 1070 c.c. (88 mm. by 88 mm.) which was originally used in the Williamson motorcycle.

In 1914, the Douglas Company used this engine in water-cooled form for a soundly conceived cyclecar of the more elaborate kind, having a 3-speed gearbox integral with the crankcase, shaft drive and a bevel-gear live axle. Other refinements, such as Riley detachable wheels and a C.A.V. electric-lighting set were also included at a price of £175. Although this was a sound and attractive design made by a reputable company, few of the Douglas cyclecars were made, perhaps because of the comparatively high price. The horizontally-opposed water-cooled engine fitted to the Adams cyclecar was mounted longitudinally in the chassis and drove the rear axle through a primary chain and countershaft, in which was incorporated a 2-speed epicyclic gear, and a secondary chain to the differential gear in the rear axle. An unusual feature was the underslung three-quarter elliptic springs for the front axle, and the single transverse half-elliptic spring for the rear axle.

PROPRIETARY FOUR-STROKE ENGINES

Although a number of the numerous cyclecar manufacturers which appeared from 1910 to 1914 designed and built their own engines, a large proportion depended upon the supply of various types of proprietary designs. These types derived both from the motorcycle as well as the motor car industries; with the former, it was generally a case of making the design somewhat more robust and in water-cooled form, with heavier flywheels; and with the latter, the adoption of a policy of scaled-down car practice and a lesser number of cylinders was adopted. Single-cylinder engines, and twin-cylinder engines with a variety of cylinder arrangements, were developed in both air and water-cooled forms. The average output of these units was about 10 h.p. per litre capacity at speeds up to 2000 r.p.m., although some engines could run up to 3000 r.p.m.

The single-cylinder type of engine, largely used at the beginning of the century for simple cars such as the De Dion-Bouton and others, was also used in cyclecars of the simplest kind.

The 500 c.c. J.A.P. side-valve motorcycle engine was perhaps the simplest and best known of this type, and was used in the lightest monocars. A more powerful form of single-cylinder motorcycle engine was the 750 c.c. (85 mm. by 132 mm.) Rudge-Whitworth engine, with side exhaust valve and overhead inlet valve. The 746 c.c. (89 mm. by 120 mm.) Buckingham engine was still more advanced, having overhead inlet and exhaust valves, operated by push rods and rockers.

One of the engine units most generally used in the early cyclecars was the 8 h.p. vee twin-cylinder J.A.P. motorcycle engine; this side-valve unit had a bore and stroke of 85 mm., a capacity of 964 c.c., and cast-iron cylinders with integral heads. The Precision engine of the same general characteristics was also used to some extent. From these were developed specialised cyclecar engines, of the same side-valve arrangement, but water cooled, of more robust construction and somewhat larger capacity, such as the Blumfield and Dalman engines. The Blumfield design had the then unusual features for the cyclecar type of engine of an integral oil-sump and a pressure lubrication system supplied by means of an engine-driven pump.

Still more specialised and powerful cyclecar engines of this form appeared in the 838 c.c. (90 mm. by 77·5 mm.) J.A.P. (Plate 9) air and water-cooled design, having its cylinders set at 55° to one another, and with overhead inlet and exhaust valves; and the 1095 c.c. (89 mm. by 88 mm.) Buckingham design, with overhead inlet and exhaust valves. Other proprietary engines of this type included the American Wizard and Spacke De Luxe and the Swiss M.A.G. designs. A four-valve per cylinder example of the latter was produced in 1914 which, fitted to a Morgan, was capable of 70 m.p.h.

A few two-cylinder units of this type were produced on car lines, which were used for some of the more elaborate cyclecar designs. Of the more important were the 1098 c.c. (80 mm. by 108 mm.) Dorman engine, which

Plate 9

Autocarrier engine: 1910

G.W.K. engine: 1913

J.A.P. engine: 1914

Jowett engine: 1916

Plate 10

Jowett: 1906

Humberette cyclecar: 1914

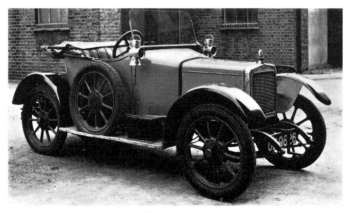

Perry: 1914

Plate 11

Morris Oxford: 1914

Austin: 1922

Plate 12

Saxon: 1914

Bugatti Type 13: 1914

A.C.: 1914

Plate 13

White and Poppe engine: 1912

Bugatti Type 13 engine: 1914

Stellite engine: 1914

Wanderer engine: 1914

Plate 14

G.N. cyclecar: 1920

Rover cyclecar: 1922

Morgan Aero cyclecar: 1923

Plate 15

Peugeot: 1915

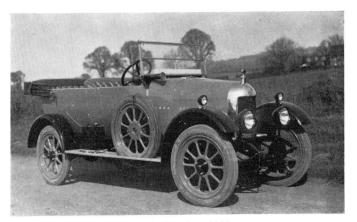

Morris Cowley: 1923

Wolseley: 1924

Plate 16

Morris Cowley engine: 1925

Austin engine: 1926

Riley engine: 1927

Bugatti engine: 1928

developed 20 h.p. at 2500 r.p.m., and the 1070 c.c. (86 mm. by 92 mm.) Coventry-Simplex engine, which developed 9 h.p. at 1500 r.p.m., and weighed 120 lb. The 1088 c.c. (94 mm. by 60 mm.) Alpha engine was another example of the same kind; this unit developed 11·5 h.p. at 1500 r.p.m. and weighed 178 lb.

The chief example of the horizontally-opposed twin-cylinder form of engine in proprietary supply was the 1070 c.c. (88 mm. by 88 mm.) Douglas, which was used in water-cooled form.

TWO-STROKE ENGINES

The few years before 1914 had seen the establishment of the simple crank-case-compression or Day type of two-stroke engine as a successful motorcycle unit, and its simplicity of manufacture, smooth running and high torque recommended it for cyclecar propulsion. Although some few interesting designs were built and encouraging performances obtained with them, it was not adopted for production to any significant extent, owing to lack of basic development which was manifested in particular by poor slow running, high specific fuel consumption and a tendency to overheat.

The most advanced and efficient design of cyclecar two-stroke engine of this period was produced by H. R. Ricardo. This was a 773 c.c. (72 mm. by 95 mm.) two-cylinder vertical water-cooled unit, with piston-controlled exhaust ports in the cylinder walls, and flap-valve controlled inlet ports in the head. Separate pumping cylinders on the Clerk principle, having a bore of 100 mm. and a stroke of 80 mm. which were also provided with flap valves to control the outlet ports, provided positive fresh-gas charging. This efficient, yet essentially simple arrangement, permitted a more positive and powerful operation of the two-stroke cycle than was possible with the simple crankcase-compression designs, as was demonstrated by the good performance, high torque and flexible running that were obtained with the engine fitted in Hampton and Weston light cars of this period. This Ricardo 'Dolphin' design was the forerunner of some of the later two-stroke engined light cars which followed after the 1930's, particularly on the Continent. The 1950 Trojan engine was substantially the same basic design as the Ricardo of 1913.

Other two-stroke engines of this period included such designs as the horizontally-opposed M.I.P. with rotary delay valves in the transfer ports, the water-cooled 690 c.c. (72 mm. by 85 mm.) Cycaren twin-cylinder vertical unit, and the French Côte water-cooled twin-cylinder vertical unit which used stepped pistons for fresh gas charging to avoid the use of crankcase-compression. A three-cylinder vertical engine, using crankcase compression, was proposed by Dr. A. M. Low. There were also the Vox twin-cylinder (72 mm. by 95 mm.) car, the C.I.D. 'Baby', and the Medinger designs. In America, a cyclecar was produced fitted with a small single-cylinder two-stroke engine which drove an air propeller.

ACCESSORIES AND ANCILLARIES

Since the cyclecar was basically an evolution of the motorcycle and many motorcycle standard components and assemblies were employed in its

47

construction, motorcycle type accessories and ancillaries were similarly adopted where practicable. These items are described in separate Science Museum publications.[1]

CYCLECAR PERFORMANCE

The performance and general reliability to which the light car had attained by 1914 were demonstrated in such events as the London–Edinburgh, London–Land's End and, in particular, the 1913 Scottish Six-Days' Trials. In the latter event in the Scottish Highlands, the 1000 miles course included some of the worst roads and most severe hills in Britain such as Amulree, Cairn-o'-Mount, Glendoe, and Tournapress. Reliability under severe racing conditions was effectively demonstrated in such events as the French Grand Prix and various races at Brooklands.

[1] See *The History and Development of Motor Cycles* (Parts I and II). Published by H.M.S.O.

Light Cars: 1912-1918

Concurrently with the development of the cyclecar, described in the previous chapter, there was also evolved the light car as defined by the specification promulgated by the A.C.U. in 1912, by which engine capacity was limited to 1500 c.c. The development of the cyclecar owed much to motorcycle design and proprietary units and fittings, whereas the light car derived largely from the current larger forms of motor car and to some extent from the earlier voiturette, so they were in general scaled-down versions of their larger prototypes. Most of the numerous light car designs which appeared during this period had four-cylinder engines of capacities of between 1000 c.c. and 1500 c.c., although a few early designs of this kind had capacities as small as 800 c.c. These latter vehicles were, by A.C.U. definition, cyclecars; examples such as the Baby Peugeot of 1912 were, however, miniature cars in the later sense of this designation and they may justly be considered as the true forerunners of the successful ultra-light or baby car, such as the Austin Seven and Citroën 5 c.v. designs of the early 1920's.

The essential requirement which brought this class of motor car into being and fostered its commercial development was the demand for more comfortable and convenient motoring than was possible with the cyclecar, without sacrificing operational economy. The first light car designs retained as much as possible the completeness, comfort and versatility of the larger motor car designs of 1912, so far as these qualities had progressed at that time. As a result, they were, within their limitations, practical vehicles serving the needs of average middle class individuals such as the business man and the doctor; they were also used as auxiliaries to larger cars in a fuller and more adequate manner than had been possible with the earlier voiturettes. The 1000 to 1500 c.c. capacity designs, in particular, which appeared before the end of 1914 effectively laid the foundations for the future vigorous development and wide use of this class of economical light car.

Apart from the wide range of cubic capacities of these four-cylinder light car engines at this early period in their development, there was also revealed a versatility of detail design involving push-rod or camshaft-operated overhead valves, and even the use of four valves per cylinder for the purpose of increasing specific outputs. Other fundamental developments, such as dynamo-lighting systems and hand, foot and electric engine-starting devices were also becoming available and being adopted in a limited manner.

By the end of 1914, the light car had established itself in a new and potentially large market. A great variety of types were in fairly large production—Morris-Oxford cars, for instance, were being built at the rate of forty a week—by a large number of manufacturers, and the 1915 designs in particular showed considerable improvement in both general and detail design. The Ministry of Munitions order of 3rd November, 1916, however, restricted the manufacturing resources of the country to war requirements, and abruptly terminated this vigorous cyclecar and light car development for the next three years.

LIGHT CARS: to 1000 c.c.

There were few examples of the very small four-cylinder light cars at this period, but those which did appear were sound and of reliable design and performed well within their capacities. They are of interest since they clearly foreshadowed the successful and popular models of similar type and capacity of the 1920's. These engines to 1000 c.c. capacity were unprecedentedly small for their time, and owed their inception to some extent to the few successful four-cylinder air-cooled engines of similar capacity then being used for motorcycles. This was one of the few contributions which motorcycle design made to the light car as distinct from the cyclecar.

A notable and successful example of the smallest form of four-cylinder light car produced during this period was the 855 c.c. Baby Peugeot. The first production version, designed by Ettore Bugatti, appeared in 1911; it soon gained a reputation for its sound design and reliable operation for both touring and racing purposes. It had a wheelbase of only 6 ft. and weighed 8 cwt.; the comparatively roomy two-seat body on the short wheel-base chassis located both driver and passenger immediately over the rear axle. This Baby Peugeot (Plate 15) with various modifications continued to be produced up to the early 1920's.

Apart from the small capacity of this early four-cylinder light-car engine, the original features of this design were mostly in the engine and transmission details. The cylinder block, head and crankcase were cast in one piece, and the valves were arranged in T-head form, with separate camshafts for the inlet and exhaust valves. The engine was mounted on an undershield, which formed a sub-frame. Cooling water was circulated by a pump, and lubrication was effected by means of a motorcycle type sight drip-feed from a tank mounted on the dash. A Peugeot carburettor and a Bosch magneto were used.

The clutch was of the inverted cone leather-lined type, and the gearbox and back-axle gears provided three forward speeds and a reverse. The second and third gears were direct from the engine, through two enclosed concentric shafts and alternative pairs of bevel gears on the rear axle. Reversed cantilever springs, a characteristic of later Bugatti designs, and semi-elliptic springs were fitted respectively to the rear and front axles. Steering was by worm and worm-wheel gearing. Pedal-operated internal-expanding brakes and hand-lever operated band brakes were incorporated with brake drums on the hubs of the small-diameter (550 mm. by 65 mm.) wire wheels.

A larger example of this small class of light car was the 992 c.c. Horstmann; it weighed 8 cwt. and was of generally normal layout with a 3-speed and reverse gearbox, and shaft and bevel drive to a live rear axle. A foot-starting mechanism, consisting of a large quick-thread formed on the shaft connecting clutch and gearbox, and a nut actuated by a pedal, permitted the engine to be rotated from the driver's seat. Such devices indicated the growing desire at this time to make even the smallest cars as flexible and convenient as possible before the development and general adoption of electric starters for light cars.

French examples of this small four-cylinder type of light car included the Rontiex and Cummikar, both of which fitted engines of 966 c.c. capacity. The 950 c.c. Bayard (55 mm. by 100 mm.), adopted the current policy of a long stroke, as well as the unusual features of a crankshaft carried on two ball-bearing races, an oil pump of the plunger type, combined oil filter and crank-case breather, a large single valve cap covering both inlet and exhaust valves, and a spring-loaded aluminium-alloy radiator fan. The Bayard, in addition to having some novelty in design, was of sound and solid construction which made it one of the more important Continental forerunners of the ultra-light car.

The D-Ultra design was an example of the cyclecar type fitted with a Lister 995 c.c. water-cooled engine.

The few designs, generally of the cyclecar type, such as the Wilkinson, the Winter and the American Lavigne, which were fitted with four-cylinder air-cooled engines, were of interest but little used. Their additional complication enhanced neither the cyclecar nor light car types at this particular stage of development, since they were essentially hybrids of no particular value.

LIGHT CARS: to 1250 c.c.

The medium size of light car was the most potentially important and also the best represented by individual designs, and it was from this category that there was evolved the successful and popular 8–10 h.p. light car of the 1920's. The development of this type was perhaps the easiest and most logical course for designers to have taken, since the size permitted the essential features of the larger car to be adopted and used effectively, and also provided a formula which ensured economy in first cost, operation and maintenance. After two years of somewhat indeterminate development, the medium-size light car attained, by the end of 1914, the status of a proved and practical type which broke away decisively from the cyclecar formula and emerged in its own right as a reliable light car in fairly large production and in increasingly wide use. By the middle of 1914, there were some seventy different models of light cars on the British market, and at least as many more on the Continent. The majority of these were well-matured and complete designs in relation to their period, with practical and well-proportioned bodies and comfortable upholstery, fitted radiators, blended dash-boards, detachable spare wheels and, in some cases, electric lighting and even electric-starting systems. This relatively high standard of quality and completeness of light cars at this early stage was largely due to the fact that they were based upon the estab-lished principles of the larger forms of motor car, rather than being, as in the case of cyclecars, economic compromises evolved from less related forms.

The medium size of light car instituted what was then called the 'lower middle class' form of motoring, and was related to and influenced by the quickening of social development which has already been noted in connection with the development of the cyclecar. Light, handy and practical designs of this kind, which weighed from 10 to 13 cwt., and which could cover 35 to 40 miles in the hour and the same distances on a gallon of fuel with comfort and reliability, became increasingly useful for such duties as tenders to large cars, town or country runabouts for doctors and professional men, and family vehicles for both long and short journeys. In addition, models fitted with 5 cwt. van bodies were beginning to be used by salesmen and for commercial delivery purposes. These medium-size light cars cost between £175 and £225.

One of the most rational and successful of this type was produced at Oxford by William R. Morris, who had built cycles and later motor cycles before he embarked upon his life work as a motor car manufacturer. The first Morris-Oxford light car appeared late in 1912, and was remarkable for its sound and robust design; it formed the basis for the classic Morris Cowley car, which was first made in 1915, and produced in large numbers during the 1920's. This prototype of 1912 was essentially a light motor car, without in any way entering the field of the cyclecar; it was, moreover, constructed with a thoroughness and care that was then given to the larger and higher priced cars. It weighed 12½ cwt. and was capable of a maximum speed of 55 m.p.h., and of covering 50 miles on a gallon of fuel. By the end of 1914, some 40 of these cars were being produced each week and retailed at a price of £175.

So progressive and typical of the best type of small light car was the Morris-Oxford (Plate 11) of this period, that a somewhat detailed description of it is warranted to indicate its importance in relation to later development. The chassis frame was of pressed-steel girder construction, mounted on semi-elliptic springs in front, and on three-quarter elliptic springs in rear. The drive to the live worm-gear rear axle was by an enclosed propeller shaft. Both hand- and foot-operated brakes were of the internal-expanding type incorporated in the rear axle drums. The engine, multi-plate clutch and sliding-pinion type of 3-speed and reverse gearbox were of unit construction; the whole unit was supported within the chassis upon a simple three-point suspension. A light yet well designed and constructed two-seat body, with hood and windscreen, was blended with the bonnet and a rounded radiator. The steering was of the worm-gear type, the column being well raked to provide a comfortable driving position. The detachable Sankey pressed-steel wheels were fitted with 700 mm. by 80 mm. beaded-edge tyres, and a spare wheel was included in the specification. One of the improved 1914 models included a dynamo-lighting system.

The 1018 c.c. capacity (60 mm. by 90 mm.) White and Poppe four-cylinder monobloc water-cooled engine (Plate 13), with inlet and exhaust valves arranged in T-head form and a stiff crankshaft carried in three bearings, was of robust and straightforward design. Detachable cover plates enclosed the valve stems, springs and tappets; lubrication was effected by the flywheel dipping into a wet sump and dispersing the oil to various catch pits, whence it drained to the moving parts. Ignition was by means of a Bosch high-tension magneto, and mixture was supplied by a White and Poppe carburettor.

In this period should also be noted the appearance of the prototype Morris Cowley design of 1495 c.c. (69 mm. by 100 mm.), which was put into large and sustained production from 1919 to the early 1930's in substantially the same form. It was recognised during its prototype trials in 1916 as a 'car of superlative merit'[1] for its period. It is interesting to note that its logical design and sturdy construction, together with its economy and excellent road performance and driving characteristics, were immediately recognised from the prototype some four years before it appeared in quantity production and was given general acclaim.

Another design of this period, which had evolved from earlier designs, was the 10 h.p. Austin four-cylinder car of 1911. It represented a form that was then passing rather than, as in the case of the Morris-Oxford, a new one that was in process of evolution. It is of interest, however, in showing the ancestry of later Austin light cars. Another sound although less progressive British design was the four-cylinder version of the Perry car produced in 1914 which was the ancestor of the Bean design of 1919. With a standard specification, and an engine of 1244 c.c. capacity, it was, like the earlier twin-cylinder model, a sound example of current light car design and construction.

The first A.C. light car, produced in 1913 and fitted with a 1094 c.c. Fivet four-cylinder water-cooled engine, was designed by J. Weller to be light and fast. The car weighed 10 cwt. and had a top speed of 45 m.p.h. It also had the unusual features of a 3-speed gearbox integral with the rear axle, and a disc brake on the propeller shaft.

Other important British designs of this general type at this time included the Singer, Standard, Lagonda, Riley, Calthorpe, Deemster, Swift, Stellite, J.B.S., Marshall-Arter, Alldays, Marlborough, Enfield and Day-Leeds, as well as several others of lesser merit. The majority of these designs were generally of the Morris layout already described, but with detail variations intended to provide advantages.

Some of these features, however, merely added complication and detracted from reliability, in proportion as they departed from the robust and logical simplicity of the general light car prototype formula which by 1914 was well established. For instance, the gearbox incorporated in the back axle with the differential unit, as used by Singer, A.C., Marshall-Arter and Stellite, while being more compact than the separate gearbox, added considerably to the unsprung weight of the rear axle; in addition, the flexing of the gear controls tended to upset selection adjustment and, in extreme cases, to engage two gears at once. Other features were sounder, such as the arrangement of inlet valves over exhaust valves and the operation of them by push rods and rockers, which was adopted in such designs as the Lagonda and Stellite to improve volumetric efficiency by increasing the effective size of the valves. The Swift, Perry and Autocrat designs used the separately-mounted gearbox, an arrangement which was then in favour with larger cars.

Unorthodox examples of medium-sized light cars with four-cylinder engines, some of which even employed cyclecar features, such as friction drive, included the Pilot and Cumbria designs.

[1] *The Light Car and Cyclecar*; 18 September, 1916. pp. 385–388.

In France, the pioneer firms of De Dion-Bouton, Renault, Clément and Charron produced good examples of this progressive form of medium light car. In addition, certain other firms which later established reputations in the light car field also appeared at this time, such as the Mathis, Nardini, Corre-la Licorne, Buchet and Averies designs. One of the most elaborate of these designs was the 1914 1182 c.c. De Dion-Bouton, which was soundly constructed on advanced orthodox lines, with a neat unit-construction four-cylinder engine and gearbox. This car, however, weighed about 15 cwt., and, fully laden with four people, its fuel consumption was little better than 30 m.p.g.; it compared unfavourably, in spite of its pedigree, with such advanced newcomers as the Morris-Oxford. The 1206 c.c. Renault and the 1049 c.c. Charronette, both distinguished by the rounded form of bonnet and the radiator placed behind the engine were good examples of orthodox French practice. The Clément Bayard car had a 1131 c.c. capacity engine designed in accordance with the policy, then in favour for larger cars, of using a long stroke, namely 100 mm., with a bore of 60 mm. It was comparatively light, 10 cwt., and of advanced orthodox design; it was one of the more important forerunners of the efficient French light cars of the 1920's. The Charles Fournier design, fitted with a 1130 c.c. (60 mm. by 100 mm.) Buchet four-cylinder engine, was equipped with friction drive.

In addition to the Mathis car, there were also produced in Germany at this time other designs of merit, such as the 1163 c.c. N.S.U., which was a good example of the advanced type of light car of the Morris variety. The 1058 c.c. Mathis 'Babylette' was produced at Strasbourg, and the successful Mathis light cars which were subsequently produced, under French nationality after 1918, proceeded from this example of 1913. The 1140 c.c. Wanderer (Plate 13) was a well-designed example with overhead inlet-valves. The Püch light car was one of the best examples from Austria.

The Apollo type B had a 1030 c.c. (60 mm. by 92 mm.) engine which developed 12 h.p. at 2400 r.p.m. and had overhead valves and pressure lubrication. Engine and gearbox were in one unit. The 12 h.p. Wanderer had overhead inlet and side exhaust valves.

This medium class of light car was also given some attention in the U.S.A., and among the few designs produced was the friction-driven Ajax.

LIGHT CARS: to 1500 c.c.

A considerable number of light car designs, in which full advantage was taken of the maximum limit of light car engine capacity of 1500 c.c., appeared before the end of 1914. This tendency is comprehensible when it is remembered that the designs of this size were nearer to the medium size car of that time, and the large light car could be conveniently evolved by scaling-down the larger prototypes. This policy resulted, in the majority of cases, in the production of designs which were not very different in size, weight and characteristics from the accepted practice of the motor car proper, and the distinction, so far as it went, became less and less real as the specific output of the 1500 c.c. engine was increased. This general tendency continued so

54

that by mid-century a car of this size had in fact, if not by definition, ceased to be a light car.

The details of the designs of this largest category which appeared before the end of 1914 are nevertheless worth considering as light cars, not only because they were created under the limits of the A.C.U. light car definition of 1912, but also because some remarkable and original designs were produced, the immediate successors of which had an important influence on later design during the 1920's. As may be expected, this largest category of light car included a wider variety of detail design than was economically possible with the simpler and cheaper category, with in general, side-valve engines limited to 1250 c.c. capacity.

The high performance and reliability of these early voiturette engines were of particular significance, and perhaps the real development of the light car proper and its power unit can be dated from the first few of the Coupe des Voiturettes and the Grand Prix des Voiturettes Races. A contemporary comment in the *Autocar* of the 14th May, 1910, emphasised the importance which the small car was now assuming: 'There is no longer the same demand for powerful and costly touring cars, for these have given way to the lighter class of vehicle, which fully satisfies requirements in speed and comfort and is, besides, much more economical'.

What may be considered the more orthodox examples of this so-called 10–12 h.p. class included such side-valve engine designs as the 1593 c.c. Humber, 1357 c.c. Hillman, 1456 c.c. Calcott, 1327 c.c. A.C. (Plate 12), 1313 c.c. Belsize, 1496 c.c. Chater-Lea, 1496 c.c. Phoenix and 1453 c.c. Vulcan. Among these should also be mentioned the 1616 c.c. Austin which, although it was of somewhat greater capacity than that set by the light car limitation, was nevertheless the forerunner of the notable Austin 10's and 12's of the following two decades. Generally, these cars weighed about 15 to 18 cwt., and employed the orthodox layout of a four-cylinder side-valve, water-cooled engine, integral or separately mounted 3- or 4-speed gearbox, shaft drive by bevel or worm gear to a differential rear axle, with internal-expanding brakes on the rear wheels and a separate transmission brake. Additions which made for greater convenience of use such as dynamo lighting, engine starter, electric horn, speedometer, watch and spare tyre rim or detachable wheel were beginning to be added as optional extras, although these were not yet all included in car specifications as standard items. The engines were generally of robust and sound design, with three-bearing crankshafts, aluminium-alloy crankcases, monobloc cylinder castings with fixed heads and detachable valve caps, gear or chain-driven camshafts, magneto ignition, and efficient induction system, which was sometimes equipped with a vaporising hot-spot, and one of the now well-developed carburettors which provided reliable and economical operation. The side-valves were now generally arranged in L-head fashion.

There were several examples of this class of light car in Europe and a few in the U.S.A., a proportion of which followed generally the orthodox design and layout already indicated. In some other foreign designs, however there were manifested more originality and versatility; the technical advances so gained helped to lay the basis of the high-performance sports-touring type of car which began to be produced and used in the 1920's.

In France, there were the 1327 c.c. Aries, 1357 c.c. Clément-Bayard, 1539 c.c. Berliet, 1527 c.c. Brasier, 1244 c.c. Charron, 1460 c.c. Delage, 1460 c.c. Sizaire-Naudin, 1357 c.c. Sirron and 1505 c.c. Vermorel. In Germany, there were the 1500 c.c. N.A.G., 1301 c.c. Opel, 1295 c.c. Sperberette 1300 c.c. Brennabor and 1300 c.c. Adler. In Belgium, there was the 1244 c.c. F.N., and in Italy, the 1244 c.c. Bianchi. In the U.S.A., where engine capacities were already comparatively large, there was in particular the 1438 c.c. Saxon (Plate 12), which was, perhaps, the most successful and representative American light car of this period, and a few others such as the Carnation, Grant and Little Princess. In general, American four-cylinder light cars tended to have large capacity engines, such as the 2300 c.c. Briscoe, but they also had the advantages of being exceptionally light and cheap.

Although these side-valve engined designs in general differed little in detail, they constituted collectively a sound basis which contributed to the future growth of the light car. It was also of significance that several of the pioneer motor car firms were now considering the commercial and technical possibilities of the light car.

In addition to the side-valve engine formula which the majority of the larger light car designs followed, there also appeared during this early stage of development a tendency among a few designers towards additional complexity and experimental novelty for the purpose of increasing specific outputs.

The chief of these innovators was Ettore Bugatti, who produced his first light car in 1907, and soon after established his factory at Molsheim in Alsace. The first important success of the Bugatti light car was in the 1911 Grand Prix de France race at Le Mans, when a small car weighing only 6 cwt. and equipped with a 1456 c.c. (65 mm. by 110 mm.) sixteen-valve overhead-camshaft engine, gained first place at an average speed of 46 m.p.h. From this prototype was developed the 1327 c.c. (65 mm. by 100 mm.), Types 13, 15 and 17 (Plates 12 and 13) light car of 1914 which, apart from a high performance, also had the advanced characteristics of a 4-speed and reverse gearbox with a remote-control gate-change, multiple-disc clutch, large-diameter internal-expanding brakes and inverted quarter-elliptic leaf-springs at the rear which were claimed to eliminate body-roll. The large-diameter valves were operated by high-lift cams, and the whole valve-operating mechanism was enclosed and pressure-lubricated by a mechanical oil pump. General engine lubrication was effected by a separate high-pressure pump.

The Type 22 of 1453 c.c. capacity (68 mm. by 100 mm.) appeared in proto-type in 1913; the engine had four valves per cylinder. This advanced and elaborate design was the forerunner of a series of later Bugatti light cars which were notable for their progressive and original technical characteristics blended with an individual artistry of design. These inherent qualities were typified by the combined grace and effectiveness of the characteristic heart-shaped Bugatti radiator.

The German M.A.F. design of 1913 was fitted with a 1310 c.c. (68 mm. by 90 mm.) four-cylinder engine, which was air cooled by means of ducts and a forced draught. The Stellite and Wanderer engines (Plate 13) had overhead inlet valves.

One of the most elaborate and unusual designs was the Eagle light car, made in 1914 in the U.S.A. This was equipped with a Macomber five-cylinder swash-plate rotary air-cooled engine of 1250 c.c. capacity (65 mm. by 76 mm.).

An early example of a light car equipped as standard with electric lighting and starting systems was the Salvador made in 1914 in the U.S.A. This was a normal reflection of large car practice, when such advanced equipment was becoming general practice, particularly in the U.S.A. where electric lighting and in particular starting originated.

TWO-STROKE ENGINES

Two-stroke cycle engines were not used in production for the largest type of light car, and those examples which did appear were of the experimental category such as the twin-piston Trojan and Lucas Duplex designs, the Record stepped-piston and piston-valve design, and the simpler Low crank-case-compression three-cylinder design. Of all these, only the Trojan of 1910 proved to be the forerunner of a future considerable individual development and production which began in 1922.

ACCESSORIES AND ANCILLARIES

By the beginning of 1914, there was an increasing tendency to elaborate the light car, as distinct from the cyclecar, by the addition of numerous accessories for the purpose of making it more flexible in operation and convenient in use. Such additions included efficient lighting systems, mechanical and electrical engine starters, detachable wheels, coupé and saloon bodies, side curtains for use with folding hoods, and similar provisions which even large cars had only begun to adopt a few years before. This process of refinement helped to popularise the light car more rapidly, and provide it with the essentials of comfort and convenience required by motor cars of this class. This trend was, however, only the initiation of such fittings and appliances and some of the more advanced items were as yet employed on relatively few light cars and then only as special items. New accessories such as starting and lighting electrical equipment were comparatively heavy, cumbersome, and not too efficient; but they did initiate refinements which became sufficiently developed for general use by the 1920's.

Engine Accessories

Engine ignition was supplied almost wholly by the now thoroughly developed and dependable high-tension magneto, and the majority of these instruments were supplied by German manufacturers such as Bosch, Eisemann and U.H. British types included the C.A.V., B.T.H., E.I.C., and Thomson-Bennett designs. The Splitdorf, Berling and Dixie magnetos were perhaps the best known examples developed in the U.S.A. at this time.

This was an important period in the development of the automobile carburettor because of the appearance of a number of new and progressive types, which not only effectively replaced the older and less efficient forms, but also served as the prototypes from which the modern carburettor has since been developed. Orthodox automatic instruments, employing main, compensator and slow-running jets were represented by the Claudel, Zenith and Solex designs. The S.U. design used an induction vacuum-operated piston which controlled a tapered needle for the purpose of varying automatically the mixture strength with the throttle opening. The Smith 4-jet and the Binks 3-jet designs used a series of jets which came progressively into action to maintain the correct mixture strength as the throttle was opened. The Polyrhoë instrument had a multiple series of jets, formed by slits in brass strips, which came into action progressively.

The inconvenience of swinging the engine by hand for starting had, by 1910, introduced various mechanical and electrical appliances for performing this function without trouble to the user of the car. Engine starters commended themselves in particular to such users as doctors and women drivers. By 1913, some of these systems were tentatively applied in smaller forms to the light car, but although there were a number of types available at this period, their use was the exception rather than the rule.

A few car designs incorporated hand or foot-operated mechanical starters. The Brennabor unit consisted of a hand-operated rack-and-pinion assembly incorporated in the rear of the gearbox. The Horstmann had a foot-operated thrust nut which operated on a robust quick-thread formed in the drive shaft between engine and gearbox. The F.N. foot-operated starter engaged directly with pegs on the flywheel. The Jackson device used a foot-operated rack-and-pinion mechanism. The F. and G. design employed a free-wheel unit incorporating wedging rollers by means of which the engine could be rotated. The Deemster hand starter operated a quadrant in the gearbox, which engaged directly with the layshaft. The Herzmark hand starter consisted of a ratchet ring mounted on the flywheel which was operated by means of pawls.

Electric-starting systems for light cars included a number of primitive yet promising arrangements. The Lucas unit consisted of a four-pole motor with a friction pulley by means of which the flywheel was rotated through an epicyclic reduction gear. The Brolt starter was more advanced and used a pinion carried on a quick-thread shaft, which automatically meshed with a ring of teeth on the flywheel. The Rushmore starter achieved the same result of meshing by arranging for the armature and shaft to slide longitudinally. Another method employed a simple friction-wheel which could be brought directly into contact with the flywheel periphery.

Body and Chassis Accessories

Oil lamps survived until 1920 as side and tail-lamps for both light cars and cyclecars, and were generally provided in sets of miniature design by such manufacturers as Lucas, Powell and Hanmer, F.R.S. and Miller. Illumination of the road for extended night travel, as was now quite practical, required a more powerful source of light, which was generally provided by acetylene lamps supplied from a gas generator of from a dissolved-acetylene cylinder. Acetylene lamps usually used the open-flame 'bats-wing' burner which, because of its large size of flame, did not provide an ideal light source for use with the Mangin mirror reflector. A more efficient method was provided by the Fallolite incandescent pastille, by means of which the light intensity was increased several times. The Low pressure generator used a special lining which permitted the gas to be stored at a pressure of 30 p.s.i.

Simple electric-lighting systems employing an accumulator, which required to be charged periodically from exterior sources, were used to some extent as an alternative to the acetylene system, but this form was never considered really convenient. Electric-lighting sets, employing an engine-driven generator for battery-charging in conjunction with a cut-out, were developed from the larger car systems, which had appeared first about 1910. These were produced by such makers as C.A.V., Rotax-Leitner, Brolt, Bosch, Lucas, S. Smith and F.R.S. The generally rather large and heavy generator was usually driven by belt and pulley; but in the case of the Kemco unit, the generator was incorporated compactly in the radiator fan assembly. The switch-box and fuse panel was mounted as a separate unit on the dashboard. At 6 to 8 volts, outputs were from 40 to 60 watts, and headlamps, sidelamps and tail lamps, and even a dash light and electric horn were included in the equipment. A complete electric-lighting set for addition to a light car cost about £16.

Brakes consisted for the most part of a foot-operated brake on the transmission shaft behind the gearbox, and two hand-operated brakes, of either the internal-expanding or external-contracting varieties, on the rear wheel hubs. More advanced designs such as the Morris-Oxford and the Perry employed two separate sets of internal-expanding brakes incorporated in wide brake drums on the rear wheel hubs. Each set of brakes was operated respectively by a foot pedal and hand lever. The more efficient and better protected internal-expanding type of brake was, by 1914, largely replacing the external-contracting type. The A.C. light car had a disc brake acting on the propeller shaft in rear of the differential gear.

Although fixed wheels, of either the wooden-spoked or wire types, were generally used before 1914, detachable wheels of the wire Rudge-Whitworth and Riley types or the pressed-steel Sankey artillery type, were also being fitted as standard to some of the more advanced light cars.

Improved riding comfort was provided by the early adoption of spring buffers such as the Hobson, shock absorbers such as the Houdaille and J.M., or snubbers such as the Gabriel, by means of which the action of the road springs was controlled to some extent, and road shocks absorbed and consequently minimised. The poor condition of some roads, as well as the current small-section high-pressure tyres in common use about 1914, made devices of this sort desirable if not essential.

Apart from the general use of the folding hood and the windscreen, as well as the partial adoption of side screens for weather protection, the totally-enclosed two-seat coupé and four-seat types of body were also being tentatively used to some extent, particularly by doctors and professional men who required to use their light cars continually and in all weathers.

Cyclecars: 1919-1939

Although the true miniature car, as exemplified by such designs as the Austin Seven, was a production reality by 1923, the earlier and more primitive cyclecar continued to evolve in both its simple and more elaborate forms until about 1935. After this, the improved and highly practical forms of light car including, in particular, the miniature or ultra-light car, almost completely replaced it and, as a type, it virtually disappeared. Of all the several basic types and the great numbers of individual designs of cyclecar which had appeared since the beginning of the movement in 1910, only two continued until the mid-century in full commercial production and popular use: the Morgan three-wheeled and the Jowett four-wheeled designs.

This decline of the cyclecar was due to inherent deficiencies of this form of car, which were engendered by the hybrid nature of its constitution which rendered it incapable of achieving full development within the limitations of its period. The technical advances of the next thirty years substantially removed these limitations, and in the form of the minicar of 1950 and later the basic conception of the cyclecar was more fully achieved than had been possible before 1930.

Nevertheless, this period of the 1920's was active in the production of various types of new cyclecars, as well as improved versions of some of the more important designs which had appeared before 1915. These later designs were efficient and practical within the essential limitations of their formula, and some of them served as the basis for more elaborate designs which could be considered to be true light cars. The chief general tendency in this development was the departure from motorcycle standards and the approach to motor car standards, as was now proved possible with the smallest cars having relatively elaborate specifications.

This later cyclecar development proceeded in both the three-wheeled and four-wheeled forms; moreover, these new models provided increased passenger-carrying capacity by the use of bodies having up to four seats. The majority of them used four-stroke engines, either air or water-cooled, and of from one to four cylinders. There was also an increased interest in the possibilities of the simple two-stroke engine and a number of two-stroke engined cyclecars of varying types appeared. The three-wheeled type continued to progress in a variety of makes, which established it as the strongest competitor to the successful ultra-light car. In addition, the three-wheeler was generally more economical in first cost and road tax, and these factors during this period helped to offset the intrinsic inadequacies of the type. Four-wheeled cyclecars, on the other hand, competed more directly with the miniature and medium light car forms, and they were therefore the first to disappear.

The three-wheeled chain-driven cyclecar, of the general type pioneered by H. F. S. Morgan, was adopted by a number of manufacturers both in this country and on the Continent. Apart from the simplest designs with single-cylinder engines, the three-wheeler tended to become larger and heavier;

it was equipped with more powerful multi-cylinder engines and provided with better coachwork, weather protection, brakes and transmission. With the major exception of the Morgan and, later, the front wheel-driven B.S.A. three-wheeler, it reached the peak of its development by 1930. The simpler types of cyclecar, of both the three- and four-wheeled varieties, remained vehicles essentially for the young and adventurous in this country, but they continued to serve more utilitarian purposes on the Continent where economy was still of the first importance.

The heavier and more elaborate four-wheeled cyclecars of this period tended more and more to conform to conventional motor car practice, with comfortable bodies, unit-construction gearboxes, shaft drive and live rear axles. The eventual and logical adoption of four-cylinder engines in four-wheeled chassis for many of these designs merged them finally with the light car class.

These improved cyclecars, besides being used for touring and racing, still further demonstrated their increasing capabilities by successfully competing in various long distance trials such as the English and Scottish Six Days, the London–Land's End and the London–Edinburgh Trials, as well as in various Continental events.

MONOCARS

The simplest forms of cyclecar which had appeared before 1915, consisting of the essentials of body, wheels, engine and transmission, survived for a short while after 1918 because of the appeal which economy, simplicity and to some extent performance made to an impoverished yet adventurous younger generation of users. Chief among the few existing designs was still the four-wheeled Carden monocar with its vee-twin air-cooled J.A.P. engine, placed in rear, which drove the rear wheels through a chain and a motorcycle-type gearbox equipped with a kick-starter. Later models were arranged with two seats in tandem and alternatively side-by-side, but in general this simple type was produced with only one seat. The Tamplin was somewhat more complex, having a vee-twin air-cooled engine in front which drove the rear wheels through a primary chain and countershaft and two secondary belts, generally in the manner of the earlier Bedelia arrangement. An alternative model had a second seat arranged in tandem.

Of greater simplicity still was the Grahame-White 'Buckboard' which was produced for a short while soon after 1918. This vehicle was essentially a platform mounted on four wheels, which was driven by a 350 c.c. Precision air-cooled two-stroke engine; a bucket seat was provided for the driver and an abbreviated bonnet enclosed the engine. It was at first rather in the nature of a novelty, and foreshadowed the motor-scooter or monocar rather than the miniature car, but in a later model it was developed into a two-seat runabout. Various other economical arrangements were tried during this period to provide the practical alternative to the motorcycle, including such designs as the Automette, Xtra, Euston and G.B. three-wheelers which were virtually sidecar adaptations driven by 350 c.c. single-cylinder two-stroke engines. Variants of this latter type were now also beginning to be used in considerable numbers both here and on the Continent as small delivery vans. This simple form of commercial vehicle was quite successful and continued to be used in much the same form for many years. The A.C. Autocarrier single-cylinder delivery vehicle, although no longer produced, continued to be used during this period. French examples of this type included the Monitor.

One of the first 'city runabouts', intended to provide light economical transport for one or two persons in congested traffic conditions, was the Scootacar of 1933. A light tubular chassis, mounted on four wheels without springing, was powered by a 98 c.c. Villiers Midget two-stroke engine mounted in unit with the back axle; the drive was through a centrifugal clutch and chain. The clutch operated automatically at 800 r.p.m. Although little more than a toy at this time, a substantial number were built and used for sport, town work and even light goods transportation. Later and larger models employed a larger $2\frac{1}{2}$ h.p. Villiers engine and a three-speed and reverse gearbox which incorporated a kick-starter. One of the first 1 h.p. ungeared models was restored and driven round the world in 1966 at an average speed of 10 m.p.h. The Scootacar foreshadowed the tendency to adopt 'city runabouts' in the congested traffic conditions of the 1960's.

THREE-WHEELED CYCLECARS

A considerable variety of three-wheeled cyclecars of advanced features appeared after 1918 which included four-seat family touring models of the greatest utility and economy, as well as two-seat sporting models and single-seat racers. Basically, these vehicles were two-seaters with some small provision for the carrying of luggage, but in a few cases alternative bodies were provided incorporating three and even four seats. A few compact coupé and saloon bodies were also produced for the purpose of greater comfort and weather protection but, in spite of these elaborations, the three-wheeled cyclecar remained in the category to which it was best suited, namely, the two-seat open sports vehicle of light weight and comparatively high performance.

The engines remained of the same average capacity, namely, about one litre; they were, however, of increased specific outputs, and overhead-valve units were more frequently adopted. These were usually vee twin-cylinder units, either air or water-cooled, with side-valves, push-rod operated overhead valves, and, in a few cases, overhead camshaft-operated valves. A few horizontally-opposed twin-cylinder engines were also used and, later in the 1920's, still greater flexibility and a hitherto unattained refinement of operation were obtained by the use of small four-cylinder water-cooled engines of about one litre capacity. The average fuel consumption of these 8–10 h.p. three-wheeled vehicles was about 50 m.p.g. at cruising speeds of 50 m.p.h. Later developments included such advances as the drive being applied to the two front wheels, as in the case of the B.S.A. three-wheeler. This was an improvement on the more usual method of driving the single rear wheel, although the latter system remained the more generally used for reasons of economy in production costs.

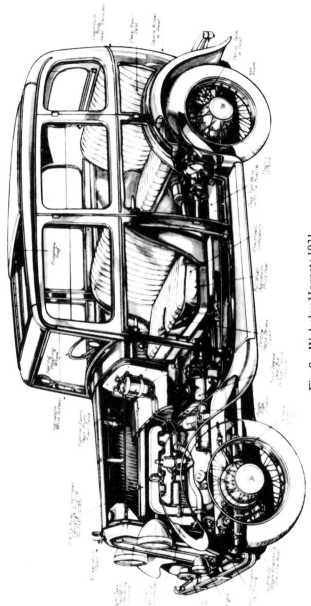

Fig. 9   Wolseley Hornet: 1931

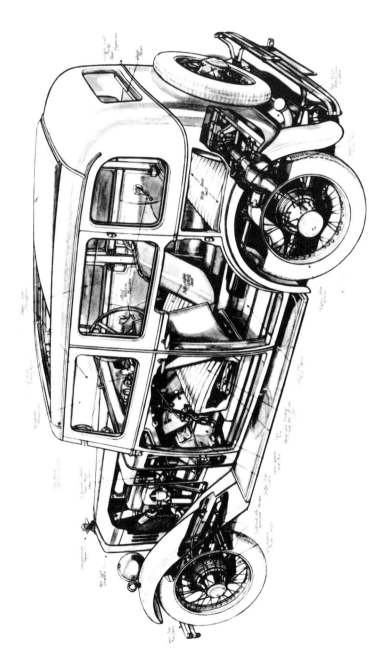

Fig. 10   Morris: 1931

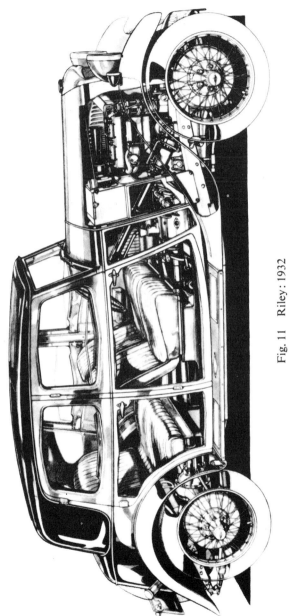

Fig. 11   Riley: 1932

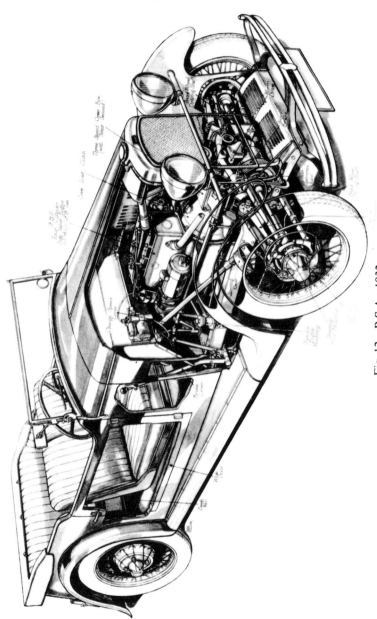

Fig. 12 B.S.A.: 1932

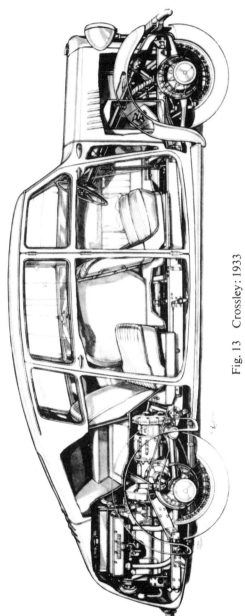

Fig. 13   Crossley: 1933

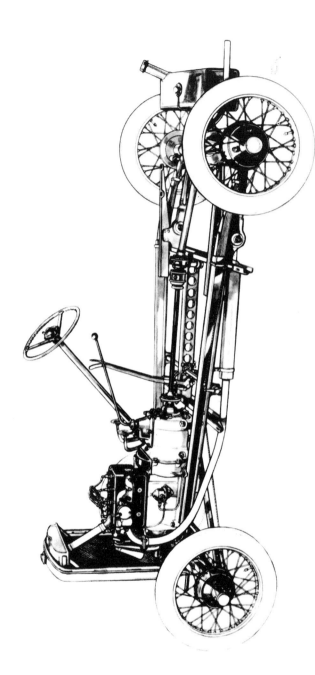

Fig. 14   Austin chassis: 1934

Fig. 15 Mercedes chassis: 1934

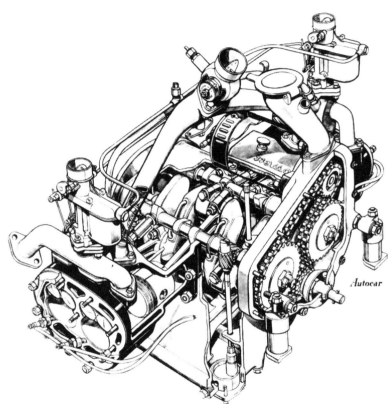

Fig. 16   Jowett engine: 1935

The Morgan three-wheeler (Plate 14), while retaining its original basic layout, began by 1925 to incorporate various improvements. Different models such as the Family four-seater, the Grand-Prix and the Aero were in normal production with air- or water-cooled J.A.P., Anzani, M.A.G., Matchless or Blackburne vee twin-cylinder engines. Special racing models were also produced on the same general lines, but employing overhead camshaft vee twin-cylinder engines, which established many world records and won many races. The weight of 5½-cwt. made the Morgan the lightest 8–10 h.p. three-wheeler in production. The transmission still consisted of a leather-faced cone clutch, primary shaft, a 2-speed dog-clutch type of gearbox with ratios 4½ and 8 to 1, and two final chains to the rear wheel. The steering was direct, and independent hand and foot brakes of the external-contracting type acted ln the rear-wheel hub.

The detail improvements now incorporated in the later Morgan design comprised such items as electric lighting and even electric starting, front hand starter, front-wheel brakes, shock absorbers, steering reduction gear and a reverse gear. Some of these features were from time to time added to the official specification either as standard or as optional additions, and some were produced as proprietary accessories; but, in spite of this modernisation procedure, the Morgan three-wheeled cyclecar up to about 1930 continued to remain in essence the same as when it was first produced.

A 3-speed gearbox in place of the 2-speed dog-clutch gear and double driving chains and a single-plate dry clutch in place of the leather-lined cone-clutch, were adopted in 1932. The basic model was elaborated still further in 1933 by the adoption of 8 or 10 h.p. four-cylinder water-cooled Ford engines which provided the new models with a smoothness of operation that made the economy of the Morgan still further appreciated. In this model, a pressed-steel frame chassis was adopted in place of the former tubular frame.

Of the later forms of three-wheeler cyclecars, the B.S.A. and the Raleigh were the most important, not only because they were commercially successful but also because they embodied progressive ideas which brought the three-wheeled cyclecar in its original forms to its ultimate development. The B.S.A. three-wheeler was introduced in 1932; it employed the unusual feature of front-wheel drive through two De Dion-Bouton type flexibility-mounted half-shafts to the front wheels. A 1021 c.c. vee twin-cylinder air-cooled engine was mounted in front of a simple channel-section chassis which was formed in rear with a large-diameter central tube; the single rear wheel was mounted on a hinged arm having as an extension a leaf spring which was enclosed within the central chassis tube. In 1933, following the trend towards smoother and more comfortable operation, the B.S.A. cyclecar was produced with a 1075 c.c. four-cylinder water-cooled engine; the details of the general layout were otherwise substantially unchanged.

The Raleigh cyclecar, although it appeared as a family four-seater model, was also largely used as a commercial delivery runabout. It was substantially a normal cyclecar, having a 742 c.c. vee twin-cylinder air-cooled engine and gearbox unit which drove through a cardan shaft to a bevel and pinion rear axle. The single front wheel was centrally placed and was mounted in conventional motorcycle type spring forks; steering was effected by means of a wheel.

Apart from the miniature three-wheeled monocars, mostly fitted with small two-stroke engines, there was a slightly larger class fitted with single-cylinder four-stroke engines of up to 500 c.c. capacity, which conformed broadly to the Morgan layout. These included such designs as the Royal Ruby and the J.M.B., and although their bodywork and external appearance were of advanced cyclecar form, engines, gearboxes and transmissions consisted generally of proprietary motorcycle items. The usual means of starting the engines of these machines was by an adaptation of the normal motorcycle type of kick-starter incorporated with the gearboxes.

The economic depression of the early 1930's provided the smaller type of cyclecar with a further lease of life, particularly in Germany. This trend was aided by the continuing improvement in engine efficiency and specific power output, so that now relatively small-capacity engines were used to propel vehicles of lighter construction and more streamlined bodies. These designs significantly foreshadowed the trend of development of the Continental mini-car after 1945.

The German Hercules three-wheeler had a streamlined coupé body, a 200 c.c. two-stroke engine and a 4-speed and reverse gearbox. The 250 c.c. Goliath single front-wheel steering cyclecar was produced in five models, varying from an open roadster to a sunshine saloon. The Tamag Zepp was a front-wheel driven cyclecar, to which was fitted a 600 c.c. D.K.W. two-stroke engine. In France, the Sandford concern adopted the same progressive policy and in 1935 produced a small high-performance three-wheeled cyclecar, having a 950 c.c. air-cooled horizontally-opposed engine which was capable of producing 26 h.p. at 3800 r.p.m. The weight of this car was under $6\frac{1}{2}$ cwt.

FOUR-WHEELED CYCLECARS

The decade of the 1920's was a period of development and transition, in which the earlier and simpler types of cyclecar tended in general to approach and in some cases to merge with, the heavier and more complex light car formula. There were consequently few four-wheeled cyclecars worthy of the name at this time which retained the motorcycle-type engine units, chain transmission and gearboxes. Although these new designs on the whole tended to retain the simplicity of the two-cylinder engine unit, yet they soon began to be equipped with unit-construction gearboxes, universally-jointed cardans shafts and live differential axles; at the same time, chassis and bodywork also became larger and more comfortable and fittings in general more elaborate. Some of these later offshoots of the cyclecar formula approached, by 1925, so near to the light car formula that, except for their two-cylinder engines, they hardly came under the original cyclecar definition. So vigorous was the four-cylinder light car development at this time, however, that it is convenient to classify these later two-cylinder engined designs as cyclecars. After 1925, the new cyclecar types became less numerous, because they were being effectively replaced by the four-cylinder light car in all capacities from 750 c.c. to 1500 c.c., and the cyclecar had to depend more than ever on its essential merits of simplicity, lightness and economy. The quality of economy, in particular, gave it continued life in new and smaller forms during the difficult period of the early 1930's.

An industrial aspect of some note of the early 1920's was the entry into the motoring or motorcycling spheres of a few aeronautical firms which, during the first world war, were fully occupied with aeroplane production, but which afterwards had to find other work for their factories. Among such names were the Sopwith, the A. V. Roe and the French Blériot concerns the latter of which, in 1920, produced the Blériot Whippet. This was a light two-seater four-wheeled cyclecar, which weighed under 6 cwt. and mounted a 998 c.c. Blackburne air-cooled vee-twin cylinder engine. A primary chain-drive connected the engine with a countershaft, which incorporated a Zenith Gradua variable-pulley gear, used for some years with Zenith motorcycles the final drive was by means of a vee belt to a fixed pulley mounted on the rear axle. The gear ratio was raised by means of an interconnecting linkage which brought the halves of the countershaft pulley together and thus increased its effective diameter, and simultaneously moved the rear axle forward to maintain correct belt tension; the opposite procedure lowered the gear ratio. The Whippet was a practical cyclecar for its period and, in spite of its high price of £250 during this post-war inflationary period, it achieved some popularity in spite of the excessive belt wear inherent with the use of the Gradua gear. A later model had a normal gearbox and shaft drive to a live rear axle.

The two original four-wheeled cyclecars, the Bedelia and the G.N., also progressed along the lines of their original designs until about 1925. The G.N., in particular, was much used for both sporting and touring purposes, and some eight different models were produced during the period 1919 to 1924, besides being built under licence by the Salmson Company of Paris, who produced about 3000 G.N. cars in two years. The standard model of 1920 (Plate 14) had the normal 1087 c.c. 90° vee-twin air-cooled engine, mounted in a strengthened chassis, which carried a much improved two-seat body; in addition, the multiple chain-gear system used four separate chains which provided three forward speeds and a reverse, an arrangement which was used for all but one of the remaining G.N. models. The Vitesse model had push-rod operated overhead valves and aluminium-alloy pistons; the Legere model was generally the same as the Standard model, but had a tuned engine fitted with aluminium-alloy pistons. The still later Vitesse model had an engine (Fig. 3) fitted with chain-driven overhead-camshafts, ball-and-roller main bearings and large inclined valves. The unit developed about 35 h.p. with a compression ratio of $5\frac{1}{2}$ to 1.

The special long distance racing Akela twin-cylinder engine of 1920 to 1921 had four valves in each cylinder operated by shaft-driven overhead camshafts, dual ignition and heavily finned bronze cylinder heads. This car, driven by H. R. Godfrey, won the first 200 miles race at Brooklands in the 1100 c.c.

class in 1921. The later Akela model was an improved version of the original of the same name, which had fully justified its ability to continue at full throttle for long periods. Geared at $3\frac{1}{4}$ to 1, these later Akela models were capable of nearly 100 m.p.h. The G.N. also performed with great success in competitions, particularly during 1921 when 112 firsts were gained at speed trials, and 28 gold medals were won in reliability trials.

The last two G.N. models, produced between 1923 and 1925, were both four-cylinder designs, thus departing from the two-cylinder policy which this firm had maintained since its foundation in 1910; moreover, the 1923 model with an 1100 c.c. overhead-camshaft engine had a normal gearbox and shaft and bevel drive to a solid rear axle. The last model, produced in 1925, was equipped with a 1500 c.c. Anzani four-cylinder engine, but reverted to the four-chain gear drive; this was the design which was the basis for the later Frazer-Nash cars.

The Bedelia design continued to be built in France in various improved models until 1925, after which, in company with most of the other original cyclecars of 1910, it gave place to new ideas and advanced designs.

Examples of the very simple four-wheeled cyclecar were also made in the early 1920's, such as the Gibbons and the Lecoy, which were fitted with proprietary single or twin-cylinder motorcycle engines, such as the J.A.P., Coventry-Victor, Precision and Blackburne units.

A somewhat more advanced series of four-wheeled cyclecars appeared after 1918, fitted with vee or horizontally-opposed twin-cylinder engines, which constituted an intermediate development between the cyclecar and the light car since they employed more of the chassis characteristics of the latter, while still retaining the simple two-cylinder engine unit of the former, as had the earlier Humberette and Swift designs of 1914. These new types had only about five years of commercial existence, yet their contribution to the evolution of the light car was not without importance.

The Crouch, fitted with a 1022 c.c. water-cooled vee twin-cylinder engine set across the chassis, which drove through a 3-speed and reverse gearbox and a final chain drive to a solid rear axle, was virtually a four-wheeled version of contemporary chain-driven three-wheeled cyclecars such as the Coventry Premier and Omega designs. Later models incorporated a positive shaft and bevel-gear drive to the rear axle. The 998 c.c. Rover 8 (Plate 14) and the 1198 c.c. A.B.C. designs of 1924 were still more advanced with air-cooled horizontally-opposed twin-cylinder engines, 3-speed and reverse gearboxes and shaft drive to live rear axles as used in normal car practice. Both these original and successful cars established individual reputations for the comparatively short period before they were eclipsed by the fully evolved type light car. The former was a light and handy runabout-tourer, and the latter was a sports car whose light, highly efficient overhead-valve engine was based upon the latest static air-cooled aero engine practice in which the designer, Granville Bradshaw, had been one of the pioneers.

Other examples of the advanced air-cooled cyclecar of the early 1920's were the 1080 c.c. B.S.A. and the overhead valve 998 c.c. Stoneleigh, built by Armstrong-Siddeley Ltd., both of which had 90° vee twin-cylinder engines, 3-speed gearboxes and shaft and gear drive to live axles. The Stoneleigh was a three seater car, having the unusual arrangement of a single centrally-positioned driver's seat in front and two seats behind.

Still more advanced designs appeared fitted with water-cooled horizontally-opposed engines which, in chassis detail and body design, approached almost to the current formula of the light car. The 938 c.c. 7 h.p. Wolseley, in particular, was perhaps the best example of this type; in addition, there was the latest model of the 815 c.c., later increased to 907 c.c., Jowett. The Ariel, a product of an established mororcycle firm, was less well known. There was also an improved version of the Douglas design equipped with a 1223 c.c. engine, which had a very complete specification.

Perhaps the most unorthodox and original of this type of later cyclecar was the Belsize-Bradshaw design, which was fitted with a 1289 c.c. (85 mm. by 114 mm.) oil-cooled vee twin-cylinder engine. In this design, the plain cylinder barrels were completely enclosed in the crankcase and only the detachable cylinder heads, which carried the push-rod operated overhead valves, were air-cooled. The finned crankcase sump carried a large volume of oil, 1½ gallons, which was pressure circulated in large quantity, so that the exterior as well as the interior of the cylinder barrels were continually washed in oil for cooling purposes. Air cooling had, however, by now become efficient enough to make this comparatively complicated system of cooling unnecessary, and relatively few of this design were made.

TWO-STROKE ENGINED CYCLECARS

During this period there was a vigorous prototype activity with the two-stroke engined cyclecar, a movement which had started in 1913 with a few interesting designs. In spite, however, of the many different forms evolved, few went into commercial production. The essential qualities of simplicity and smooth torque of the two-stroke engine were particularly attractive to the cyclecar designer. Inadequate materials, as well as lack of commercial development and use, with which the four-stroke engine was now well provided, prevented the majority of these new two-stroke designs from becoming technically reliable and commercially successful. The small-capacity single cylinder two-stroke engine, which had already had considerable development as a motorcycle unit and had reached an adequate stage of reliability, was used to some extent with the smallest cyclecars.

In spite of this failure to establish the two-stroke engine in production form as a suitable cyclecar engine, an event which did not happen until the 1930's and then on the Continent rather than in this country, the various two-stroke engined cyclecar designs of this period were of importance in showing the interest with which economical motoring was now being regarded. This was the result, on the one hand, of the stringent economic conditions created by the world war and, on the other hand, of the ever increasing use of the motor car by nearly all classes of users.

The simplest form of two-stroke engined cyclecars were the small three-wheelers already mentioned in this chapter, which were fitted with either single-cylinder air-cooled motorcycle engines of not more than 350 c.c. capacity, or twin-cylinder engines of about 500 c.c. capacity, arranged to drive a single rear or front wheel in the simplest manner through a gearbox and chain drive. The majority of such designs in this country used the now well-developed Villiers engines, and this type of vehicle found a convenient use, both here and on the Continent, as a light delivery van as well as a simple tourer and occasional runabout car. Among such designs were the Royal Ruby in this country; and the Hanissard, the 342 c.c. Nomad, the 350 c.c. front-wheel driven Villard, and the G.M. on the Continent. A few examples, such as the 200 c.c. Excelsior and 500 c.c. Claveau employed twin-cylinder engines; the 500 c.c. Villard used a four-cylinder duplex-piston engine, which drove the front wheel through a friction gear. The French Major, designed by M. Violet, used an engine fitted with a rotary inlet valve, from which high specific outputs were claimed.

A few more advanced designs, of either the three or four-wheeled categories, incorporated more complex engine units and methods of drive in the attempt to improve performance and so use the essential qualities of the two-stroke principle to the best mechanical and commercial advantage. The 808 c.c. German Grade was friction driven. The French Benjamin four-wheeled car employed a twin-cylinder vertical water-cooled unit in which the fresh-gas charging was effected by means of stepped or double-diameter pistons, as had formerly been used in the Côte design. The Sima-Violet was produced by M. Violet, who had made a successful debut in cyclecar design with the Violet-Bogey of 1913. This four-wheeled cyclecar mounted a 496 c.c. air-cooled horizontally-opposed engine between the front wheels, and the drive was taken through a 2-speed gearbox and cardan shaft to a worm gear in a fixed axle. This car was used by the designer himself with considerable success in various racing and trials events during the 1920's.

Some of the most interesting two-stroke designs of this period were produced in this country. J. V. Carden, the designer of the Carden monocar, turned his attention immediately after the war to the development of a very simple two-seat cyclecar to be sold for £100. The body was a light and simple shell mounted on four wheels, the front pair of which were independently sprung on coil springs. A 698 c.c. twin-cylinder air-cooled engine and a 2-speed gear and multiple-plate clutch were incorporated as a complete unit in the rear axle, thus concentrating all the mechanism at the rear and underneath the body. Although this arrangement was simple and compact, it had the disadvantage that the whole of the engine unit weight was unsprung and was thus exposed to vibration and road shocks. The engine could be started from the driver's seat by means of a hand-lever. The total weight of this two-seater car was only $3\frac{1}{2}$ cwt.

The Scott Sociable three-wheeler (Plate 7) was produced by A. A. Scott, who had already established a reputation for unorthodox but well engineered two-stroke motorcycles using twin-cylinder water-cooled engines. A similar engine of 578 c.c. capacity, incorporating a 3-speed gear and clutch unit, was mounted midway in a complex chassis constructed on a system of triangulated tubes. The engine drove the off rear wheel by means of a shaft and worm gear and the single front steering wheel, positioned on the off side, was mounted on a stub axle and steered by means of a hand wheel. This offset front wheel gave the vehicle an awkward appearance which no doubt helped to prevent this design from becoming popular. A two-seat body, with hood and windscreen, provided a certain degree of comfort and weather protection. This design had such embellishments as rotary inlet valves to improve volumetric and thermal efficiency, and a hand-starter by means of which the engine could be started from the driver's seat. The engine and drive unit was very accessible, being enclosed by a detachable panel in the off-side of the body. The Scott Sociable was designed in 1916, and contemporary opinion held that if it had been made as a four-wheeler and thus avoided the sales resistance due to its unorthodox appearance, it might have become the first family ultra-light car. As it was, in spite of excellent reliability, adequate performance and a low weight of 5½ cwt., relatively few of these cyclecars were made.

The Constantinesco cyclecar, which was fitted with a 494 c.c. twin-cylinder engine was notable, not so much for the fact that it used a two-stroke engine, but rather for the novel and ingenious mechanical 'torque-converter' drive that was incorporated in it. It was produced only as a prototype.

The Lincoln design incorporated a two-cylinder vertical engine which used crankcase-compression for scavenge air only. Fuel, in the form of a rich mixture for adding to the scavenge air to form a combustible mixture, was supplied by a separate pumping cylinder.

LATER CONTINENTAL CYCLECARS

The need for economy in motoring was greater before 1939 on the Continent and particularly in Germany, than in this country and, as a result, quite a number of new German designs appeared which were both advanced and novel. Considerable use was made at this time of the simple two-stroke engine, the design of which was now making considerable progress at the hands of German engineers.

The Tempo cyclecar of 1936 was driven through all four wheels by means of a twin-cylinder two-stroke engine mounted at each end of its chassis. The Framo was an open three seater, with a very large-section box member forming the chassis. The two-cylinder 600 c.c. water-cooled two-stroke engine drove through a solid rear axle which incorporated a 2-speed gear, in conjunction with the normal 3-speed gear; six different gear ratios were thereby provided, thus making the vehicle capable of going anywhere with its small capacity engine. The Czechoslovak Jawa concern, a descendant of the pioneer firm of Laurin and Klement, produced a 615 c.c. two-cylinder two-stroke ultra-light car.

The simple three-port crankcase compression two-stroke engine, with its three moving parts, power stroke every revolution and good torque characteristics, was greatly improved in 1929 by a loop-scavenge system, invented by Dr. Schnuerle, which provided a more rational sequence of gas charging and exhausting, and so make possible higher specific outputs and thermal efficiencies. This invention was acquired by the Deutsche Kraftfahrzeug Werke A.G., which was later incorporated in the large Auton-Union A.G. combine. Consequently, this phase of two-stroke engine development and its commercial application to light cars was essentially a German achievement, and was largely applied initially to German designs. The Schnuerle system was of considerable importance, not only because of the technical advances it made possible in two-stroke engine development, but also because it initiated the large-scale research and production which the small two-stroke engine had previously lacked.

The 8 h.p. D.K.W. two-cylinder engined front-wheel drive car was the first production design which employed this new and efficient two-stroke engine; it also embodied the combined and self-contained engine and drive unit which has since become a modern characteristic. The D.K.W. design itself hardly comes under the classification of a cyclecar because of weight and size, for it weighed 14½ cwt. and had a full four-seat body. Yet, on the score of small engine capacity and extreme simplicity of engine and drive layout, it was one of the most straightforward and effective cyclecar engine units to be produced at that time. The twin-cylinder water-cooled engine had incorporated with it in one unit a 3-speed and reverse gearbox, a multi-plate clutch and a differential unit from which the front wheels were driven through two flexibly mounted half-shafts. This compact engine and drive unit was located under the bonnet; the rest of the body was unencumbered with mechanism and was therefore low and commodious. The power developed by the 684 c.c. (76 mm. by 76 mm.) engine was 20 h.p. at 3500 r.p.m., which enabled the car to cruise at speeds up to 50 m.p.h. at a consumption of up to 50 miles to a gallon of fuel.

CYCLECARS ENGINES

Cyclecar engines during this period were notable, apart from their ever improving specific output and reliability, because of the wide variety of types in which they were produced. The tentative adoption of the two-stroke engine was of importance to future development.

The superior balance characteristics and smooth running of the horizontally-opposed twin-cylinder engine recommended itself for use in the later cyclecar. A few three-wheel designs, such as the Wooler Mule and Corona, employed horizontally-opposed engines of special design, and others, such as the Coventry-Victor, fitted proprietary engines. A larger version of the four-wheel Douglas design was produced in 1919, having a 1223 c.c. (92 mm. by 92 mm.) capacity water-cooled engine, and electric-lighting and engine-starting systems.

Designs using vee twin-cylinder engines included the New Hudson, L.S.D., T.B., Omega, Merral-Brown and Coventry Premier. The T.B. incorporated the unusual feature of shaft and bevel drive to the rear wheel. The Merral-Brown fitted a double rear wheel to improve the drive and riding-comfort; in general, however, this expedient was unnecessary. The Coventry-Premier used a single rear driving chain enclosed in an oil-bath chain case. Accessibility to the rear wheel for the repair of punctures was assisted by a hinged body tail in the case of the Morgan, and a removable panel in the case of the Coventry Victor. Interchangeable wheels were difficult to arrange with single rear-driven wheels; some experimental solutions were evolved, but they were not generally adopted in production.

One of the notable developments in automobile engineering of the 1920's was the successful development and wide commercial production of the small four-cylinder water-cooled engine, the majority of the production units of which were used for light cars proper. Some of the most elaborate forms of cyclecars fitted these engines in the interests of smoothness of operation, although inevitably some of the cyclecar characteristics of these designs were modified thereby; in particular, the longer wheel-base that was necessary to accommodate the larger engine increased the chassis weight and modified the handling qualities of the car as a whole. The first model of the Morgan so equipped appeared in 1933, fitted with a modified 8 h.p. (933 c.c.) Ford engine, a 3-speed gearbox mounted at the rear, and a single chain drive to the rear wheel. A 10 h.p. (1172 c.c.) Ford engine was later used for a yet more advanced model, which served as the basis of the four-wheeled Morgan type 4–4 light car which appeared in 1936.

There were, however, some four-cylinder cyclecars being produced considerably before this period. One of the first examples was the elaborate Castle Three design of 1921. The more important of the Continental examples included the French D'Yrsan and Sandford three-wheelers. The D'Yrsan was similar to the Morgan in general layout, and was equipped with a 904 c.c. water-cooled four-cylinder engine, with an integral 3-speed and reverse gearbox, a plate-clutch running in oil, a primary shaft, and a final chain-drive to the rear wheel. The Sandford, a three-wheeler of high quality which first appeared in 1923, was also based upon the general Morgan layout, with a tubular chassis, a primary shaft, a separate 3-speed and reverse gearbox, and a final chain-drive. The later models were fitted with a 1075 c.c. overhead-valve Ruby four-cylinder engine, which gave the car a top speed of nearly 90 m.p.h. This design also provided the basis for a four-wheeled light car, on the lines of the Morgan, which was produced during the 1930's. The front-wheel drive Stanhope saloon three-wheeler of 1925 was an advanced design for its period.

The simple three-port crankcase-compression two-stroke engine, as already developed for motorcycles, was used to some extent at this time for small cyclecar propulsion. The considerable increase in efficiency imparted to these simple engines by the Schnuerle loop-scavenge system began to make them suitable for use, particularly in two-cylinder form, with somewhat larger and heavier light car designs.

Light Cars: 1919-1929

The decade immediately following the First World War was perhaps the most important in the evolution and development of the light car, since it was during this period that it became firmly established as an efficient and reliable form of economical personal transport which served in a practical manner the needs of a wide variety of users. As is usual in vigorous evolutionary phases of development, this period produced a great variety of light car chassis arrangements and engine forms of varying capacities up to 1500 c.c. By about 1924, the general light car specification included a front-mounted in-line four-cylinder side-valve water-cooled engine, a plate clutch, an integral 3-speed and reverse gearbox and a final shaft drive to a live rear axle. Other engine types also appeared in prototype or small commercial production, including sleeve-valve, slide-valve, barrel-rotary and static-radial forms of four-stroke engine, as well as various arrangements of two-stroke engine. Also, six- and even eight-cylinder engines were developed to some extent before 1930 for racing and such special purposes, thus creating the basis for the light six-cylinder cars which had some popularity during the 1930's.

Chassis and body development also progressed in like manner to constitute, with the advance in engine development, the really practical and reliable light car. Stiff braced channel-section steel chassis frames were generally carried on semi-elliptic or quarter-elliptic springs, which were supplemented by the addition of adjustable shock absorbers. By 1924, four-wheel brakes were becoming general practice. Adequate and reliable electric-lighting and engine-starting systems also became part of the standard specification, and not, as heretofore, optional extras. Bodies became roomier and more comfortable, with improved weather protection for the open types; in addition, the saloon and the drophead coupé types of bodies were increasingly popular and became standard models. The sunshine roof made the closed saloon still more versatile.

This period was also particularly notable for the appearance of the practical ultra-light car, as distinct from the cyclecar, which eventually proved such a boon to a great variety of users on the score of economy and general utility, and which influenced the trend of motor-car design in general, both in this country and on the Continent. The pioneers of this important development were André Citroën in France and Sir Herbert Austin in England who, in 1921 and 1922 respectively, created this new kind of motoring with their Citroën 5 c.v. and Austin Seven designs. They were soon followed in this same development by William R. Morris in this country, and Louis Renault and Peugeot in France. These manufacturers achieved in the 1920's the ideal of cheap and reliable motoring, which their many forerunners of before 1915 had initiated but only partially realised.

During the early 1920's, successful production types were established for touring and general use, with robust four-cylinder water-cooled engines in the general categories of 750 c.c., 1100 c.c. and 1500 c.c. capacities. Moreover, the large and increasing demand for light cars enabled them to be produced in unprecedentedly large quantities by means of the quick and economical mass-production system, which was now being adopted by motor car manufacturers in place of the earlier slow and expensive hand-made system. The standard touring form of car was concentrated upon during this period, but the search for higher specific output and greater engine efficiency was also continued energetically. At first, special engines and chassis of advanced specifications were used primarily for racing and competition purposes; but, before 1930, the lessons learned with them were being applied to the evolution of both the standard touring car and also the efficient high-performance sports car.

The sports car was now gaining in popularity. It had a light chassis and body, and either a specially tuned side-valve engine or an overhead-valve engine of four or more cylinders, whose relatively high specific output made possible a substantially greater performance than was obtained with the average side-valve engined tourer. The availability of high-octane fuels after 1924 fostered this search for greater engine efficiency, and compression ratios and engine speeds were increased considerably with the resulting benefits of greater fuel economy as well as greater power.

The Roads Act of 1921 introduced a tax on motors of £1 per R.A.C. horse-power rating, which was based upon the cylinder bore and took no account of the stroke of the engine. As a consequence, British designers were forced to produce long-stroke engines, with the concomitant disadvantage of high piston speeds brought about by the general trend towards increasing crankshaft speeds. This distortion of technical design policy to avoid abnormal taxation costs continued to have detrimental technical and sales effects upon British cars until the horse-power tax was repealed in 1949 in favour of a tax of £10[1] a year for all new cars, irrespective of horse-power rating.

An important innovation of this period, which helped materially to make available the popular light car in large numbers, was the system of mass production which Henry Ford had already employed with success in the production of his famous Model T design. This system rationalised the production and assembly procedures, and also standardised machining tolerances so that all individual items and sub-assemblies were made interchangeable, with a view to saving assembly time and eliminating waste as much as possible. As a consequence, substantially fewer men were required to produce the same number of cars which, before 1914, had been produced by the 'hand-made' method. The efficiency of this rational system is shown, for instance, by statistics of the Austin Motor Co. Ltd., which, in 1910, produced one car a week for every 104 employees; while in 1926 only 26 employees were required for the same result.

ULTRA-LIGHT CARS: to 1000 c.c.

This period saw the advent of the really practical ultra-light car up to 1000 c.c. capacity which quickly brought reliable and economical motoring

---

[1] Increased progressively to £12–10–0, in 1953; £15 in 1961; £17–10–0 in 1965; and £25 in 1968.

to a great number of people. The Austin Seven design was the outstanding example of this important development.

In 1922, Sir Herbert Austin designed a miniature car which was virtually a scaled-down four-wheeled car of normal size and which owed nothing to the cyclecar. Two longitudinal members of the chassis, in the form of an 'A', supported a light open four-seat body, which was equipped with a folding hood, windscreen and detachable side curtains. A transverse leaf spring supported the front axle, and two quarter-elliptic leaf springs supported the live rear axle. Compensated internal-expanding brakes were fitted to all four wheels and were operated independently by a foot pedal and a hand lever. A 3-speed and reverse gearbox, in unit construction with the engine, and a single dry-plate clutch incorporated in the engine flywheel transmitted the engine power to the rear axle. A 696 c.c. four-cylinder water-cooled side-valve engine, fitted in the orthodox position under the bonnet, developed 10 h.p. at 2400 r.p.m. This 7 cwt. car was capable of speeds up to 50 m.p.h., and of covering 50 miles on a gallon of fuel. An engine-driven dynamo-lighting system was fitted.

Six prototypes were built to this specification for testing purposes. One of these (Plate 11) was presented in 1953 to the Science Museum by the Austin Motor Co. Ltd., to represent this landmark in the evolution of road transport which provided, in the phrase of the time, 'motoring for the million'. Full commercial production began in 1923 with such improvements as a slightly larger engine (Plate 16 and Fig. 6) of 747·5 c.c. capacity, and an electric starter in place of the original hand starter operated from the driving seat. In spite of initial doubts about the durability of the small high-speed four-cylinder engine and the practicability of so small a car, the Austin Seven immediately became popular, and it was produced in large numbers. It possessed the essential qualities of economy in operation and maintenance, reliability, durability, and convenience of handling and control. Thus began a new and important phase in the development of the light car which, although it owed its inception at least partially to national impoverishment and high taxation of motor cars, was both a remarkable engineering achievement and a commercial success. Not only were these Austin Sevens purchased by the middle and lower classes as commercial, utility and pleasure vehicles, but they also served as auxiliaries to larger cars; in addition, they were used in special forms for sporting and racing events, as well as for long-distance touring, and they were eventually adopted for military purposes.

Improved models of the Austin Seven appeared from year to year, as the demand for it increased, but the essential design remained unaltered. The selling price, which had originally been £225, was, by 1930, reduced to £125, and a variety of models were made available, including the four-seat 'chummy', a metal saloon, a fabric saloon and an open two-seater. In addition, two sports models, the 'Nippy' and the 'Ulster', as well as special racing models were produced for track and road-racing events which, from 1923 onwards, were capable of remarkable performances. Thus this new miniature car, which had at first been regarded with doubt even for ordinary touring, eventually proved itself to be capable of excelling in almost all forms of motoring.

The Austin Seven won its first race, the 1933 Easter Small Car Handicap at Brooklands, at an average speed of 59 m.p.h., finishing at 65 m.p.h. It also won in the same year the Whitsun Small Car Handicap, the Whitsun Short Handicap, the Italian Cyclecar Grand-Prix and its class in the Shelsley Walsh hill climb. Moreover, in the course of making several records, the Austin Seven covered 73·5 miles in the hour, and 5 miles at 79·63 m.p.h. During its racing career, which extended over some sixteen years, its simple side-valve engine was developed by 1930 to the state when, supercharged, it could deliver 50 h.p. at 7000 r.p.m. In its ultimate development, while still retaining its essential simplicity, it produced a maximum output of more than 80 h.p.

From 1923, the Austin Seven went into continuous production until the end of 1938, and during this period some 350,000 of these cars were produced at the Longbridge Works, Birmingham. In addition, they were also made in large numbers under licence in France by Rosengart, in Germany by Dixi, and in the U.S.A. by the American Austin Car Co. Inc. The American version was called the 'Bantam'.

The 982 c.c. Humber model, known as the 8–18 h.p., was produced in 1923 and, although well made and priced at about twice the cost of the Austin Seven, its design was based upon the improved orthodox light car formula rather than upon such advanced ultra-light specifications as the Austin Seven. The 832 c.c. Triumph Super Seven was a later example of the ultra-light car which included advanced features such as hydraulic brakes on all four wheels, and balloon tyres. The 950 c.c. Clyno had a simpler specification.

In the meantime, a similar development was proceeding on the Continent and some excellent ultra-light car designs were produced. The 694 c.c. Peugeot Quadrilette succeeded the Baby of 1912 to 1915 which, but for the war in 1914, might well have been the forerunner of the first really successful ultra-light car. The gearbox was incorporated in a solid rear axle with worm-gear drive. The 550 c.c. Mathis two-seat design, the 950 c.c. Renault and the 855 c.c. Citroën all appeared in two-seater form in production in 1922, and for some years improved versions provided Continental users with economical and reliable motoring. None of these reputable designs, however, possessed the essential ultra-light car quality to the degree that made the Austin Seven paramount in its class, and none survived so long in continuous production and actual use.

In addition to these relatively simple side-valve engined forms of ultra-light car, other more complicated designs began to appear by 1925 which were intended to provide better performance and greater comfort. These cars were not primarily subordinated to economy, as were the Austin Seven and Citroën 5 c.v., and they introduced the feature of quality into this small class of light car.

The 847 c.c. Morris Minor design appeared in 1928 and was at first of a more elaborate specification since its four-cylinder water-cooled engine was of the overhead-camshaft type, on the lines of the earlier Wolseley 10. From this design was developed the first of the M.G. Midget designs. Morris Minor touring cars were produced for a short while, but by 1930 they were fitted with a simple and robust form of 847 c.c. side-valve engine, and were sold for £100 with a two-seat body. The 848 c.c. Singer 'Junior' of 1926 was another example of a low price overhead-camshaft engined car of this small size. The 970 c.c. Talbot-Darracq of 1922, which was designed by L. Coatalen, was one of the more important of this more expensive class. It had a high-efficiency engine, with push-rod operated overhead valves, mounted in a well designed and elaborately equipped chassis. An example in this class of Continental manufacture was the 998 c.c. Fiat, model 509, which had a progressive unit-type engine with overhead-camshaft-operated valves. This model was developed from the Model 500 which, with an engine of 760 c.c. capacity was produced in 1919.

LIGHT CARS: to 1250 c.c.

The medium-sized light car, having a 10 h.p. engine of not more than 1250 c.c. capacity, was also developed rapidly in the 1920's This progress was based upon the relatively advanced designs of this type which had been evolved by 1915. From this initial stage of development, there proceeded during the 1920's a great number and variety of new models which embodied the important technical advances that had been learned in the war, such as better materials generally: light pistons of aluminium alloy; tougher and more durable steels for valves, crankshafts and connecting-rods; improved carburation and ignition systems; and more elaborate and comprehensive auxiliaries and accessories. In addition to the now normal four-cylinder engine, six- and even eight-cylinder engines were also introduced for use with the larger classes of light car.

In some cases, improved versions of these earlier side-valve engined types were produced by such concerns as Humber, Swift, Hillman, Standard and Lagonda. In addition, improved designs to the same general formula also appeared, such as the Morris and Citroën, which were the first light cars to be manufactured under mass production methods, and the Mathis, Clyno and Renault.

The potentialities of this class of car having been proved by the simple side-valve type, a demand arose for better performance. This was supplied by the rapid advance of the overhead-valve engine from 1924, and new designs based upon this greatly improved technique, to which aero engine design had so largely contributed, were produced. At first, these high-efficiency overhead-valve designs were evolved as racing cars which were capable of high performances combined with a high degree of durability, as was demonstrated during the many long-distance road races which were organised on the Continent and at the Brooklands Track or on the Tourist Trophy mountain circuit in the Isle of Man. By 1925, some of these advanced models were

76

put into production as high-performance tourers and sports models, which raised the scope and status of the medium-size light car. Specific outputs were increased on an average to some 25 h.p. per litre while some of the supercharged racing models were capable of up to four times this output.

The credit for the development of the high-performance overhead-valve engined light car must go to French engineers who, by 1925, had produced at least four remarkable designs of this category which were paramount at races and speed events, and also had wide use as fast and sporting tourers. These designs were the 1087 c.c. Salmson, 1078 c.c. Amilcar, 1094 c.c. Senechal and 1100 c.c. Vernon Derby, and their features were generally similar; the compact high-speed four-cylinder water-cooled engines were of the long-stroke variety, with overhead push-rod operated valves, and short stiff crankshafts supported in two main bearings. The use of comparatively high compression ratios, up to 6·5 to 1, was made possible by the high-octane fuels which were then becoming available, chiefly through the researches of H. R. Ricardo. Sustained crankshaft speeds of up to 5000 r.p.m. and unsupercharged specific power outputs of about 30 h.p. per litre capacity were now possible with these designs. Transmissions, gearboxes, rear axle and chassis were also built to a lighter, more compact and more logical formula than had been possible with the small light car of 1914.

This efficient racing technique was also used in de-rated form for some of the more elaborate touring and semi-sports production models of this period. This development was chiefly seen in England with the appearance of such designs as the 1247 c.c. Gwynne, which had a long-stroke push-rod operated overhead-valve engine, the overhead-camshaft 1230 c.c. Rhode and the 1271 c.c. overhead-camshaft Wolseley designs. The 1087 c.c. Riley 9, which made its appearance in 1926, with a push-rod operated overhead-valve engine (Plate 16 and Fig. 5), was notable for its sound design, combined with quality construction; it provided the basis for a range of touring, sports and racing models, which had considerable popularity for ten years. Other designs of this general type during this period included the 1207 c.c. Horstmann which was developed from the smaller version of 1914, and the 1200 c.c. Th. Schneider, of French origin.

An original layout destined to set an advanced style was the Tatra Type II of 1922. The 1050 c.c. (82 mm. by 100 mm.) two-cylinder, horizontally-opposed, air-cooled engine and gearbox unit was bolted to the front end of central tubular frame and also served as chassis stiffening. The engine drive was taken to the front wheels which were independently sprung. This original and advanced layout was used for several years for later and larger Tatra designs.

Another original design was the Sascha which Ferdinand Porsche produced for Austro-Daimler in 1922 which was an exercise in extracting the maximum power possible from a small four-cylinder engine. The 1095 c.c. (68·3 mm. by 75 mm.) light alloy engine with steel liners had the M. Henry features of spherical combustion chambers, inclined valves, twin camshafts driven by kingshaft from the crankshaft, light alloy pistons, dry sump lubrication and twin ignition. An output of 45 h.p. was developed at 4,500 r.p.m. Mechanical four-wheel brakes were included in the design. This car performed with distinction in the 1922 Targa Florio race, averaging 34 m.p.h. for seven hours, 46 minutes.

The successful progress of the high efficiency overhead-valve four-cylinder engine in the medium light car category was soon extended to engine units having a greater number of cylinders. This development entailed such new problems, which were accentuated by the tendency towards higher crankshaft speeds and specific outputs, as cylinders of smaller bore, longer and more complex crankshafts and crankcases and more difficult aspects of mixture distribution. Some of these designs used a single overhead camshaft, driven from the crankshaft at half-engine speed by means of a vertical shaft and two pairs of bevel gears, or, less frequently, by means of a chain.

One of the earliest of these small six-cylinder designs was the 1145 c.c. Mathis of 1923, which had a neat monobloc engine with an overhead camshaft, the front extension of which was used to drive a radiator cooling fan. A side-valve version of this design was also produced. The 1100 c.c. supercharged Amilcar of 1927, which had a maximum speed of 123 m.p.h., and the 1100 c.c. supercharged Salmson of 1928 which developed 100 h.p. at 6000 r.p.m. were examples of the high efficiency to which these miniature six-cylinder engined light cars attained before 1930.

In addition to the six-cylinder models, a few eight-cylinder models were also produced at this time having engines of capacities less than 1250 c.c. The 1100 c.c. Bugatti was perhaps the best example; there was, in addition, the 1075 c.c. O.H.C. design. Although these complex engines of small capacity performed satisfactorily, they were costly to produce and were only used as special units for racing purposes.

LIGHT CARS: to 1500 c.c.

This period also saw the appearance of the light car proper of up to 1500 c.c. capacity as typified, in particular, by the designs of the 11·9 h.p. Morris Cowley and the 10 h.p. Citroën and, in general, by the more elaborate and expensive designs which followed them.

In spite of the varied versions of smaller categories of light car that were developed during the 1920's, the most representative light car of this period had an engine capacity of about 1500 c.c. The models produced in this category in the 1920's were based partly upon the largest examples that had appeared by 1914, and partly upon large-car practice as it had developed after 1920; they were, consequently, of considerably heavier construction and more elaborate equipment than the smaller models. They had their own individuality and were intended to be fully useful within the scope of the light car proper, and not be in any sense a compromise between other established forms.

This country and France took the lead in this particular form of development. In much the same way that Sir Herbert Austin had evolved the ultra-light car in 1922, so did William R. Morris about the same time produce the

78

Plate 17

Ford chassis: 1937

Austin chassis: 1935

Fiat chassis: 1937

Plate 18

Citroën: 1934

M.G. Midget: 1937

Vauxhall: 1938

Plate 19

Trojan engine: 1927

Wolseley Hornet engine: 1930

Morris engine: 1935

Citroën engine: 1938

Plate 20

Bond minicar: 1950

Messerschmitt minicar: 1956

Plate 21

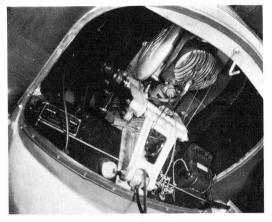

Villiers engine: 1950

Villiers engine: 1954

Anzani engine: 1955

Goliath engine: 1956

Plate 22

Citroën minicar chassis: 1954

D.K.W.: 1955

Dyna-Panhard: 1956

Plate 23

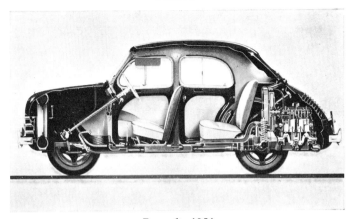

Renault: 1954

Morris Minor: 1952

Fiat: 1957

Plate 24

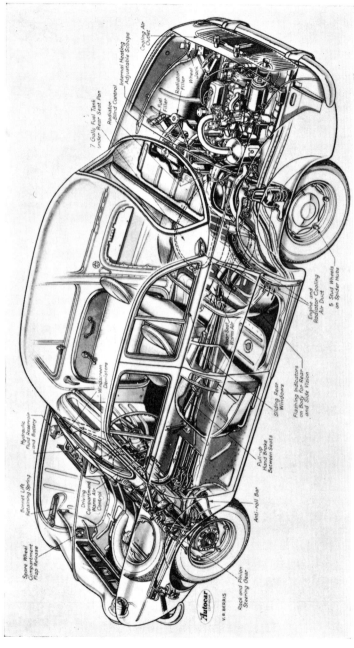

Spare Wheel Compartment Flap Release

Bonnet Lift Retaining Spring

Hydraulic Fluid Reservoir and Battery

7 Galls Fuel Tank under Rear Seat Pan

Radiator Blind Control

Internal Heating Adjustable Scoops

Cooling Air Outlet

Radiator Filler

Wheel Jack

Fuel Filler

Windscreen Demisters

Rear Seat Warm Air

Driving Compartment Warm Air Control

Rack and Pinion Steering Gear

Anti-roll Bar

Pull-up Hand Brake Between Seats

Sliding Rear Windows

Flashing Indicators on Body for Rear and Side Vision

Engine and Radiator Cooling Air Duct

5 Stud Wheels on Spider Hubs

Autocar
V R BERRIS

Renault: 1956

true light car and establish it in large production and general use. The propitious beginning that this pioneer of the light car had made before 1914 was interrupted by the war, and the first three years after the war was spent in reorganising and enlarging the works at Cowley, Oxford, for the large production of a new design on progressive and economical mass production lines. This was the classic Cowley model, the prototype of which had been made as early as 1915.

The Morris Cowley (Plate 15), although it was designed upon orthodox lines, was a remarkable and distinctive car which proved its worth by remaining in production continuously in various improved models from 1919 to 1933. It is worthy of note that the masterpieces of motor-car design such as the Rolls-Royce 'Silver Ghost', the Ford Model T, the Austin Seven and the Morris Cowley have all achieved the hall-mark of long continuous production as proof of their essential technical and commercial rightness. William R. Morris produced his new design by the economical and efficient methods of mass production and, in addition, provided a cheap and efficient service organisation. Although the Cowley was priced at £525 in 1921, it was available at £175 in 1924, in a variety of body styles including two and four-seat tourers, two-seat coupés and four-seat saloons. The chassis also became in 1923 the basis for a special sports model produced by Morris Garages Ltd., and known as the M.G., under which name was produced the long and successful range of small sports cars of the 1930's.

The Morris Cowley's chief external characteristic was a tapering bonnet and rounded or 'bull-nose' radiator with which the models were fitted until 1926; after this, a rectangular-shaped radiator was adopted. The car (Fig. 7) had a robust 1495 c.c. (69 mm. by 100 mm.), later increased to 1550 c.c., four-cylinder water-cooled engine (Plate 16), with a unit 3-speed and reverse gearbox and multiple-plate cork-lined clutch. These engines were at first built by the Hotchkiss Company at Coventry. The cylinder head was detachable and the cylinder block was cast integral with the upper half of the crankcase; the valves were placed on one side and operated by a chain-driven camshaft. Positive pressure lubrication was effected by means of a pump submerged in the crankcase sump, and a magneto supplied the ignition. A large electric dynamotor, for both charging and engine-starting purposes, was connected to the gearbox shaft by means of a silent chain. The drive to the rear axle was by an enclosed shaft, with a universal joint behind the gearbox, and a spiral bevel and differential gear incorporated in the rear axle casing. The weight of the Cowley was 16¾ cwt., and the fuel consumption averaged 25 miles to a gallon. Later improvements included four-wheel internal-expanding brakes which were at first offered as an extra, low-pressure tyres, Autovac and later pump-operated fuel supply systems, coil ignition and shock absorbers. The robustness of the design, combined with the excellent servicing facilities which were widely available, made the Cowley a car that could go anywhere with unfailing reliability.

A similar role in light car development was also played by André Citroën in France. He adopted the mass-production system and designed a 10 h.p.

utility car on rational and advanced lines for large production and general use. This simple and robust car, first produced in 1921 and fitted with a 1453 c.c. four-cylinder side-valve engine, employed an orthodox general lay-out, and it was immediately adopted for wide use on the Continent. It incor-porated such features as the 60° Citroën double-helical gear in the rear axle, and plain pressed-steel disc wheels which were cheap to produce, durable and readily detachable by the removal of three nuts. The Clyno, the product of an established English motorcycle firm, was a later attempt to produce a simple and reliable light car on the same general lines and was in production for a few years. In addition, some of the older firms continued with what may be called improved versions of their 1914 models and designs, such as Calcott, Calthorpe, Swift, Standard, Hillman, Marlborough and others. The pioneer De Dion-Bouton concern produced a 1328 c.c. four-cylinder car in 1925 which depended too much upon its ancestry, and was not a notable advance. There were also new designs on normal lines such as the Cluley and others. The Frazer-Nash, with G.N.-type chain gears, was a successful and popular sports car design. The friction-drive system was revived for a short while by such designs as the four-cylinder G.W.K. Some of these models possessed improved features and were produced and used in a relatively small way; none of them, however, attained the progress towards the new approach that Morris and Citroën had made in their attempts to achieve the best possible synthesis of current design and techniques. As a consequence, these older designs eventually declined and vanished, some entirely and some, like the Standard and Hillman, to reappear later in improved forms which were in accordance with the progressive standards of the time.

In addition to these economical designs in the largest light-car category, there were also some new designs of better quality and higher cost, such as the 12 h.p. Alvis in England, the 11 h.p. Fiat type 503 in Italy, and the 11 h.p. Peugeot and 12 h.p. Renault in France. These were all of the side-valve engine type, but they were designed with less regard for economy and were consequently more elaborately equipped. These cars, however, were heavy and by 1930 their general type tended to be replaced by lighter and more efficient designs of the same or even less engine capacity.

The Mercedes-Benz firm of Stuttgart, which usually concentrated on the design and production of medium and high power, high quality cars, pro-duced some light cars during this period. The Mercedes Type 130 developed 26 h.p. from a capacity of 1300 c.c. The Mercedes Type 150 developed 55 h.p. from a capacity of 1500 c.c. Both these models were noteworthy for being the first Mercedes cars with rear-mounted engines. (Fig. 15).

A few experimental examples of the four-cylinder air-cooled type of engine were produced during this period, which were inspired by current aero engine development and perhaps by the Franklin motor car design, then being successfully produced in the U.S.A. Air cooling, however, made little progress in connection with the larger forms of light car engine at this time, partly because of the strong predilection for water cooling which then existed, and partly because air-cooling technique, and the materials necessary for its particular requirements, were not yet sufficiently developed. Other examples of air-cooling were the static-radial forms of engine mentioned later in this Chapter.

Under the influence of the desirability of quietness and smooth torque, together with cheaper costs of manufacture which were made possible by large quantity mass-production, a small number of six-cylinder side-valve engined cars were produced, including the 1473 c.c. Renault 'Monasix', and the 1434 c.c. Armstrong-Siddeley designs, Such designs provided at little extra cost a somewhat more refined car than the normal four-cylinder engined type.

The increased outputs and improved performances made possible by the use of hemispherical combustion heads and inclined overhead valves, in conjunction with higher compression ratios and the use of high-octane fuels, were particularly applicable to the higher-priced light car, and by 1925 various examples of this category were produced with four, six and even eight cylinders. Of the four-cylinder designs, the 10 h.p. Wolseley (Plate 15) with overhead-camshaft engine and the Lea-Francis with push-rod engine were the most representative of the earlier designs. Continental examples of the two valves per cylinder overhead-valve arrangement were the 1487 c.c. Alfa-Romeo, 1480 c.c. Berliet, 1300 c.c. Bianchi, 1450 c.c. Ansaldo and 1327 c.c. F.N. designs.

A still more advanced design was the 1496 c.c. Bugatti 'Brescia' Type 23, which was developed from the advanced Type 13 of 1914, and was the fore-runner of the long range of technically excellent and artistically refined models which appeared during the next twenty years. These cars were remarkable for their progressive individuality; among the many advanced features adopted were the camshaft-operated two inlet and two exhaust valves per cylinder of the Type 23, and the two exhaust-valves and one inlet-valve per cylinder of the later four-cylinder Types 37 (Fig. 4) and 40. These arrangements, although complicated and expensive to produce, improved volumetric efficiency by providing a larger aggregate valve area than was possible with two valves. All these designs were generally standard in their chassis layouts. Examples of front-wheel drive designs were produced before 1930 by Alvis and Tracta.

Still more complication, in the search of higher power with lightness of construction, was used in the special six-cylinder designs produced by Amilcar, Donnet and Alfa-Romeo. Examples of eight-cylinder engines of under 1500 c.c. capacity at this time were the Bugatti (Plate 16), Delage, S.C.A.P. and Talbot, all of which were of the in-line variety, and the Vernandi whose eight cylinders were arranged in vee formation.

The Austro-Daimler Sascha of Ferdinand Porsche and the Mercedes 25/40 design of Paul Daimler, both of 1922, admirably demonstrated to what degree of efficiency motor car design could attain at this early period in the hands of first class designers. The Mercedes 25/40 was a scaled-down super-charged version of the 1914 Grand Prix Mercedes; it had a capacity of 1499 c.c. (65 mm. by 113 mm.) and was capable of developing 80 h.p. at 5000 r.p.m. The usual Henry formula of a hemispherical combustion chamber, four valves per cylinder and twin overhead camshafts were used.

Engines of the double sleeve-valve (Knight), single sleeve-valve (Burt-McCollum), slide-valve (Imperia), cuff-valve (Enfield-Allday) and rotary-valve (Marlborough) varieties were produced during the 1920's as part of the experimental search of this prolific period for the most efficient form of engine with which to power the light car. Although the two former types had been evolved and proved in production before 1914, their use was still limited enough to place them on a less reliable, economical and convenient level than the now rapidly developing poppet valve. These other forms of valve did not long survive and, by about 1930, they had, so far as four-stroke engines were concerned, all been abandoned in favour of the poppet valve.

The 1393 c.c. Panhard and Levassor double sleeve-valve four-cylinder and the 1496 c.c. Argyll single-sleeve four-cylinder designs were good production examples of their respective types. The 1094 c.c. Imperia was fitted with an engine whose inlet and exhaust valves consisted of separate oscillating slides; these operated in flush grooves in the cylinder bores and opened and closed respectively the inlet and exhaust ports. Rotary and cuff valves appeared only in a few unorthodox prototype designs.

DIESEL ENGINES

As early as the 1920's, the compression-ignition form of internal-combustion engine was being considered for use with light cars, as a means of obtaining maximum operational economy. The 1400 c.c. two-cylinder Held engine of this kind, made in Belgium, was one of the very few examples to appear in prototype form.

STATIC RADIAL ENGINES

The comprehensive search for efficiency combined with lightness in engine units for light cars in the early 1920's caused the static-radial form of internal-combustion engine to be considered. The compactness and light weight of this form of engine, as well as the intense development which had been given to it in aero engine production during the war, provided both the incentive and the technique to apply it to the light car.

The earliest example was produced by one of the chief firms then engaged upon the development of this form of aero engine. The 1200 c.c. three-cylinder C.A.R. design was produced in 1919 by the Cosmos Engineering Company. The overhead-valve engine was positioned under the bonnet in a conventional chassis, which carried a plain utility type open body supported on four pressed-steel wheels. The 1247 c.c. five-cylinder Enfield-Allday design was more complex and created much interest at the 1919 Motor Show at Olympia. The engine was supported in front on a girder-type chassis, and drove through a 3-speed gearbox supported in the middle of the chassis on sub-girders, to a live rear axle. One of the most interesting features of the engine was the double push-rod operated cuff valves, which performed as miniature double sleeve-valves located in the cylinder head. The five cylinders were enclosed in sheet-metal cowling, through which passed cooling air induced by means of fan blades incorporated in the flywheel. The 1750 c.c. North-Lucas design had its five-cylinder air-cooled engine mounted horizontally over the rear axle, which it drove through gearing and De Dion-Bouton type half-shafts. Another progressive feature of the North-Lucas design was its chassis-less body; it was thus contemporary with the Lancia design which originated this method of construction. Later examples of the radial-engined light car included the Rubury-Lindsay, which employed a three-cylinder 1230 c.c. air-cooled engine having push-rod operated overhead-valves; and the French Laffite, whose 900 c.c. three-cylinder engine was mounted on trunnions which permitted the flywheel periphery to move across the concave face of a friction-disc fixed to the propeller shaft, for the purpose of varying the gear ratio.

Although there are no fundamental objections against the satisfactory use of the static-radial engine for car propulsion, and authorities of the highest standing have continued to advocate its adoption, yet neither these early attempts of the 1920's nor those which were made later, have served to establish it as a production type. The special advantages of light weight and compactness which the air-cooled radial engine form provides continue to be valid recommendations for its adoption for light-car propulsion.

TWO-STROKE ENGINES

The simplicity and smooth and powerful torque, particularly at low speeds, of the two-stroke engine had given some theoretical promise but less practical realisation for light-car propulsion, as has already been indicated. As a consequence, the two-stroke engine had little of the vital development that results from large commercial production and use. Its advantages, nevertheless, continued to attract some designers and a new experimental period began in the 1920's, during which a variety of designs were produced. The most important of these were the Trojan in this country and the D.K.W. in Germany, and both survived in comparatively large commercial production. The importance of these early two-stroke light-car designs rests not only on their achievements during the time they were current, but also on the fact that they were the forerunners of future successful designs of this type.

Although the simple single-cylinder air-cooled motorcycle type of engine was generally used to power certain small cyclecars and runabouts of this period, as has been indicated in Chapter 6, the two-stroke engines intended specifically for light cars were generally more complex. The simple crankcase-compression type of engine appeared in four-cylinder in-line form, with separate crankcase compartments sealed from one another by intermediate crankshaft bearings. A. M. Low was an advocate of this simple form, and in 1920 he followed his 1914 suggestion of a three-cylinder engine with an improved four-cylinder version. Another design of this kind was the 747 c.c. Century of 1928 which developed 16 h.p. at 2600 r.p.m.

The twin-piston or duplex form is somewhat heavier and more complicated than the simple crankcase-compression single-cylinder type; on the other hand, this arrangement makes possible the use of end-to-end scavenge and the differential operation of inlet and exhaust ports, both of which considerations were important from the point of view of fuel economy and improved brake-mean-effective pressure. The French Deguingand duplex four-cylinder design was produced for a short while at this time; it had a normal crankcase, with pressure lubrication to the main and big-end bearings, and the mixture was supplied by means of a vane-type supercharger. Gas charging was effected at pressures above atmospheric and, as a consequence, high outputs were obtained with this engine.

The chief example of an English two-stroke engined light car of this period to be commercially successful was the 1529 c.c. Trojan. It was introduced in 1922 and was perhaps the most unorthodox in both engine and chassis arrangements. The chassis was mounted upon a system of long double-ended cantilever springs, which ran the length of the car, and which were flexible enough to permit the use of solid rubber tyres. A four-piston duplex water-cooled engine was mounted horizontally in the centre of the chassis, which drove through a 2-speed and reverse epicyclic gear mounted on the crankcase extension, and a single silent chain to the solid rear axle. Fuel was supplied through a mixing-valve and ignition was supplied by a coil-and-battery system. The engine could be started from the driver's seat by a hand lever. Although the top speed of the car was not high, a fair average performance could be maintained continuously by virtue of the high torque at low revolutions, a characteristic of the two-stroke engine which this design particularly exemplified. An output of 12 h.p. was developed at a crankshaft speed of 1000 r.p.m. The original 1922 Trojan design, with certain modifications such as a slightly smaller (1488) c.c. engine (Plate 19), a more commodious body, and pneumatic tyres, was in continuous production until 1929. During this period many Trojans were used for both touring and commercial delivery purposes.

The 584 c.c. German D.K.W. twin-cylinder design, introduced in 1929, was notable not only for its wide production and use on the Continent over many years, but also for its use of the Schnuerle deflectorless-piston loop-scavenge system, which made an important contribution to efficient two-stroke engine operation. The 584 c.c. engine developed $16\frac{1}{2}$ h.p. at 3500 r.p.m. The engine, gear and differential unit was compactly housed in the front of the chassis and drove the front wheels through flexibly-mounted half-shafts. This arrangement clearly foreshadowed the trend of design to be adopted for minicars and small light cars after 1945.

The 1210 c.c. Lloyd-Lord car of 1924 used a two-cylinder water-cooled engine, in which a supercharger was used for fresh-gas charging.

The Clerk type of two-stroke engine, having a separate cylinder and piston to serve as a charging pump for the working cylinder, which had been used by H. R. Ricardo in 1913 with considerable success, was adopted in the French Françon-Chedru and the German D.K.W. designs. The 622 c.c. (60 mm. by 110 mm.) Françon-Chedru twin-cylinder engine was generally on the lines of the earlier Ricardo 'Dolphin' design, but instead of employing a separate pumping cylinder and piston for each working cylinder, a single double-acting pumping cylinder of large bore and short stroke was used to serve each pair of cylinders. Loose piston rings in the pumping piston were arranged to reverse over transfer ports at the beginning of each stroke to serve as valves and direct the mixture alternately to each working cylinder. The 1500 c.c. D.K.W. design was a four-cylinder vee-type water-cooled engine; each pair of cylinders was served by a separate double-acting pumping cylinder.

The 723 c.c. Zoller eight-piston duplex engine was fed by a vane-type blower. It was designed to work with a high degree of supercharge and at high crankshaft speeds, and was capable of an output of 30 h.p. at 2600 r.p.m.

PROPRIETARY ENGINES

Although the majority of light car manufacturers at this period were making their own individual designs of engines, the use of proprietary engines continued to some extent. The chief examples of proprietary four-cylinder water-cooled engines available were the Coventry-Climax, Anzani, Meadows, Hotchkiss, Chapuis-Dornier and Ruby designs.

These designs gradually incorporated as standard such improved features as light-alloy pistons fitted with oil-scraper rings, durable exhaust valves of improved steel such as KE 965, larger bearing areas having white-metal surfaces and positive pressure lubricating systems. The trend towards overhead valves and more complex design generally was well established before 1929.

ACCESSORIES AND AUXILIARIES

In addition to the rapid development of the light car, the decade of the 1920's was also notable for the evolution and general adoption of a wide range of accessories and auxiliaries, which complemented the great technical advances made in the motor car itself and helped to complete it from all essential aspects. From then on, various devices intended to make motor cars more generally convenient and easy to use were established, such as dependable electric-lighting and engine-starting systems, and automatically-operated windscreen wipers. Also, additional safety and comfort were provided by the adoption of four-wheel brakes, low-pressure balloon tyres and improved shock-absorbed springing. Such items became inherent during this period in the essential specification of a light car.

Engine Accessories

Although a reliable and permanent source of electrical supply was now available in light cars, there was no immediate return to the coil-and-battery type of engine-ignition system. The high-tension magneto, made by such concerns as Bosch, B.T.H., Smith, Lucas, M.L. and Marelli, continued to be generally used. Sparking plugs began to be developed in various types to make them suitable for both normal engines and the more efficient engines now being developed. Plugs for the latter type had to be capable of withstanding substantially greater combustion-chamber temperatures and pressures, and higher speeds of operation.

The carburettors of the 1920's were elaborations and refinements of the types which had been established by 1914. These refinements aimed at more efficient combustion, improved thermal efficiency and lower fuel consumption, by means of better atomisation, distribution and mixture control over the operational range of the engine. These improvements were provided for in a variety of ways which included more exact choice and combination of choke and jet sizes and control of mixture strengths. In particular, instruments of the variable-jet variety such as the S.U. and Capac and the multiple-jet variety such as the Smith 5-jet and Binks 3-jet, were specially flexible in respect of the control of mixture strengths over a wide variety of operational conditions. The simpler Zenith and Solex designs achieved greater flexibility by the addition of calibrated air-bleed jets. Other types included the Cox-Amos, Degory, Amal and Stromberg designs.

The air-strangler and the separate starting jet now became an inherent part of the carburettor as a means for providing a rich mixture for engine-starting purposes. These provisions obviated the earlier haphazard methods of a rag stuffed in the intake orifice or the priming of the cylinders with liquid petrol. Air-intake cleaners to prevent abrasive matter from entering the engine were adopted by 1928. Petrol supply from rear-positioned tanks was usually effected by means of the Autovac suction device.

With few exceptions, such as the Trojan and the prototype Austin Seven designs which incorporated hand-operated engine starters, the electrically-operated engine starter was firmly established by 1925, since a reliable and adequate source of electrical power had by then become an integral part of light-car design. The more generally used type of starter unit was mounted on the crankcase or flywheel housing, from where it could couple with and free from the toothed periphery of the flywheel by the action of the inertia-operated Bendix-type pinion mounted on the starter shaft. An alternative type was the dynamotor, incorporating both dynamo and starter-motor windings, either of which could be energised separately. The Morris Cowley used this type of instrument coupled to the gearbox shaft by a silent chain. Continental practice, as exemplified by such designs as the Renault and Salmson, mounted the dynamotor at the front end of the crankcase and coupled it directly with the crankshaft.

The original cranking-handle was retained as an insurance against battery failure and cold weather. The tendency in America was to make the starting handle detachable.

Gearboxes with sliding-pinion mechanism and straight-cut gear teeth were still in use during this period. The sliding-dog constant-mesh type of gearbox with helical gears was also being introduced to facilitate gear-changing and provide quiet operation, at least on the higher gears. A common arrangement was the 'close-ratio' or 'twin-top' gearbox, with helical gears on the third speed and straight-cut gears on the second and first speeds. The still more important 'synchromesh' type of gear, which made gear-changing easier by means of integral slipping clutches which automatically matched the speeds of engaging gears, was generally adopted by 1935. Nearly all gearboxes were, by 1929, incorporated with the engine as a unit, and the separate gearbox ceased to be used.

Free-wheel devices became popular by 1928 as an aid to improved economy in fuel consumption and easier gearchanging. The types available included the Humfrey-Sandberg and the Millam designs.

Body and Chassis Accessories

Oil lamps were still used for side and tail illumination up to about 1924, but after this date the reliable, convenient and comprehensive electric-lighting system was firmly established. Current was supplied by either a 6-volt or 12-volt engine-driven dynamo and a storage battery; an automatic cut-out switch prevented the battery from discharging to the dynamo. The dynamos were capable of an output of from 60 to 100 watts and so could supply continuous current for head, side and tail lights; in addition, current was also available for dashboard and other interior lights that were now required for saloon bodies, windscreen-wipers, traffic indicators, cigarette lighters and solenoid-operated fuel pumps. This source of electric power also supplied the heavy current demands of the electric engine-starter.

Such a comprehensive electrical system transformed road illumination for night driving from the inadequate glimmer of the oil lamps and the inefficient glare of the acetylene lamps, to the positive and accurately-focused light beam which 18 or 24 watt headlamp bulbs of the gas-filled type now provided. This efficiency soon required modification since it caused glare to drivers coming in the opposite direction, and as the numbers of cars on the roads increased, so did this problem call for solution. Devices, either mechanically or electrically-operated, were accordingly incorporated in the system by means of which the off-side headlight was extinguished and the near side headlight was both dipped and deflected to the near side. This 'dipping' was action controlled by means of either a hand or a foot-operated switch.

The chief electrical systems for light cars were produced by Rotax, Lucas, S. Smith, B.T.H., Bosch, Ducellier and Marelli.

The foot-operated transmission brake was retained during this period for a few years but, with the adoption of four-wheel brakes which were generally of the enclosed internal-expanding type, the arrangement of a pedal operating all four brakes was soon established. The hand-brake lever was generally arranged to operate the rear wheel brakes or, sometimes, all four brakes as an emergency provision. Brakes were cable or rod-and-lever operated.

Bumper bars at the front and rear ends of the chassis were introduced by 1925 and became an integral part of car design.

By 1920, all wheels were detachable and a fifth wheel was provided on the car as a quick and convenient remedy for punctures. These wheels were of the wire-spoke, Sankey pressed-steel and pressed-disc types. Wooden-spoked wheels ceased to be used. Until 1924, the original high-pressure beaded-edge type continued in use, but after this date the large-section low-pressure or balloon type with wired-on edges was generally adopted.

The control of chassis spring action in the interests of greater riding comfort was improved by the evolution and general adoption of single-action snubbers or double-action shock absorbers of the friction or hydraulic types, as made by André, Gabriel, Hartford, Newton and Houdaille. A further refinement was the provision on the André shock absorber for varying the degree of friction from the driver's seat to meet different road conditions.

Side curtains, as adjuncts to the folding hood of the open tourer or two seater, were elaborated to give complete weather protection together with easy dismantling, and either partial folding or complete stowage in fine weather. The totally-enclosed saloon and coupé bodies were also developed and popularly adopted as standard types, while the open four-seat tourer became less used. The addition of the sliding sunshine-roof, which gave a greater versatility to the saloon body, was popularly adopted and became a standard feature in car specifications. Hand or, later, electrically or pneumatically-operated windscreen-wipers became essential fittings with the saloon type of body.

The various articulated points of the chassis were hand lubricated by means of a pressure grease gun and individual non-return grease nipples. Some of the more elaborate chassis were now beginning to be fitted with a system of 'one-shot' lubrication, whereby the individual greasing points were supplied from a single central pressure unit.

Chapter 8

Light Cars: 1930-1940

During the 1930's the light car, based upon the energetic development of the 1920's and aided by the relatively low initial and operational costs then obtaining, became firmly established as the form of motor car that could most economically and with the greatest convenience transport up to five people on journeys ranging from short trips in towns to trans-continental expeditions. The cost of operating a light car varied from between 1*d*. to 3*d*. a mile for petrol and oil, depending upon the size of the car. The Austin Seven 'Ruby' saloon car of 1935, for instance, could transport four people and 56 lb. of luggage for the price of a single railway ticket. Prices varied from £100 to as much as £600, but the great majority of light cars produced during this period cost under £200, while the cost of a good second-hand car two or three years old was about a half of its first cost. Purchases were, moreover, considerably facilitated through hire-purchase, and the price of petrol varied from 1*s*. to 1*s*. 6*d*. a gallon, according to quality. Economical motoring thus became available to still greater numbers of users.

Various important general and detail improvements were made at this time in car design which contributed to the ever increasing acceptance and use of the light car. Aided, in particular, by the availability of improved fuels, materials and design technique, the specific output of engines increased some 20% from 1930 to 1940, so that while performances consequently increased, engine capacities tended to become smaller. For instance, the performance which had been formerly provided by the 750 c.c. engine developing about 17 h.p. at 4000 r.p.m., was now obtainable with four-cylinder four-stroke or twin-cylinder two-stroke engines of less than 600 c.c. capacity. Conversely, engines of 1500 c.c. capacity were now able to provide the performance which formerly had required engine capacities of 2 litres or more, and so 1½ litre engined cars tended to move outside the reasonable definition of a light car.

With higher specific power output was also linked lower specific fuel consumption, which was achieved by the judicious use of high-octane fuels, efficient combustion-head designs, in particular those produced by H. R. Ricardo, and improved carburation technique which, for instance, enabled a 10 h.p. (1200 c.c.) car to cover as much as 40 miles on a gallon of fuel at steady speeds up to 30 m.p.h. Maximum speeds for the average light car increased to more than 60 m.p.h., while standard production sports cars, having 1250 c.c. high-efficiency engines developing more than 50 h.p. at 5500 r.p.m., were capable of 80 m.p.h. Specially designed 1500 c.c. racing cars, with normally-aspirated engines, were capable of speeds up to 130 m.p.h. The increasing popularity of the sports car revived the use of the open two-seat and close-coupled four-seat types of body, fitted with folding hood and side curtains for weather protection. The use of six-cylinder engines also increased to some extent for both touring and sports models. The very few eight-cylinder models, in particular the Bugatti and Delage, were special developments intended for racing purposes. The use of air cooling was revived, particularly in the case of the Volkswagen design which, with the D.K.W., foreshadowed the principle of 'driving the pair of wheels immediately adjacent to the engine', as it was more widely adopted after 1945.

As had happened in 1914, light car development ceased abruptly at the end of 1939, and the application of the nation's industrial output to war needs interrupted light car production for civilian use. The 1940 designs did not appear in production until after 1945, and then only for a time as stop-gaps to serve promptly an uncritical world-wide demand.

ULTRA-LIGHT CARS: to 750 c.c.

The small four-cylinder engined light car, which had become well established in the 1920's with engine capacities of about 750 c.c., continued to be developed and used to an increasing extent. The progress achieved in engine development enabled the simple side-valve type of engine to improve continually in performance so that there eventually emerged a trend, which had been foreshadowed by the Peugeot Quadrilette of the 1920's, to use even smaller engines in the interests of still greater economy. This policy was successfully achieved, together with good reliability and a relatively high performance, by various new models having engines of both two-stroke and four-stroke varieties of between 500 c.c. and 650 c.c. capacities.

The most important of this new kind of baby car was the Fiat 500 three-seat saloon (Plate 17) which first appeared early in 1936. It was light, weighing only 9 cwt., and was constructed on advanced but orthodox lines. One of its chief features was the mounting of the four-cylinder side-valve water-cooled engine in front of the front axle, thus making available extra space in the diminutive streamlined body without having to extend the wheel base. This was one of the first examples of a principle which was adopted with advantage for the minicars developed after 1950. The original 570 c.c. engine developed 13 h.p. at 4000 r.p.m. Other advanced features, such as independent front suspension, 4-speed and reverse synchromesh gearbox, hydraulic brakes on all four-wheels and small-diameter (4·00 in. by 15 in.) low-pressure tyres were employed. It was sold at about £120. Another foreign example of small capacity was the 725 c.c. Datsun of Japanese manufacture.

A still more advanced design which, in spite of its interesting features, remained little more than an experimental production, was the French front-wheel drive Villard of 1931. This car was fitted with a 500 c.c. Chaise narrow-angle (14°) four-cylinder vee-type engine, which was constructed under Lancia licence.

Of the more normal versions of the 750 c.c. category of light car, the Austin Seven (Fig. 14) continued to maintain its lead by adopting some of the advanced features of the period. In 1935, an improved version of the original design appeared in the form of the Ruby model (Plate 17), which had a longer wheel base and larger body space, rear fuel tank, low-pressure tyres (40·0 in. by 17 in.), a neat and convenient four-seat saloon body, and an enclosed radiator. The first of these new models retained the two-bearing engine which, with a compression-ratio of 5·4 to 1, developed 13½ h.p. at 3500 r.p.m.; the 1937 model had a three-bearing engine which, with a compression-ratio of 6·3 to 1 and a redesigned shock-absorber type combustion head, developed 17 h.p. at 4200 r.p.m. This later model also incorporated Girling brakes.

There were relatively few overhead-valve engines of the 750 c.c. category of importance during this period. One of these, in particular, deserves special note because, although only six were specially built for racing in 1936, the design summarised the ultimate which could then be achieved in this category. This was the Austin racing car which, while in no sense based upon the original Austin Seven, its conception was partially inspired by it. Its 744 c.c. (60 mm. by 65 mm.) four-cylinder supercharged double overhead-camshaft engine was designed to run at the unprecedentedly high maximum speed of 12,000 r.p.m.; it developed 80 h.p. at this speed with special fuel of high anti-knock rating. Although the design in this form had little relationship to the commercial ultra-light car proper, yet this and other similar achievements at this time made important technical contributions to later high-performance production designs.

More normal designs of this category of high performance sports car included, in particular, the 746 c.c. (57 mm. by 73 mm.) M.G. Midget Q and R models of about 1935. Supercharged at 25 p.s.i., 100 h.p. was developed at 7300 r.p.m., which gave the car a speed in excess of 120 m.p.h. Many world records were established at this time with these special M.G. designs, and they helped in the development of the more standard unsupercharged M.G. Midget designs which followed.

LIGHT CARS: to 1000 c.c.

The remarkable Austin Seven design ceased to be produced in 1938, due to a growing demand for a larger body which, in turn, required a bigger engine. This demand was supplied by the 900 c.c. Austin Big Seven model, which developed 25 h.p. at 4000 r.p.m., and soon afterwards by the slightly more powerful Austin Eight model. Light cars such as these were capable of speeds up to 60 m.p.h., and of covering 40 miles on a gallon of fuel at a steady speed of 40 m.p.h.

In the same way, other small capacity designs, which had served a useful purpose from about 1930, also tended to become larger by virtue of the advantages then existing of relatively low production and fuel costs. The 847 c.c. Morris Minor gave place in 1934 to the 918 c.c. Morris Eight (Fig. 10), which continued to be made with the addition of improved technical features and body form until it was replaced in 1948 by the redesigned Morris Minor. Other designs of this category, however, had appeared in the early 1930's with the larger size engine; one of the most notable of these was the Ford Eight (Plate 17), which had a straightforward and robust side-valve engine of 933 c.c. capacity. This car was of sound design, in the best Ford tradition; it was intended for economical mass production and use in conjunction with a cheap and well-organised maintenance service. Other makes of this latter type included the 1005 c.c. Standard Little Nine design.

High-performance cars with engines of 1000 c.c. capacity and having overhead valves were produced to a small extent, both in this country and on the Continent, and included the famous M.G. Midget range, the 972 c.c. Singer Le Mans model, the 995 c.c. Fiat Balilla, the 995 c.c. Triumph Junior, the 995 c.c. Skoda Popular, the 788 c.c. B.M.W., the 995 c.c. Praga Piccolo, and the 955 c.c. Adler designs. The M.G. Midget which, from the original overhead-camshaft model of 1929, was developed through the 847 c.c. (57 mm. by 83 mm.) J type of 1932 and P-type of 1934 and the 939 c.c. (60 mm. by 83 mm.) PB-type of 1935 to the larger 1287 c.c. T-type of 1936 (Plate 18). These and other M.G. models were essentially sports cars and were produced in a factory devoted to this type of car. They were therefore thoroughbreds which had the advantages of specialised and continuous development, with the result that they combined high performance with reliability in conformity with the Company's apposite slogan of 'Safety Fast'. Apart from the many successes in sporting events which M.G. cars achieved during the 1930's, a continuous series of world-speed records was established with special supercharged versions in the hands of such drivers as G. E. T. Eyston and A. T. G. Gardiner. The 972 c.c. Singer Le Mans replica model was capable of 90 m.p.h.; the specification of this design included hydraulic brakes and a 15 gallon fuel tank.

Somewhat more progressive and unorthodox versions of this size of light car appeared on the Continent such as the 984 c.c. Steyr of Austrian manufacture, which had a water-cooled four-cylinder horizontally-opposed engine, and the Stoewer-Tatra design of the same formula but having an air-cooled engine.

LIGHT CARS: to 1250 c.c.

By 1930, the 10 h.p. car having an engine capacity of about 1250 c.c., had evolved into a useful and flexible type which was produced in many forms and in large numbers for a variety of purposes. Moreover, its continually improving performance was now giving it the scope and capabilities which formerly belonged to the 1500 c.c. category of light car. Overall weight decreased and specific output increased; for instance, the Morris Cowley of the 1920's, whose 1550 c.c. engine developed 28 h.p. at 3400 r.p.m. and consumed a gallon of fuel every 25 miles, was replaced in 1932 by the Morris Ten-Four whose 1292 c.c. engine (Plate 19) developed 30 h.p. at 3200 r.p.m., and covered 32 miles on a gallon of fuel. The same comparative advance was made by several other firms at this time, with new side-valve models such as the 1125 c.c. Austin Ten, the 1172 c.c. Ford Ten whose engine developed 32½ h.p. at 4300 r.p.m. and which was identical to the one used in the Ford Eight except that the bore was increased by 0·25 inch, the 1267 c.c. Standard Ten, the 1185 c.c. Hillman Minx and many others. A more elaborate design of this type was the 1185 c.c. Talbot, which developed 40 h.p. at 4400 r.p.m. Later Standard models were equipped with independent front suspension and high output engines.

The straightforward 1¼ litre side-valve engines of this period retained in general their essential simplicity and general robust construction with a three-bearing crankshaft, detachable cylinder head which was now some-times of aluminium alloy to permit a higher compression ratio to be used, and unit-construction 3- or 4-speed gearbox. By 1935, the car designs to which they were fitted began to incorporate various up-to-date improvements and embellishments, such as synchromesh gearboxes which greatly facilitated gear-changing, electrically or mechanically-operated fuel pumps, totally-enclosed and pressure-lubricated valve gear, and oil-fume extractors. In addition, air cleaners and secondary oil filters were more generally used as a means of preventing abnormal engine wear by the exclusion of abrasive matter from the bearing surfaces of the engine, and flexible engine moun-tings resulted in smoother running.

A development of some significance in this category of light car was the appearance of four-wheeled versions of various three-wheeled cyclecar designs which had been popular and successful in the previous decade, such as the Morgan and Sandford, and later examples such as the B.S.A. (Fig. 12). The Morgan 4–4, introduced in 1936, was built upon progressive sports-car lines, with a low-slung chassis, a 1122 c.c. four-cylinder Coventry-Climax engine, with overhead-inlet and side-exhaust valves, and a separately mounted 4-speed gearbox. Some of the basic features of the classic three-wheeled model were retained, in particular, the arrangement of coil-sprung independent front-wheel suspension. The 1122 c.c. Coventry-Climax four-cylinder engine developed 34 h.p. at 4500 r.p.m., and gave the car a maximum speed of over 70 m.p.h. The French Sandford four-wheeled model was on generally the same lines, and was fitted with a special sports 1100 c.c. Ruby engine. The B.S.A. Scout four-wheeled car also owed something to its predecessor, the B.S.A. three-wheeler fitted with a four-cylinder water-cooled engine; it employed the same arrangement of front-wheel drive and the same 1075 c.c. engine, which drove the front wheels through a 3-speed gearbox and final worm-gear to the open flexibility-mounted half-shafts. The Morgan, in particular, continued in production, and progressively larger engines were fitted to provide improved performance in the sports-car tradition. Perhaps-the first three-wheeled car to adopt four wheels was the Merrel-Brown three-wheeler, which had a composite double rear wheel for the purpose of strengthening the rear support of the car and improving road grip.

More elaborate and expensive versions of the medium form of light car fitted with overhead-valve engines were also developed to provide better acceleration and higher maximum performance than was possible with the simple side-valve type of engine. These better class models had engines of four, six or even eight cylinders, and the overhead valves were normally operated by means of overhead rockers and push rods, although some had overhead camshafts. Chassis, body and accessory design were also all of a higher quality which, combined with the higher performance, generally put this category of light car in the £200–£400 class, although some of the lower priced models were little more expensive than the higher priced side-valve models. By about 1938, progressive developments such as independent front-wheel suspension which improved riding comfort and control, light stressed-skin bodies which eliminated the weight of the separate chassis frame, and engines of improved economy still further added to the general high quality of this type of light car.

The Riley Nine, with its 1089 c.c. four-cylinder push-rod operated overhead-valve engine (Plate 16 and Fig. 11), which had first appeared in 1926, was one of the most typical and best examples of this category. Based upon the original model, this design was produced during the following eleven years in considerable numbers and a variety of models, including the Merlin, Kestrel, Sprite and Monaco models. The Imp sports model version, with twin carburettors and high compression-ratio, had a power output of 37 h.p. at 5000 r.p.m. Specially low-built racing models of the same basic design, with tuned engines capable of developing still higher outputs, were also produced which established many important records. Other designs of this general layout, but mostly employing three-bearing crankshafts, were the 1232 c.c. Triumph Gloria, 1069 c.c. Wolseley Wasp and the 1122 c.c. Crossley Regis (Fig. 13). The 1166 c.c. Jowett (Fig. 16) was an example of the four-cylinder horizontally-opposed type.

A later and more advanced design of this general type was the Vauxhall Ten (Plate 18) which first appeared in 1938 and was a pioneer of its type. Although built upon up-to-date mass-production lines, which permitted its sale at only £168, it embodied many advanced features and was, moreover, capable of a good and economical performance. Weight and production costs were both reduced by the use of a stressed-skin steel saloon body which eliminated the separate chassis frame; the car weighed 18 cwt. Efficient independent suspension of the front wheels by means of torsion-bar springing improved riding comfort and lessened maintenance. Powerful hydraulic brakes and synchromesh gears facilitated driving. The 1203 c.c. four-cylinder overhead-valve push-rod operated engine, which developed 34·5 h.p. at 3800 r.p.m., had an efficient shock-absorber type of combustion head which permitted the use of a high compression ratio; a 6-jet carburettor was used which provided the most economical cruising mixture and enabled some 40 miles to be covered on a gallon of fuel at 30 m.p.h. A top speed of 60 m.p.h. was obtained.

Of the more elaborate designs of foreign construction, the most notable were the Lancia 1196 c.c. Augusta and 1352 c.c. Aprilia, the 1100 c.c. Opel, the 1100 c.c. Hansa with independent suspension, De Dion-Bouton half-shafts and backbone-type chassis, and the 1097 c.c. Hotchkiss designs. Continental designs at this time included various interesting and progressive features, such as the compact narrow vee (less than 20°) engines of the Lancia models, the front-wheel drive of the French Georges-Irat fitted with a 1100 c.c. Ruby engine, and the front-wheel drive Austrian Stoewer-Tatra fitted with a horizontally-opposed four-cylinder engine. The first three prototypes of the Volkswagen designed by Ferdinand Porsche in 1935 had two interesting forerunners. Three years before Porsche had designed for Zundapp a 1 litre rear-mounted, water-cooled, five-cylinder, radial engine which developed 25 h.p. Then Porsche designed for N.S.U. a 1·4 litre flat four-cylinder, air-cooled engine which developed 30 h.p. Neither of these designs were put into production. When Porsche received the Government order for the Volkswagen, the N.S.U. forerunner assisted the rapid production of the three 1 litre prototypes; the engine was enlarged to 1,134 c.c. after the war for mass production. Its advanced and rational design, with an air-cooled four-cylinder horizontally-opposed engine positioned in rear and driving the rear wheels, was in accordance with post-1945, rather than pre-1939 principles of design and manufacture. A basic VW engine enlarged to 1100 c.c. and tuned to give 40 h.p. intended for the Berlin–Rome race in 1939 but not used because of the war, provided the prototype from which the post-war range of Porsche cars proper evolved.

Although light car and cyclecar sporting and speed events had been popular for many years, the vehicles used for these purposes before 1925 were generally special models of standard designs with tuned engines. Towards 1930, however, the idea of the sports car as a separate and specialised form of production light car, as originated by the Bugatti Type 13 of 1914, began to be developed and a general specification emerged which included such features as high specific output, good acceleration, low build and weight, light and compact open body and good road-holding, braking and steering qualities. Some few designs to this formula appeared before 1930 such as the Bugatti, Salmson, Senechal, Vernon-Derby and M.G., which have already been noted, but after this date the sports car began to take concrete form as a standard production type and appear in several specialised designs both in this country and on the Continent. Engines were generally of the four-cylinder overhead-valve form, but six- and even eight-cylinder models were also made.

The successful series of four-cylinder M.G. Midget designs of capacities up to 1292 c.c. have already been noted. In 1936, the T-type design appeared which, with a 1292 c.c. (later 1250 c.c.) engine developing 52 h.p. at 5200 r.p.m., was an improved and slightly larger version of what had by then become the general M.G. Midget type. The layout was standard, but the co-ordination of each individual assembly into a well-balanced whole was individual in the highest sense, and the rightness of the design was proved over many years of long-distance touring, hill-climbs, trials, record-breaking and racing. This car, at its normal setting and tune, had a top speed of 80 m.p.h. and a fuel consumption of 30 miles on a gallon of fuel at a cruising speed of 40 m.p.h. Other degrees of standard tune were also available which gave the T-type car even greater performances. Of special interest was the supercharged 1100 c.c. six-cylinder M.G. which, in November, 1938, achieved a maximum speed of 186½ m.p.h.

Another efficient sports car on similar lines was the H.R.G. designed by H. R. Godfrey. This design was originally fitted with a 1497 c.c. Meadows engine with push-rod operated overhead valves, specially modified to obtain increased output. The body was of particularly neat and convenient sports form; the total weight was under 14 cwt., and the car was sold with a guaranteed speed of 90 m.p.h. A feature linking this new design with the

G.N. design of twenty-five years before was the short stiff cantilever leaf-springs upon which the front axle was carried. A characteristic item of the sports car form now evolving was the large-capacity slab fuel tank carried in rear, as a continuation of the short body, to provide the car with a long range of action.

The Lagonda Rapier was the product of an old-established firm which had specialised for some time in the design and production of high-performance cars. Of normal chassis layout, it had a 1104 c.c. engine of double overhead-camshaft type, a feature that was unusual in this size of production car. It had a 4-speed pre-selector gearbox. It weighed 17 cwt., and its four-seat body provided more seating accommodation than was usual with the sports car. The Rapier was in production for only two years and, at the high price of £368 relatively few were made.

LIGHT CARS: to 1500 c.c.

One of the chief general features of the largest form of light car during the 1930's was that the type, in its utility form of family car, tended to become so large and heavy that by reasonable definition it ceased to be in fact a light car. This was due to the continually increasing specific output of the 1500 c.c. capacity engine and the elaboration of body design, which enabled the type to perform the class of duty and carry the loads which in 1914 had required at least twice the engine capacity. Moreover, these duties were achieved with a better performance, improved economy and all-round roadworthiness which indicated the considerable technical advances that had been achieved within two decades. The high-performance sports types in this category, however, kept both size and weight low and some remarkable designs of high power-weight ratio were made for racing purposes and even, in de-tuned versions, for sporting and fast touring purposes. Individual examples were produced before 1940 which, with a weight of 15 cwt. and an unsupercharged output of some 80 h.p., were capable of speeds up to 100 m.p.h., and special record-breaking designs were capable of considerably higher performances.

The standard four-cylinder side-valve engine, while retaining its essential simplicity, had an average output of some 35 h.p. at 3500 r.p.m., which provided it with a maximum speed of about 60 m.p.h. This was the class which was most affected by the tendency to increase the body size and overall weight, so that a normal model at this time could weigh as much as 24 cwt. unladen. These cars were, moreover, not so rigidly built to a low price, as was necessary with the smaller models, and they were accordingly not unduly limited in their quality of workmanship and equipment. Among the more important of these standard models were the Austin 12, Morris Twelve-Four, 1343 c.c. Standard and others. Continental models of this kind included the 1496 c.c. Citroën, and the 1463 c.c. Renault. There was now, however, a tendency to abandon the side-valve engine for the larger forms of light car, and concentrate on the overhead-valve engine as was indicated by such examples as the 1496 c.c. Alvis Firefly, 1389 c.c. Rover Ten, 1444 c.c. Lanchester Eleven, 1550 c.c. Morris Twelve-Four, and the 1452 c.c. Bianchi which had a five-bearing engine. More progressive chassis arrangements were also adopted, as in the case of the 1493 c.c. Fiat and the 1628 c.c. front-wheel drive Citroën which first appeared in 1935. The 1495 c.c. Aston Martin, whose engine developed 80 h.p. at 5250 r.p.m., Alvis and E.R.A., were British examples of the larger and more expensive sports and racing cars of which this period was so prolific.

The more important development in this class was the four-cylinder overhead valve type which, during the whole of this decade appeared in many new and progressive forms and, by 1940, had developed to the extent that the 1940 models, in view of the interruption of the war, served as precedents for the next decade. Of the more normal type, some examples of which were developments of the earlier forms of the 1920's, were the 1629 c.c. Alvis and 1629 c.c. Lea-Francis, whose engines were capable of developing a normal output of some 70 h.p. These designs were made with streamlined saloon bodies as well as open sports bodies.

Among the most original of the utility types were the front-wheel drive 1628 c.c. Citroën (Plate 18) and the 1530 c.c. Vauxhall 12 designs, the latter of which was a larger version of the Vauxhall 10 already mentioned. The advanced feature which these two designs had in common, and which was increasingly adopted after 1945, was the use of independent front suspension, and a stressed-skin body. The front-wheel drive Citroën made possible the full use of the body space by the elimination of the propeller shaft, and also permitted a low centre of gravity. The Mercedes 130 (Fig. 15) had a side valve four-cylinder engine of 1308 c.c. capacity (70 mm. by 85 mm.) installed at the rear end of a central tubular chassis; the output was 26 h.p. at 3200 r.p.m. The 150H model was a development of this design, and carried its engine ahead of the rear axle.

Some examples of the six-cylinder engine in side-valve form were also produced at this time, to combine simplicity with improved evenness of torque, as represented by such designs as the 1496 c.c. Austin Light Twelve-Six, 1378 c.c. Morris Ten-Six, 1474 c.c. Renault Monasix and 1434 c.c. Armstrong Siddeley Twelve designs. In general, these six-cylinder models were somewhat lighter than the heavier four-cylinder models of the largest capacity, and they had a certain popularity for a few years. By about 1937, however, they were discontinued because of a return to favour of the robust four-cylinder form, which continued to increase in power and refinement.

New types of six-cylinder cars included the 1458 c.c. Riley, based to a certain extent on the earlier 'Nine' model, and the 1640 c.c. Crossley with automatic clutch and self-changing gearbox. Still more elaborate were the 1378 c.c. Lanchester and B.S.A. Light-Six models which incorporated the Daimler fluid-flywheel and the Wilson-E.N.V. pre-selector gearbox. Continental models included the 1500 c.c. Bugatti Types '37' and '40', 1500 c.c. Maserati and 1500 c.c. Alfa-Romeo; and British six-cylinder models included the 1271 c.c. (Plate 19 and Fig. 9) and the later 1376 c.c. Wolseley 'Hornet' designs with overhead camshaft, 1490 c.c. Frazer-Nash B.M.W., 1493 c.c. Singer, 1271 c.c. M.G. Magna (Fig. 8), 1287 c.c. M.G. Magnette, and 1498 c.c.

Invicta. The 1½ litre six-cylinder Maserati engine of 1935 developed about 170 h.p. when supercharged.

Still more elaborate eight-cylinder forms for special purposes were represented by such designs as the 1500 c.c. Bugatti and the 1486 c.c. Delage with twin overhead-camshafts.

In 1939 there came from Mercedes their remarkable W 163 design, which won the Tripoli Cup for that year. The engine was a 1500 c.c. vee-eight cylinder unit fitted with a two-stage supercharger which developed 254 h.p. at 8000 r.p.m. Although this prototype was only used once, it is a remarkable testimony to sure progressiveness of the Mercedes firm, particularly as it was designed and produced and built in eight months and was raced successfully after one day's testing.

TWO-STROKE ENGINES

The two-stroke light car engine, as distinct from the simple forms used with cyclecars and runabouts described in Chapters 4 and 6, was employed in particular during this period for two main designs: the Trojan in England and the D.K.W. in Germany. The 1488 c.c. Trojan, of the same basic design which had been in continuous production since 1922, was produced in improved form and was used mostly for light commercial work. A new tourer model appeared in 1930 which mounted the same form of Trojan engine vertically in a trunk in rear of the body, from which position it drove the rear wheels by means of a chain, epicyclic 3-speed gearbox, and an automatic centrifugal form of clutch.

The 1047 c.c. four-cylinder vee-engined D.K.W. model was a development of the 1500 c.c. version of the same two-port type of 1929, with separate double-acting pumping cylinders for the supply of fresh gas. The engine unit was positioned at the front end of the chassis and drive the front wheels through a chain in the fashion employed by the smaller two-cylinder models. The 976 c.c. Robertson experimental design of 1931 was a four-cylinder unit with sleeve valves.

The Czech armaments firm of Zorojovka produced during the early 1930's a range of sophisticated two-stroke racing and sports cars. The 987 c.c. (80 mm. by 100 mm.) had two cylinders and rotary inlet valves to improve volumetric efficiency. The 1 litre six-cylinder Z 2 model with opposed pistons was abandoned in favour of the 1500 c.c. Z 13 model which had an eight-cylinder duplex two-stroke engine fed by Roots or Cozette blower.

ACCESSORIES AND AUXILIARIES

Engine Accessories

Improvements in engine accessories included better induction-pipe design to improve volumetric efficiency, particularly in the case of six-cylinder engines, down-draught carburettors with special starting devices, thermostats for engine-temperature control, mechanical and electrically-operated fuel pumps, coil-ignition units with high-voltage coils and automatic ignition advance-and-retard mechanism, external oil filters, air-cooled dynamos, and air cleaners and oil-fume extractors.

The coil-and-battery ignition system virtually replaced the high-tension magneto during this period, as it was now reliable and cheap to make. Magnetos were, however, retained for racing engines, and specially advanced types in the form of the four-, six- and eight-pole Scintilla Vertex, Lucas and B.T.H. types were produced for this purpose.

Carburettors continued to be made, with minor improvements, on the efficient principles which had been established during the past decade. New features such as the separate starting jet and choke tube, and the automatic starting of the engine by the turning on of the ignition switch.

The adoption of rubber or spring engine mountings provided smoother and quieter running.

Body and Chassis Accessories

Improvements in transmission included the single- or double-plate clutch of the now established Borg and Beck type, which was smooth, reliable and durable in operation. Gearboxes became more compact and were either of the 3- or 4-speed and reverse gear types. After 1935, the 4-speed type became generally adopted, together with the synchromesh form of gear which greatly facilitated gear-changing and decreased gearbox wear. Pre-selector types of gearbox, fluid-flywheel clutches, free-wheel and even overdrive gears were also beginning to be used on a few of the more expensive light cars before 1940.

The earlier Hardy fabric universal joints used with cardan shafts gave place to the Hardy-Spicer enclosed needle-roller bearing type of universal joint. The De Dion-Bouton form of universally jointed half-shafts was adopted for some advanced designs for both front and rear wheels drives in conjunction with independent wheel suspension.

Body and chassis design features were developed to increase efficiency, improve appearance, decrease weight and provide a lower centre of gravity. The open tourer and two-seat types of bodies, which had been much used from the early days of motoring and were still retained with the growing number of sports models, were now largely replaced by the saloon with a sunshine-roof and the coupé with a drop-head hood. From the radiator rearwards, the cars of the 1930's assumed a more streamlined and graceful form, without departing radically from their individual characteristics, particularly in radiator forms. Soon after 1935, the angular bodies of the 1920's were replaced by sleeker and lower forms which had improved performance and road-holding characteristics, and which paved the way for the stylised and streamlined production cars of the mid-century period. Specially light bodies were used, constructed in the Weymann fashion of a wooden frame covered by fabric, or of sheet aluminium instead of the usual procedure of die-pressing the body from sheet steel in large sections and welding the whole together. The normal type of chassis-frame was made stiffer to sustain greater engine power and higher road performance by the adoption of such features as box-section girders and additional cross-bracing. Stiffer chassis construction was made still further necessary by the practice now being adopted of mounting the engine flexibly on rubber instead of bolting it solidly to the frame members, and also the elimination of the solid front axle and sub-stitution of independent front-wheel suspension. A still more advanced method of saving body weight was the adoption of the Lancia system, originated in 1922, which used a stressed-skin type of body to provide the necessary stiff structure formerly provided by the chassis frame.

Four doors were available in some of the later models of the smallest saloons, and the spare wheel was enclosed to improve appearance and protect the tyre from deterioration. Safety glass, of either the Triplex or the later toughened types became standard under the requirements of law.

Riding comfort was improved by the general adoption of low-pressure tyres, better shock absorbers and, just before 1940, the adoption to some extent of the independent suspension of the front wheels.

Chassis maintenance was simplified by the use of Silentbloc rubber bushes which made the mechanism quieter and also eliminated many greasing points. Grouped greasing nipples and 'one-shot' automatic chassis-lubrication were also used by some manufacturers.

Brakes were of necessity more efficient to deal with increasing engine output and vehicle performance. They were larger and acted on the wheel drums; the old type of transmission-brake disappeared. On the cheaper cars, the brakes were operated by means of compensated cable or rod-and-lever systems, but the improved Bendix and Girling mechanical types and the still more positive and expensive Lockheed hydraulic type began to be used on light cars by 1934.

Electrical systems, which supplied ignition, lighting, starting and a variety of auxiliaries were by now fully developed and universally used. Constant-voltage dynamo control was also coming into use in place of the earlier third-brush method of voltage control, and electric screen wipers with an additional blade for the passenger were now adopted.

Minicars: 1945-1955

Economical motoring is naturally attractive to the middle and lower classes of motorists, and the practical realisation of suitable designs for this purpose has brought this convenient means of personal travel at low cost within the reach of an ever widening circle of users since the cyclecar appeared in 1910. During the forty years which followed, there were special phases of economic stringency, such as the after-war periods of 1919 and 1945, and the world-trade depression of 1929 to 1930. In addition, individual national economic conditions, such as existed in Germany in the 1930's, also made the provision of cheap motoring of high importance. These happenings, as a consequence, had a considerable and fundamental influence on the evolution of the ultra-light car. The post-war periods, in particular, in which the whole economic world structure was severely disrupted and then reconstructed on new and more difficult lines, with the associated features of high costs and shortage of materials, were particularly damaging to private motoring. After 1945, this was particularly so. Not only did manufacturing costs, additionally loaded with heavy taxes, increase to three or four times their 1939 values, but also this trend towards higher costs persisted and increased over several years as a result of world-wide social readjustment and international tension.

This abnormal situation made private motoring difficult and even pro-hibitive, particularly during the years immediately following 1945. It was natural, therefore, that the idea of the most economical form of car, from both the manufacturing and operating viewpoints, should now be revived. This form—defined in 1912 as the cyclecar—was, with a few notable excep-tions, little produced after 1930, except in some impoverished Continental countries, because a real and entirely reliable miniature car, such as the Austin Seven and the Morris Eight, could be purchased for little more than £100 and, moreover, could be operated on fuel costing about 1*s*. 6*d*. a gallon. The post-war equivalents of such economy cars having engines of under 1 litre capacity, however, cost about £500 and fuel rose to nearly 5*s*. a gallon, so that the need for a car of extreme simplicity and ultra-small engine capacity became paramount.

As had happened in the evolution of the original cyclecar, motorcycle engine units, gearboxes and other components were once more adopted as the basis for some of these new designs as the cheapest and most reliable way to attain this end. The high degree of technical development, and the high specific power output of which quite small-capacity air-cooled engines of the simplest characteristics were now capable, greatly aided this policy. A simple two-stroke single-cylinder engine unit of 1950, incorporating a 3- or even 4-speed gearbox and clutch, of about 200 c.c. capacity, was capable of develop-ing some 10 h.p. Such an output had, in 1914, necessitated an engine of about four times the capacity and several times the weight; moreover, it consumed about 40% more fuel.

Such new facilities of this kind which were available after 1945 thus made possible the evolution and development of new and essentially simple light three-wheeled motor vehicles. This trend, in effect, constituted a return to the cyclecar, but with the advantages that mid-twentieth century advances in materials and techniques could give. The minicar, as this revived form was now generally called, could carry two people with luggage for some 70 miles on a gallon of fuel at speeds up to 45 m.p.h. Although the minicar was considerably less of a real miniature car than the small four-cylinder motor car of the 1930's, and cost more than twice as much to purchase, yet this form of ultra-simple three-wheeler provided in this difficult post-war period the most economical motoring possible, and it was readily accepted as part of the new economic order. Moreover, it constituted a new and advanced general type which began to develop on individual lines, and which had immediate and increasing popularity.

THE LAST OF THE CYCLECARS

Two examples of the original cyclecar formula of forty years before, the Morgan and the Jowett, had survived in full production and in their same basic forms until the mid-century. Soon after 1950, however, economic pressure and the competition of new types at last caused their disappearance after so long and successful a period of commercial production and wide use.

The Morgan three-wheeler continued to be produced until 1950 in the form of the F.4 model with a four-cylinder water-cooled engine and 3-speed and reverse gearbox. The three-wheeler model was discontinued soon after this date, and production was concentrated upon the Morgan Plus 4 model with a 2 litre Standard engine which was intended chiefly for overseas markets.

The Jowett, with the same general arrangement of a 918 c.c. horizontally-opposed water-cooled engine and a straightforward chassis specification with which it has been produced for many years, continued in production until 1954 as the Bradford and was fitted with either a commodious van or station-waggon type of body.

THE MINICAR AFTER 1945

The widespread financial and material poverty of the world immediately after 1945, as well as the added difficulties brought about by the instability of national and international affairs, created a general need for strict economy. In the few years immediately after the war this condition was most acute and, in the motoring sphere, it resulted in the establishment of a simple yet modern formula for a three-wheeled miniature car, which adopted some of the methods that had been used for the production of cyclecars forty years before. In particular, motorcycle engines of small-capacity but high specific output with integral gearbox units, which had been highly developed over many years and were in full economic production, were used for some of the smaller of these new vehicles with considerable success. Such self-contained engine units constituted the major functional part of the design, and permitted the simplest forms of drive, such as chain or even belt, to be taken to either the front or the rear wheels.

The body, mounted on three wheels arranged with either a steerable single front wheel or pair of wheels, was a light and simple shell, with a simple folding hood or a fixed saloon top for weather protection. Forty years of concentrated general progress in design, materials and production techniques enabled the inadequacies of the cyclecar designs of 1914 to be substantially eliminated and the practical success of these new minicars to be ensured. Although of the simplest specification, these direct descendants of the simpler cyclecars of 1914 quickly gained a growing popularity by reason of their economy and reliability in operation, remarkable capacity for long-distance touring and convenience as handy runabouts.

One of the most remarkable aspects of this new form of ultra-light car was the use with them of engine units of quite small capacity—100 c.c. to 400 c.c. With actual outputs ranging from 4 to 15 h.p., these engines were comparable with the 500 c.c. to 1000 c.c. units of the first voiturettes. They, however, were operating at about four times the crankshaft speeds and were much lighter than their forerunners; moreover, the overall weight of the complete cars was about half that of comparable voiturettes. The minicar of 1950 therefore had twice the performance and half the relative running costs of the earlier vehicles.

The first example of this form of minicar to appear in this country was the Bond design (Plate 20) which appeared in 1948 fitted with a 123 c.c. Villiers two-stroke engine unit (Plate 21), incorporating a 3-speed gear and clutch. The engine unit, which developed 4·8 h.p. at 4400 r.p.m., was mounted on the centrally-positioned front steering-fork, and drove the single front wheel by means of a chain. The front wheel itself was mounted on a trailing arm, suspended on a hydraulic shock-absorbing coil spring. The two rear wheels were mounted on separate stub-axles which were supported by independent bonded-rubber units; the wheels themselves had an outside diameter of only 8 inches, thus providing an exceptionally low centre of gravity. A 6-volt electric-lighting system was energised from the additional generator coils incorporated in the Villiers flywheel-magneto, and the engine could be started from the driving seat by means of a hand lever. The later Mark B model of 1952 employed a 197 c.c. Villiers 6E engine unit, which developed 10 h.p.; the car had a total weight of little more than 4 cwt. Two persons could be carried with additional luggage. Cruising speeds of up to 45 m.p.h. were possible, and up to 90 miles could be covered on a gallon of fuel. An alternative model was produced as a miniature truck, with a carrying capacity of 3 cwt. The price was £275.

The Gordon was another example of the same general arrangement equipped with the 197 c.c. Villiers 6E engine and gearbox unit, except that the engine was mounted at the side of a Y-shaped chassis frame and drove the off-side rear wheel by means of a chain. The integral kick-starter was used for engine starting. The Pashley and the Progress Tourette designs also fitted 197 c.c. Villiers 6E engine units.

The E.E.C.C. 'Worker's Playtime' design incorporated the more powerful and smooth running 250 c.c. Excelsior vertical twin-cylinder two-stroke engine which had been successfully used for some time as a motorcycle unit. A later and more elaborate design was the Astra which was made by the

British Anzani Co. Ltd. It was equipped with this company's 322 c.c. (60 mm. by 57 mm.) twin-cylinder two-stroke engine unit. The car was a 7 cwt. four-wheeled design with a light station waggon type of body. The engine developed 15 h.p. at 4800 r.p.m. and drove through an integral 3-speed and reverse gearbox and a differential gear unit, from where the drive was taken through two flexibly-mounted half-shafts to the front wheels. A feature of the engine was its crankshaft inlet ports, which improved crank-case volumetric efficiency by providing longer and more efficiently-phased port opening than is possible with the simple piston-controlled port in the cylinder wall. The commodious Powerdrive design was also equipped with the 322 c.c. Anzani engine (Plate 21).

Examples of Continental manufacture of this small-capacity type of three-wheeled minicar included the German Messerschmitt Kabinenroller and Dobler Inter, and the Italian Mi-Val designs. The Messerschmitt design (Plate 20), had its two seats arranged in tandem and incorporated a hinged aeroplane-type hood giving good weather protection as well as an all-round view. It was powered by either a 174 or 200 c.c. Fichtel and Sachs single-cylinder two-stroke engine, flexibly mounted in a tubular-steel triangulated structure behind the passenger's seat. The drive to the single rear wheel was taken through a 4-speed gearbox. The maximum speed was 50 m.p.h., and cruising speeds up to 40 m.p.h. could be maintained. The Dobler Inter was of similar specification fitted with a 175 c.c. Ydral single-cylinder two-stroke engine. The 191 c.c. Bruetsch design was of the same general layout, but had a top speed of about 60 m.p.h.

One of the smallest minicars at this time was the Bruetsch Mopetta design, which was equipped with a 50 c.c. single-cylinder two-stroke air-cooled engine. The drive was taken through a 3-speed gearbox to the single front wheel. The total weight of this vehicle was only 120 lb., and 135 miles could be covered on a gallon of fuel.

The Heinkel was an example of the 'front-entry' type of saloon minicar, having the whole of the front of the body hinged to form a door to provide access. This design was powered by a 175 c.c. overhead-valve four-stroke engine and was fitted with a 4-speed and reverse gearbox. The German Lloyd used a 386 c.c. engine which drove the front wheels.

An Austrian version of this general formula, which appeared in 1954, was the Frankel and Kirchner three-wheel runabout, fitted with a 199 c.c. single-cylinder two-stroke engine, which was located behind the two side-by-side seats and which drove the single rear wheel. The vehicle weighed 420 lb. and had a top speed of 50 m.p.h. and a fuel consumption of 100 miles a gallon. It was fitted with such advanced features as independent wheel suspension, hydraulic brakes, electric starting and 'winking' traffic indicators.

A somewhat more powerful and elaborate single-cylinder engined design was the A.C. 'Petite' three-wheeled minicar which, with a saloon-type hood, weighed 7½ cwt. The single front wheel of this car was steerable, and the 346 c.c. Villiers Mk. 29B two-stroke engine was mounted in the rear and drove the two rear wheels through an integral 3-speed gearbox and primary drive of triple vee-belts; the final drive to a differential-gear unit incorporated with the rear axle was by means of a chain. The drive from the differential to the rear wheels was by two flexibly-mounted half-shafts. All three wheels were independently sprung on coil springs. As well as an electric-lighting system, an electric-engine starter was also employed, and hydraulic brakes were fitted to both rear wheels. Up to 70 miles could be covered with a gallon of fuel. The Allard 'Clipper' was another example of this larger form of three-wheeled minicar. It also employed the 346 c.c. Villiers Mk. 26B two-stroke engine (Plate 21) and 3-speed gearbox, triple vee-belts for the primary drive, and final chain drive. The weight was 6 cwt.

The most powerful and elaborate of these new three-wheeled minicars which appeared after the war was the Reliant 'Regal' (Plate 29) of British manufacture. The weight of the Reliant was just under 8 cwt., and it was built on the same general lines as was used, for instance, by the Austin Seven 'Ruby' design. It had a stout channel-frame chassis, a 750 c.c. four-cylinder water-cooled engine which was based upon the earlier Austin engine of that capacity, a 3-speed unit gearbox, and shaft drive to a live rear axle. The single front wheel was mounted on a long stub axle and was steered by means of a normal steering wheel. This chassis was used both for a two-seat coupé body and a delivery-van body made of fibreglass.

This modern form of a minicar was also produced in a variety of four-wheeled designs by various countries in the search of economical road transport. The British-designed Rodley was equipped with a 250 c.c. twin-cylinder two-stroke Excelsior air-cooled engine. The German Fulda-Mobil was fitted with the reliable proprietary 360 c.c. Fichtel and Sachs single-cylinder air-cooled two stroke engine. This design had such advanced features as an aluminium coupé body, rubber-mounted pendulum-type independent suspension on all four wheels, hydraulic shock absorbers and interior heating.

British designs in this category which fitted the efficient 322 c.c. Anzani two-cylinder two-stroke engine unit, equipped with Siba Dynastart flywheel-dynamotor, included the Unicar, Fairthorpe, Atom, Astra and Berkeley designs. The latter was one of the first examples of the minicar to be specialised as a sports car; it had a maximum speed of 70 m.p.h..

The Italian Iso-Isetta design had its two rear wheels arranged with a narrow track, and had fitted a 236 c.c. twin-cylinder duplex two-stroke engine, and 4-speed and reverse synchromesh gearbox. The engine was mounted in the rear, and was cooled by means of a fan and cowling. This design was also made in Germany as the B.M.W. Isetta (Plate 29 and Fig. 23) with the same general specification except that the engine (Fig. 22) was a 245 c.c. (68 mm. bore and stroke) four-stroke single-cylinder air-cooled unit which developed 12 h.p. The chain drive to the rear wheels was enclosed in an oil-bath case.

The Goggomobil (Plate 29) was, to external appearances, a four-wheeled car in miniature. With independent suspension on all four wheels and hydraulic brakes, together with a top speed of over 60 m.p.h. with a 293 c.c. engine, it represented one of the most advanced of its class at this time. The

Bruetsch 350 and the 400 c.c. D.K.W. designs were further examples of this same general category. The Champion coupé design was fitted with a proprietary 398 c.c. Heinkel twin-cylinder two-stroke engine. The Italian Panther design was fitted with a 480 c.c. twin-cylinder compression-ignition engine which still further enhanced the essential operation economy of this class of car.

A Japanese four-wheeled design, the Datsun 'Flying Feather', had a 350 c.c. air-cooled vee twin-cylinder four-stroke engine which developed $12\frac{1}{2}$ h.p. at 4500 r.p.m., and gave this 8 cwt. minicar a maximum speed of 46 m.p.h. and a fuel consumption of 80 miles to a gallon of fuel. The engine was positioned in the rear and drove the rear wheels.

ULTRA-LIGHT CARS AFTER 1945

A more elaborate, and consequently more generally useful, form of small car which was of the ultra-light rather than the minicar type, also appeared at this time which, while retaining economy in operational costs as its chief feature, also incorporated the requisites for better performance and comfort in its essential design. This policy made the modern ultra-light car an attractive proposition to those users who required better comfort and performance than the minicar could provide.

This particular form of light car was designed to carry a relatively large load and, at the same time, to have a comparatively high performance combined with low fuel consumption. This policy has in general been achieved by a judicious combination of the most appropriate modern features of motorcycle and light-car practice, later combined with an individual technique specialised in respect of modern minicar evolution. The designs which conformed to this formula were mostly of French or German origin and had either two or four-stroke engines, usually of the twin-cylinder variety, with capacities ranging from 350 c.c. to 700 c.c. The actual designs which appeared during the decade after 1945 were all four-wheeled cars, having engines of high specific outputs and advanced methods of engine mounting and drive, which tended to provide the most economical mechanical arrangement in the interests of low weight and cheap production. Air cooling, assisted by an engine-driven fan and cowling, was also generally used for the same reason. The engine unit was located either in front or in rear of the vehicle, depending upon whether the front or rear wheels were to be driven. This arrangement provided simplicity of mechanical layout and also, by avoiding long propeller shafts and concentrating the essential mechanism at one end of the car, permitted the use of a low-positioned body having maximum passenger and luggage space.

The four-stroke engines were generally of the overhead-valve type, and the two-stroke engines were based upon the Schnuerle loop-scavenge system. A few even had the additional aid to efficiency of solid-fuel injection pumps. These units were capable of high specific outputs which, with light chassis weight, gave these small cars high touring and maximum speeds with full passenger and luggage loads, together with good fuel economy. Continuous high-speed touring, made possible by the good quality autobahn type of road, introduced overdrive gears for some of the smallest of these ultra-light cars. The average weight of these more elaborate minicars varied from 9 to 15 cwt.

The French 2 c.v. Rovin design appeared in 1947; it was one of the first of this new type and was generally based upon the Grégoire design which had appeared in 1939. The 425 c.c. short-stroke horizontally-opposed side-valve air-cooled engine was mounted at the rear of the chassis and drove the rear wheels through separate flexibily-mounted half-shafts. The engine developed 11 h.p. at 3000 r.p.m. The car had a maximum speed of 50 m.p.h., and a fuel consumption at cruising speeds of 75 miles to a gallon of fuel.

A more elaborate and powerful example which appeared in 1946 was the French Dyna-Panhard design (Plate 22 and Fig. 20); this was a product of the pioneer automobile firm of Panhard and Levassor. In this case, the 610 c.c. horizontally-opposed twin-cylinder overhead-valve air-cooled engine was mounted in front and drove the front wheels through separate flexibly-mounted half-shafts. The engine developed 23 h.p. at 4000 r.p.m., and the car was fitted with a 4-speed and reverse gearbox; the fourth speed was an overdrive gear to permit economical cruising. A comfortable four-seat saloon body was employed, together with hydraulic brakes and a full touring equipment. A 745 c.c. model was introduced in 1951. In 1952, a still more powerful version of this design was produced which retained the essential features of the earlier model. An 850 c.c. engine which developed 40 h.p. at 5000 r.p.m. was used; this engine, while giving the car a maximum speed of 80 m.p.h., consumed only a gallon of fuel every 40 miles at high cruising speeds. This latter model demonstrated its reliability under high operational speeds in 1953 when it was placed first in the 'Index of Performance' in the arduous 'Twenty-Four Hours' race at Le Mans.

One of the most ingenious designs of this type of minicar, which first appeared in 1948 and which proved most generally useful and economical, was the French 2 c.v. Citroën (Plate 22). It was designed to be mass produced as economically as possible. The 375 c.c. horizontally-opposed, overhead-valve engine (Fig. 21), which was air-cooled by fan and cowling, was throttled to develop a maximum of only 9 h.p. at 3800 r.p.m. to ensure maximum durability at continuous operation. A 425 c.c. engine was later fitted to improve performance. The drive was taken through a 4-speed and reverse synchromesh gearbox, the high gear of which was an overdrive for economy cruising, and thence through two flexible half-shafts to the front wheels.

A large four-seat body of stressed-skin construction was mounted upon an independent hydro-pneumatic suspension system, interconnected front and rear by long compression coil springs, in conjunction with inertia dampers, which automatically conditioned the damping control to the degree of road shock. Hydraulic brakes were fitted to all four wheels, and small-diameter, large-section tyres (400 mm. by 125 mm.) gave additional riding comfort. The maximum speed was 40 m.p.h. and fuel consumption was about 60 miles to a gallon of fuel. The weight of the car was under 10 cwt.

The simple three-port crankcase-compression two-stroke engine continued to be used in commercial production in Germany after 1945, particularly by the Deutsche Kraftfahrzeug A.G. division of the Auto-Union combine. Post-war models of the successful D.K.W. Meisterklasse design had their engine units mounted forward of the wheel centres, and the compression ratio was raised to 7·2 to 1, which increased the output to 23 h.p. and the maximum speed to 62 m.p.h. This new chassis arrangement was also used for the new three-cylinder Sonderklasse model mentioned in Chapter 10.

Of the same general arrangement of power-plant and transmission as the D.K.W. design, the Argentine Justicialista was somewhat more complicated since, in the interests of greater thermal and charging efficiency, a four-cylinder duplex design was used. Hanomag of Germany also produced a engine which drove the front wheels. This design was not put into production.

The German Gutbrod design, with a 20 h.p. two-cylinder water-cooled engine of 660 c.c. (Plate 25), was of the same general layout and performance as the D.K.W. when the engine was fitted with a normal carburettor. An alternative solid-injection fuel pump system could be fitted; the output was increased to 30 h.p. at 4300 r.p.m. The elimination of fuel loss through the exhaust ports, together with the more efficient combustion due to the better atomisation of the fuel which the solid-injection system provides, resulted in an output of 27 h.p. and an improvement in thermal efficiency and fuel consumption of up to 20% compared with the performance of the carburettor-equipped engine. The solid-injection system permits the simple three-port two-stroke engine to operate to the best advantage, and it is likely to become a standard fitting when the production cost of the fuel pump has been reduced.

The Goliath design was another example of this type, which was available with twin-cylinder two-stroke engines of either 688 c.c. or 866 c.c. capacities, which drove the front wheels. The latter unit, fitted with a Bosch solid-injection fuel pump, developed 40 h.p. at 4000 r.p.m. With this installation, the car had a speed of 76 m.p.h. The Goliath model was fitted with a multi-seat utility body, and was a remarkable example of how these small-capacity-engined vehicles could deal economically with a large load. A 493·5 c.c. Goliath engine unit, with fan cooling, is illustrated in Plate 21.

The Lloyd was a British twin-cylinder two-stroke design of 650 c.c. capacity, with separate pumping-cylinders for fresh-gas charging.

The initial model of the Swedish Saab, the 92, was fitted with a two-cylinder two-stroke water-cooled engine. This model was the forerunner of later very successful Saab designs using three-cylinder two-stroke engines of high power outputs.

CHASSIS AND BODY DESIGN

Innovations in design were applied to the development of the minicar for the purpose of saving weight and making full use of available body space. For instance, not only did the front opening door of the Heinkel and B.M.W. Isetta designs economise in space but it also resulted in a saving of some 90 lb. compared with the normal two-door saloon type of body. Again, the adoption of small-diameter large-section (21 in. by 5 in.) low-pressure (15–20 p.s.i.) tyres resulted in a saving of total wheel weight of some 65 lb.

Light Cars: 1945-1955

The difficult production and supply situation immediately after 1945, mentioned in the last chapter, was still further complicated by the fact that, in this country, up to three-quarters of the new production cars were exported in order to obtain the foreign currency necessary for the nation's economic survival. The world-wide need for new cars at this time ensured that the majority of the production were exported, even in the face of American competition in world markets, and consequently during the first few years immediately after the war there were relatively few motor cars for the home market.

This situation had two major effects: the continued use of existing pre-1940 models whose second-hand value rose to some three times their original selling price, and the continued production of 1940 models with superficial improvements as the quickest and cheapest method of supplying new cars to a buying public which was, for the time being, importunate and uncritical. As world conditions slowly improved even the defeated countries, in particular Germany and Japan, began to compete for world trade, and the models based upon ten-year old designs were by 1950 replaced by new and improved designs with which a new era was begun in light-car evolution.

The emphasis on economy directed attention to the possibilities of the modern ultra-light car, not only in the minicar form with single and twin-cylinder engines, as described in the previous chapter, but also in the more elaborate small-capacity four-cylinder form of car. The considerable increase in specific output which had been substantially aided by intensive war research, together with progressive ideas concerning compact transmission and light body-chassis arrangements, produced a variety of new models which were substantially lighter, more versatile and of greater performance and improved handling qualities than the 1940 models. By 1950, several new designs ushered in this important new phase of light-car development. As a result of this technical advance, ultra-light cars were capable of performances equal to, or even better than, those of cars of twice the engine capacity of twenty years before; while, at the other end of the scale, the largest category, particularly in the heavier saloon forms, still further outgrew the definition of a light car.

Although the large numbers of standard 1940-type British cars exported during the five years immediately after the war were out of date by current European standards, they were still suitable for the smooth-surfaced and easy-graded roads of this country. But when they were exported in large numbers and used under 'colonial' conditions, they proved to be less satisfactory. Within a short while, British manufacturers had to accept policies involving drastic redesign to produce models conforming to modern standards which would meet international, rather than national, conditions of operation. Such items were adopted as large-section and small-diameter tyres, heavier-gauge steel for wheels, more efficient and durable brakes and the elimination of the condition known as brake-fade, and deep-action coil or torsion-bar independent springing on all four wheels, together with shock absorbers of increased capacity. The long stretches of travel at high cruising speeds, now characteristic of 'continental' travel because of the autobahn and autostrada types of highways now available on many Continental routes, necessitated the short-stroke, low piston-speed engine to lessen engine wear, with the additional assistance of an overdrive gear to improve fuel economy. As a concession to this policy, the horse-power tax based upon the diameter of the cylinder bore which, since 1921, had forced the adoption of the long-stroke high piston-speed engine in British cars, was rescinded and a £12 10s. 0d. per annum tax for all sizes of cars substituted. The modern British car of 1950 was thus at last based on the requirements of global rather than national conditions of operation.

The bodywork of British cars was also radically altered under the same influence. The somewhat angular but still individual body of 1940 gave place by about 1950 to the stylised full-width, envelope form of body with wholly-submerged headlamps and integral mudguards, which reduced both wind resistance and production costs. Sealing against draught and dust and loss of interior heating was also improved. As a result of this foreign demand, British cars after 1950 were better sprung, better braked, more robust mechanically, better able to sustain high speeds with reasonable fuel consumption, and more comfortable over a wide range of climatic conditions.

On the other hand, foreign buyers also learned something from British cars of even the older types, particularly in America. The capabilities of the relatively small British cars and their general high quality of finish proved their suitability and even desirability as short-distance touring or town cars. In particular, British sports cars with their excellent design and good power-weight ratio and performance were something of a relevation to motorists who for a generation had used the large and heavy American type of car for all purposes. A minor cult for sports cars was created for both touring and competition purposes, and American manufacturers even began the production of their own models, or even arranged for British manufacturers to build special designs for them.

One of the prices paid for this 'continentalising' of British designs was the loss of individuality of design, particularly in the abandonment of the characteristic radiator forms which had been preserved for so many years and which had constituted a link with tradition. This break with a historic past may be regretted for sentimental if not technical reasons. A few makes, such as Riley, Wolseley and M.G., equipped with the new form of stylised bodies, still contrived to retain modernised radiators of the traditional forms.

LIGHT-CARS: to 750 c.c.

One of the most notable examples of the ultra-light four-cylinder car to appear after 1945 was the Renault 750. This design had a progressive specification which created a wide appeal so that in six years half-a-million cars of this type were produced. In the 1954 'Mille Miglia' Race, there were 95 Renault 750 cars in the special series touring class in which they took the first five places; the winner's speed was nearly 66 m.p.h.

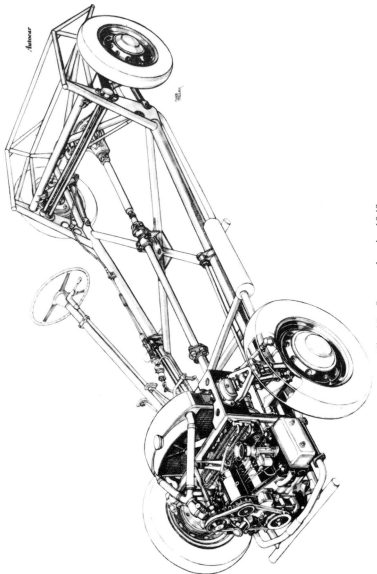

Autocar

Fig. 17   Jowett chassis: 1949

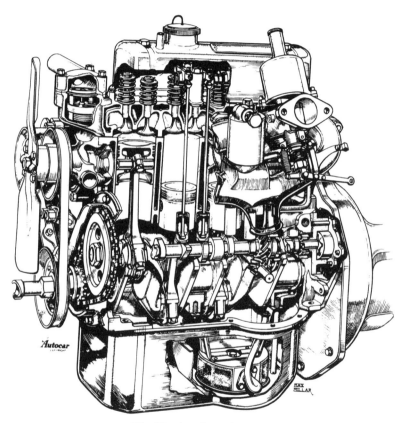

Fig. 18   Austin engine: 1952

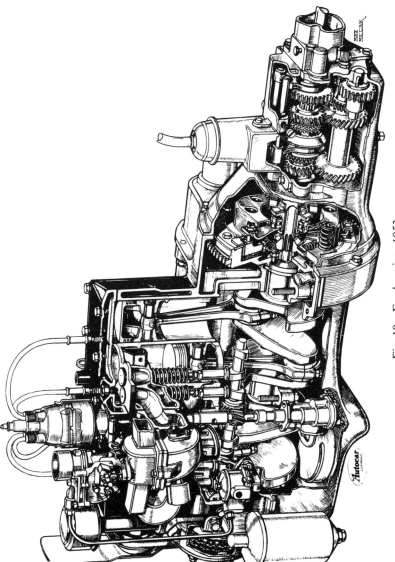

Fig. 19   Ford engine: 1953

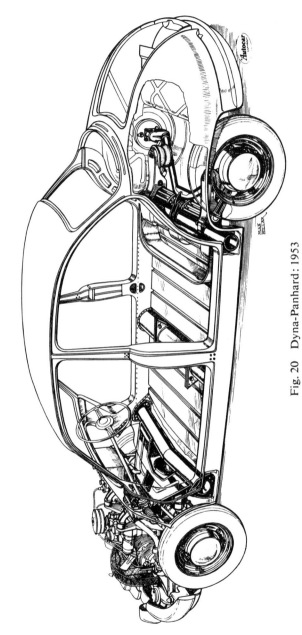

Fig. 20   Dyna-Panhard: 1953

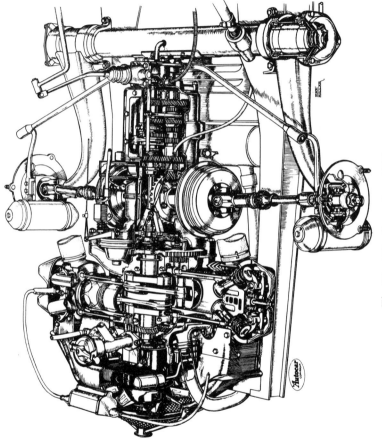

Fig. 21   Citroën engine: 1953

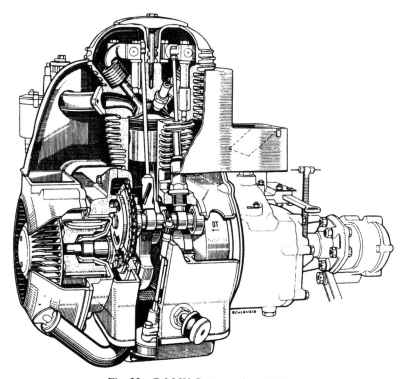

Fig. 22   B.M.W. Isetta engine: 1956

Fig. 23   B.M.W. Isetta minicar: 1956

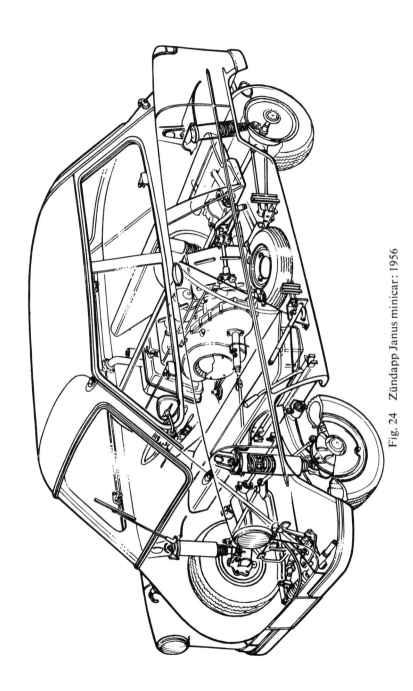

Fig. 24   Zündapp Janus minicar: 1956

The Renault 750 (Plate 23) was a saloon with four seats and four doors; it was built on the body-chassis construction principle, and its unladen weight was 11 cwt. The body was mounted on independently-sprung front wheels, of small diameter and large section (5·20 in. by 15 in.) tyres; all four wheels were equipped with Lockheed hydraulic brakes. The 748 c.c. overhead-valve four-cylinder engine (Plate 25), with a compression ratio of $7\frac{1}{4}$ to 1, developed 21 h.p. at 5000 r.p.m. The engine was mounted longitudinally at the rear of the chassis and drove, through a 3-speed and reverse gearbox and a spiral-bevel final drive, universally-jointed half shafts which connected with the rear wheels. This logical location of engine and drive unit adjacent to the pair of driving wheels, which had begun to be used tentatively in the 1930's was now being increasingly adopted; it made possible a simpler and lighter construction and permitted all the available body space to be used. The Renault 750 was of that class of design whose essential rightness from all aspects was proved by its continued large production over a long period. The 845 c.c. Renault Dauphine (Plate 24) was an improved and somewhat larger version derived from the same design.

Another important example of this small type was the improved model of the Fiat 500 which had been in successful commercial production since 1936. The 500C model of 1952, with an unladen weight of 12 cwt., had a maximum speed of 60 m.p.h., and covered 56 miles on a gallon of fuel. The 570 c.c. four-cylinder overhead-valve engine, with a compression-ratio of $6\frac{3}{4}$ to 1, developed $16\frac{1}{2}$ h.p. at 4400 r.p.m. A refinement of this design was the aluminium-alloy cylinder head with special durable valve-seat inserts which, with the additional progressive features of a high-compression ratio overhead-valves and a combustion-chamber designed to improve combustion, and lessen detonation, were now being employed by the smallest cars to maintain engine tune under sustained high operational speeds.

The later Fiat 600 model (Plate 23) followed the modern trend of driving the pair of wheels adjacent to the engine. The 633 c.c. four-cylinder engine (Plate 25), which was mounted in rear, had a compression ratio of 7 to 1 and developed $21\frac{1}{2}$ h.p. at 4600 r.p.m. The rear-mounted radiator was cooled by a large fan. The complete engine, gearbox, drive and independent-suspension rear wheels comprised a readily-detachable assembly which, with the chassis-body, was extremely simple, light and easy to maintain. High cruising speeds, economical operation and excellent road-holding characteristics were features of this progressive design.

LIGHT CARS: to 1000 c.c.

In spite of the general tendency which now existed in light-car design to use engines with overhead valves, the side-valve form of engine was retained by some manufacturers in the interests of economical production. The chief of these was the Ford Company which continued with their 933 c.c. engine design. The model, known as the Anglia, although it was of the simpler specification and produced on highly efficient mass-production lines, had a good performance combined with extreme reliability. In 1953, this basic design appeared as the 933 c.c. Popular model, which was the cheapest four-cylinder car then in production. In 1954, this model was being produced at the Dagenham factory at the rate of 350 a day.

The various Sevens and Eights of the late 1930's, which had been continued in slightly improved forms for a few years after 1945, reappeared as entirely new models by 1950. The Morris Minor, with a 918 c.c. side-valve engine which developed 29½ h.p. at 4400 r.p.m., had a modern semi-stylised saloon body of the body-chassis form of construction. The specification was typical of this advanced stage of light-car design, and included such items as independent-suspension of the front wheels, semi-floating rear axle with a hypoid gear which provided a more efficient and durable gear and a lower-slung construction, and small-diameter large-section tyres (14 in. by 5 in.). The Austin A30 Seven followed the same general design, but was fitted with an efficient overhead-valve engine of 803 c.c. capacity (Fig. 18), which developed 28 h.p. at 4800 r.p.m. On the merging of the Austin Motor Co. Ltd. and Morris Motors Ltd. into the British Motor Corporation in 1953, this engine was also standardised for the Morris Minor (Plate 23) in the interests of technical efficiency, production economy and standardised maintenance. The weight of these new Sevens was about 13 cwt.; they were still capable of covering 50 miles to a gallon of fuel as had their simpler predecessors of the 1930's and, in addition, they possessed considerably improved cruising and top speeds of 50–55 m.p.h. and 60–65 m.p.h. respectively.

To accommodate a demand for more power with the Austin A30 and Morris Minor as well as to take advantage of the 100 octane fuel which became commercially available in 1956, the 948 c.c. Austin A35 engine was produced with a compression ratio of 8 ·3 to 1, and a power output of 34 h.p. at 4750 r.p.m.

Another British example of this form of advanced small type of car was the Standard 8, which first appeared in 1953. It was of the same general specification as the Minor and A30 designs, having an 803 c.c. four-cylinder engine which developed 26 h.p. at 4500 r.p.m. A feature of this design, intended to reduce the purchase price in the trade competition which was now appearing, was a lack of embellishments such as radiator grille, internal upholstery on door panels and various accessories which did not affect the operation of the car, but which could be purchased separately as extras.

This category of light car was not much catered for by Continental manufacturers.

LIGHT CARS: to 1250 c.c.

This medium class of light car of up to 1250 c.c. capacity was by 1950 represented by many new models, which ranged from the simple side-valve four-cylinder type to the high efficiency overhead-valve four- and six-cylinder types. These designs were, moreover, produced in a variety of versions which served various needs.

The simplest and cheapest side-valve design of this category was produced by the Ford Motor Company Ltd. in their later Popular, Anglia and Prefect

(Plate 26) models. In 1953, the two latter models appeared in redesigned form, with the styled Consul-type of saloon body, and with an improved version of the simple 1172 c.c. capacity engine (Fig. 19) which developed 36 h.p. at 4400 r.p.m., and which gave these cars a performance that was little inferior to contemporary models having overhead-valve engines. A more elaborate example of the side-valve four-cylinder engined car was the 1185 c.c. Hillman Minx saloon, which was a development of the pre-1939 models. The Sunbeam-Talbot 80 was originally the same basic model as the Minx and was equipped with the same engine in more efficient form and of greater output. After 1945, this model was equipped with an overhead-valve version of the same engine which was also used for the Minx.

The more advanced models followed the general formula which had been foreshadowed as long ago as 1937 by the Vauxhall 10 design, described in Chapter 8. The 1200 c.c. Austin A40 conformed generally to the modern standard formula and, combining good and reliable performance with quiet and comfortable operation, became much used both at home and abroad as one of the best of the medium light cars. A similar design of Continental manufacture was the French 1221 c.c. Simca Aronde which, with an unladen weight of 18¼ cwt., was capable of a top speed of 75 m.p.h. Of still better quality and performance was the Wolseley 4-44 which was fitted with the 1250 c.c. M.G. T-type of engine, having an output of over 50 h.p. at 5500 r.p.m.

Such designs as these, in spite of their light overall weight and mass-produced construction, demonstrated that the latest formula which had evolved from world-wide use was capable of sustained and reliable operation under a wide variety of climatic and physical conditions. In 1951, for instance, an Austin A40 car was driven nearly 10,000 miles around the world in three weeks, averaging 441 miles a day without any mechanical trouble.

Still further progress was made with the medium-capacity engine, with the aid of the technical advances achieved during this period. The most remarkable were perhaps the Italian 1090 c.c. Lancia Appia and the 1100 c.c. Fiat 103 designs, whose small engines developed some 40 h.p. at 5000 r.p.m. The Lancia Appia (Plate 27) was in the direct tradition of the many previous models of this make which fitted engines of the narrow vee form; it had a top speed of 75 m.p.h. Besides the standard model of the Fiat 103, a sports version was also produced whose engine developed 48 h.p. at 5200 r.p.m., and which had a top speed of 80 m.p.h.

Still more elaborate forms of this medium size of light car were the 1287 c.c. Lanchester 'Eleven' which, in addition to being built to Daimler standards, included a fluid flywheel and a pre-selector gearbox.

One of the most revolutionary, both from the technical as well as the commercial aspects, was the German Volkswagen design (Plate 26) which, although it had been announced in 1937, did not go into full commercial production until 1948. This car was designed to be produced as cheaply as possible and in great numbers, and it combined simplicity and advanced layout with utility and reliability. The 1955 model was fitted with an 1192 c.c. four-cylinder horizontally-opposed push-rod operated overhead-valve engine which developed 36 h.p. at 3700 r.p.m. This engine was air-cooled, of substantially smaller stroke than bore (77 mm. by 64 mm.), and it was located at the rear of the body-chassis. It drove the rear wheels through a single dry-plate clutch and a 4-speed and reverse synchromesh gearbox, with a top gear of 4·43 to 1. Hydraulic brakes and independent torsion-rod springing were features of its advanced specification. It covered up to 38 miles on a gallon of fuel, and had a top speed of 68 m.p.h. Moreover, it was quiet in operation, a quality which had heretofore usually been lacking in air-cooled engines. The wide commercial demand for the Volkswagen caused 180,000 cars to be built in 1953, and arrangements were made to manufacture or assemble them in various countries. Some 200,000 Volkswagen cars were produced in 1954, which constituted about half of the total German production of cars.

The sports type of car, the majority of which were of the medium-capacity fuel, and had a top speed of 68 m.p.h. Moreover, it was quiet in operation, a category, included the 1250 c.c. M.G. Midget, the 1100 c.c. H.R.G., the 1100 c.c. Morgan 4–4, and the 1100 c.c. Singer designs. The M.G. Midget, in the latest TD and TF models, was, in particular, greatly improved in chassis and body details by the adoption of the modern specification of independent front suspension. The same 1250 c.c. four-cylinder engine, developing in standard form 53 h.p. at 5500 r.p.m., was still retained as the power unit for both these new sports models, as well as the M.G. saloon and Wolseley 4–44 saloon models. In addition, two additional degrees of tune were now available, by means of which higher output without supercharging were obtained The Morgan 4–4 was continued for some time after 1945 in its original form but by 1950, the production of the Morgan Company was concentrated upon the 'Plus Four' model which fitted a 2 litre Standard engine.

LIGHT CARS: to 1500 c.c.

A considerable selection of advanced models were available soon after 1950 which embodied in full measure the progressive features that had now been established as being essential to the modern car. With overhead-valve engines having outputs varying from 35 h.p. to 80 h.p., they possessed a high average performance and load-carrying capacity, together with efficiency and reliability. Examples ranging from the economical mass-produced types to those of the most complicated and special types, were produced in considerable numbers and sold in world-wide markets for use under all conditions of operation.

The lowest priced examples of this category included such models as the larger 1390 c.c. Hillman Minx (Plate 30), the 1508 c.c. Ford Consul (Plate 27), the 1507 c.c. Vauxhall Wyvern, the 1489 c.c. Morris Oxford and the 1500 c.c. Austin A50 models. These had four-cylinder high-efficiency engines of the push-rod operated overhead-valve type, which were capable of developing 40 to 50 h.p. at engine speeds between 4000 and 4600 r.p.m., and which permitted road speeds of up to 75 m.p.h.

Of more solid construction and elaborate design were the Riley 1500 and 1489 c.c. M.G. Magnette models. Besides being representative examples

114

of their class, they were also embodiments of the standardisation of basic design, since both employed the same 1489 c.c. Riley four-cylinder push-rod operated overhead valve engine produced under the combined activities of the British Motor Corporation. The M.G. Series A sports car was equipped with this engine which developed 68 h.p. at 5500 r.p.m. and gave the car a speed of nearly 100 m.p.h. The 1497 c.c. Singer with overhead camshaft engine was in the same category. The 1486 c.c. Jowett Javelin (Fig. 17) was an advanced design having the horizontally-opposed form of engine which this firm had concentrated upon since 1906. The compact four-cylinder engine was mounted in a forward position and was readily accessible for servicing purposes; it developed 52 h.p. at 4300 r.p.m. and gave the car a top speed of 80 m.p.h. and a fuel consumption of 30 m.p.g. A sports model of the Javelin was available with a top gear of 4·44 to 1, and was also fitted with a Laycock-de Normanville overdrive gear which increased the top gear to 3·46 to 1, thus making possible a reduction of engine speed and an improved fuel economy for high-speed cruising. The H.R.G. car was fitted with the improved 1497 c.c. Singer engine, which developed 50 h.p. in normal tune; in special tune and with an H.R.G. cylinder head, 90 h.p. was developed. The 1955 design of H.R.G. car (Plate 28) was an up-to-date version of the advanced streamlined sports car of high-power-weight ratio, low build and high performance.

The first version of the Rover 60 model, produced soon after 1945, besides having all the inherent excellence of Rover design and manufacture, also had a new type of four-cylinder engine, the chief feature of which was a cylinder head incorporating high-efficiency combustion chambers, and side-exhaust valve and inclined overhead-inlet valve. This arrangement of cylinder head was an example of the most modern practice for improving volumetric efficiency, and ensuring more thorough combustion of fuel in the interest of higher power and lower fuel consumption. The later version of the Rover 60 had an engine of 2 litres capacity.

Continental versions of this category were in general of the more elaborate and expensive types. The Peugeot 203 was one of the smaller designs having an overhead-valve engine of 1290 c.c. capacity, which developed 45 h.p. Its unladen weight was only 17½ cwt. The German Porsche type 356 light car (Plate 28) had a short-stroke (80 mm. by 74 mm.) four-cylinder horizontally-opposed engine (Plate 27) of 1500 c.c. capacity which, with the two carburettors which this form of engine required, developed 55 h.p. at 4400 r.p.m. Although this car had a fuel consumption of up to 35 m.p.g., it was capable of a maximum speed of 100 m.p.h. With a higher compression ratio of 8·2 to 1, this car developed 70 h.p. at 5000 r.p.m., which increased its top speed to 110 m.p.h.

Of still higher quality and performance was the 1290 c.c. Alfa-Romeo Giulietta which weighed only 16 cwt. and was an outstanding example of the chassis-body makers' art in reducing structural weight to the minimum with adequate strength. The four-cylinder engine developed 65 h.p. at 6000 r.p.m., which gave this model a maximum speed of 100 m.p.h. An alternative power unit, consisting of a List twin-cylinder two-stroke Diesel engine of 1158 c.c. capacity which developed 30 h.p. at 2800 r.p.m., was also available.

An example of the use of a sleeve valve engine for light car propulsion at this time was a prototype design produced by Sir Roy Fedden in 1948. This was a three-cylinder radial engine of 1580 c.c. capacity (86 mm. by 91 mm.) which used the Burt-McCollum single sleeve valve, and developed 68 h.p. at 4700 r.p.m. This design had behind it the many years of intensive development which had produced the wide range of Bristol sleeve-valve aero engines.

Two-Stroke Engines

The English firm of Trojan Ltd., which had concentrated upon the production of two-stroke engined cars of novel design since 1922, produced in 1947 a still more advanced design, which was nevertheless based upon old established forms. The Trojan type 15, fitted with this type 65 engine, was produced solely as a trade van. The 1186 c.c. (65.5 mm. by 88 mm.) engine (Plate 27) was of the four-cylinder duplex type with each pair of cylinders having a common combustion chamber. A maximum of 23 h.p. was developed at the low speed of 2100 r.p.m. The fresh-gas charging was effected by means of two separate pumping cylinders, having a total capacity of 1293 c.c. and arranged at 90° to the working cylinders to assist balance. The transfer and exhaust ports were controlled by the pistons in the power cylinders. Each pair of working pistons had their connecting rods mounted on a common crankpin, and the cylinders were spaced to provide a differential movement of the two pistons, so that the exhaust port opened and closed before the transfer port. This arrangement assisted scavenging and minimised loss of fresh charge through the exhaust port. The capacity of each pumping cylinder was some 9% larger than the respective working cylinder it supplied, so that good volumetric efficiency and high torque at low engine speeds were ensured. The transfer valve between pumping and working cylinder was originally of the rotary type, but was later changed to an atmospherically-operated flap-type of valve in the interests of simplicity. The engine was of a compact vee-cylinder arrangement and was mounted in the front of the chassis in normal manner.

After 1945, the development and use of the larger and more complex forms of two-stroke light car engine progressed, particularly on the Continent. The most important type in this category was the three-cylinder in-line unit which, while retaining the essential simplicity of its three-port, crankcase-compression arrangement, assumed the performance, scope and characteristics of considerably more complicated six-cylinder four-stroke engines. Having an average cylinder capacity of under one litre, light cars equipped with these engines had maximum speeds approaching 80 m.p.h., and fuel consumptions of over 30 m.p.g.

The most important development on the Continent was a new front-wheel driven D.K.W. design, known as the Sonderklasse model (Plate 22), which had the same chassis and body as the two-cylinder Meisterklasse, but which had its engine arranged longitudinally in the chassis. The new engine was an

896 c.c. three-cylinder in-line unit (Plate 25), incorporating in compact form a clutch, 3-speed and reverse synchromesh gearbox and differential unit. This engine, which developed 34 h.p. at 4200 r.p.m., was originally designed as early as 1939, but did not appear in production until 1953. In spite of its small and simple engine, the D.K.W. Sonderklasse car cruised at about 60 m.p.h. and had a top speed of 70 m.p.h.

The Swedish Saab 93 was of similar design, with a three-cylinder engine of 748 c.c. capacity (66 mm. by 73 mm.) which developed 38 h.p. at 5000 r.p.m. fitted with a carburettor.

Another example of the three-cylinder two-stroke light-car engine was the proprietary 677 c.c. Heinkel engine, which developed 26 h.p. at 4000 r.p.m. It was used, in particular, to power the German Tempo one-ton truck and light bus vehicles. The 900 c.c. Eisenacher design developed 37 h.p. at 4000 r.p.m. The 886 c.c. Lloyd Goliath was fitted with a 10-seat coach body.

The Italian 236 c.c. three-cylinder Isos cars demonstrated the power and reliability of the smallest form of the three-cylinder two-stroke engine for use in cars, by winning the Index of Performance classification in the 1954 Mille Miglia road race at an average speed of 30 m.p.h.

ACCESSORIES AND ANCILLARIES

Accessories such as lighting and starting systems tended to remain as they had evolved in the 1930's. There was, however, a fundamental change in the nature of such ancillaries as bodies and suspension systems and drive systems, which were designed to meet the new trends of development which had materialised after 1945.

The bodies of light cars after 1945 were generally of the body-chassis type, which lessened both the weight and the production costs of the structure. They were usually of the saloon type with deep windows giving clear vision all around, a factor which was becoming more and more essential in the congested traffic conditions now becoming common. Some open two and four-seater types with folding-hoods were also produced, particularly in sports-car form. Detachable hard-top covers converted the open sports car quickly and conveniently into a saloon when required. More thought was given to the conservation of power provided by streamlined body form. The sliding or sunshine roof, which had been so popular with saloons during the 1930's, now tended to disappear because it complicated the stressed-skin form of body construction, and also because the problem of making it watertight when closed had never really been solved. Another form of body which now gained in public favour was the versatile station-waggon type which, with its smart appearance and large carrying capacity, could serve business as well as family requirements. Still lighter and cheaper methods of body construction, such as the use of fibreglass and reinforced plastic construction, were being adopted by 1955. A disadvantage of the body-chassis construction was the higher cost of repair.

There were two main phases in the development of the body-chassis construction from the original separate body and chassis frame. The first stage, originated in general production by about 1937, was the building into the body of a light form of chassis frame which, in the case of an 8 or 10 h.p. car, resulted in a saving of weight of about 1 cwt. The second stage, which was in general use by 1950, discarded the chassis frame and instead strengthened the body shell by the incorporation in its structure of various box and girder sections. This method of construction saved another 1 cwt. of body-chassis weight.

The increasing tendency to arrange the engine unit to drive the pair of road wheels adjacent to it began to abolish the long propeller shaft, and thus to permit a low centre of gravity and increased body space.

Minicar bodies were, in particular, designed to conserve space and lessen weight. The front opening door, in particular, assisted these two aspects.

Tyres tended to become of smaller diameter both to lessen wheel weight and to accommodate the lower enveloping body forms now being used; they were also of increased section and lower pressure to assist riding comfort. By 1954, the tubeless tyre was introduced both as a simplication and to make punctures less likely. The use of tough and durable rayon and even nylon cord was in some cases being adopted to replace the cotton cord which had been used since the invention of the pneumatic tyre.

Wheels also decreased substantially in diameter as a consequence of the new forms of tyre being used. They were also simplified in construction and were either of the stamped-steel spoked-disc type which was secured to the wheel-hub by nuts, or of the stamped-steel rim type which was attached by studs and nuts to an aluminium-alloy hub-spider by nuts. The wire-spoked wheel ceased to be used except in highly developed forms for racing, not only because of its comparative high cost of manufacture, but also because its drilled rim could not hold air pressure when used with a tubeless tyre.

Although some designs still continued to use fixed rear axles with the usual pair of semi-elliptic leaf springs, the trend of design was now strongly towards the independent suspension of all four wheels. Front wheels were now generally independently suspended, usually on coil springs or transverse leaf springs with wishbone-type radius arms, but also to some extent on swing arms mounted on torsion rods. The interconnected front and rear swing-arm suspension system, working in conjunction with inertia-type shock absorbers of the 2 c.v. Citroën, was an outstanding example of advanced chassis suspension design.

Rear-suspension systems which were independently sprung employed both the coil spring and radius arm and the swing arm systems, in conjunction with coil springs, transverse-leaf springs or torsion-rod springs. Rear axles used with independent rear-suspension systems were necessarily of the divided type incorporating some suitable arrangement of the De Dion-Bouton split axle, which permitted the heavy differential and drive casing to be secured to the sprung body and transmitted power to the driving wheels through two universally-jointed half shafts. In some cases, the gearbox was now also incorporated with the differential unit, as had been in some use in 1914, with the important difference that both gearbox and differential units were now both supported by the suspension system.

By 1956, independent rear suspension was beginning to be adopted even for minicars. Because of the improved riding and road holding it provides, this type of suspension later became general practice for most forms of light car.

The considerably higher performance of which cars of this period were capable in conjunction with increasing traffic congestion, particularly in large towns, necessitated still more powerful and positive braking systems. Improved and larger capacity brakes of the mechanical Girling or the hydraulic Lockheed, Girling and Bendix types were therefore produced and standardised for current production cars. In addition, advanced types such as the efficient disc form of brake, which was positive and powerful in action and was also immune from some of the weaknesses of the drum-type of brake, were developed experimentally for racing. By 1954, this form of brake was beginning to be fitted as standard on some of the more expensive large cars.

The electrical dynamo and starter-motor system, with improvements such as constant-voltage control, continued to be used in standard production for the great majority of cars. Exceptions to this standardisation consisted of special requirements, such as the Siba Dynastart flywheel-dynamotor used with the D.K.W., Villiers and Anzani two-stroke engines.

Minicars: from 1956

The decade after 1960 was notable for the wide variety of new car models of increasing elaboration and performance capability, from the smallest runabouts having engines of from only 50 c.c. capacity to the largest light cars having engines up to 1600 c.c. capacity. This proliferation of all types and sizes of runabouts, ultra-light cars and minicar models as well as the larger light cars was still mainly a European initiative, although a few other countries further afield were now entering this market, notably Japan which rapidly produced a wide variety of efficient and progressive designs of cars of all kinds, and to a lesser extent Russia. Actual production of light cars was not established in America which remained wedded to the large 'continental' car, although considerable quantities of light cars were imported from England, Germany, France and later Japan.

This perfection and proliferation of the small car in the 1960's began to have the effect of reducing the average accepted size of motor cars in general, by demonstrating the redundancy of the large expensive car whose function, except for special purposes, could now be adequately and with greater economy performed by the modern medium-size car. This trend was illustrated by the marked increased demand for such cars as the Rover 2000 and the significant decline in demand for larger 3-litre cars.

What may be called the descendants of the simple and crude cyclecars of 1912–14 appeared during the 1960's in three main categories: the motorised runabout, the ultra-light car and the minicar. The motorised runabout was the ultimate in simple personal transport, especially in stripped racing form, being usually for one or two persons and powered by simple two-stroke engines of from 50 c.c. to 200 c.c. capacities; the ultra-light car was more elaborate and powerful with efficient single or twin-cylinder engines of up to 500 c.c. capacity, and capable of carrying two to four passengers in compact coupé bodies with interior heating and full weather protection; and the minicar which, in its fully-equipped form was a true motor car in miniature propelled by efficient two- or four-cylinder engines of up to 750 c.c. capacity and capable of carrying four passengers and luggage on extended touring runs.

Whereas the cyclecar of 1912–14 materialised from the prime need of economy and the related necessity of simplicity, its descendant of the more affluent and technically capable 1960's had a social rather than an economical reason for its existence, although cheapness in both first cost and operation was still of importance. The simplicity and resulting cheapness of the early cyclecars made them available to unaffluent customers whose chief desire was to become motorists, however humble. The compactness and mechanical reliability of the modern ultra-light car, rather than its simplicity and economy, considerably widened the scope of its social capabilities. The ultra-light car of this later period being now a thoroughly developed practical and reliable vehicle could be used with confidence for daily transport uses. These uses for the most part implied urban travel, with the implicit problem of urban parking in increasing traffic congestion, the inevitable result of general prosperity. The lightness, inherent compactness and ease of handling of the ultra-light car mitigated this problem of urban parking and, while its technical dependability was now established, its general concept provided at least a partial answer to a social problem of growing importance and urgency.

This particular aspect of urban traffic conditions called into prototype consideration a simple motorised vehicle suitable for such requirements which were termed 'city runabouts'. Essentially, they provided such transport with weather protection for one or two persons with parcel accommodation without the addition of unnecessary embellishments. As, however, the smallest minicars were nearly as compact as these stripped runabouts and, at the same time, were capable of both urban and long-distance duties with up to four passengers, the case for specialised vehicles was not wholly sound. In general, the larger minicars met the social needs of compactness and easy handling, and thus perhaps contributed as much to the solution of the problems as the simpler, less versatile alternative. Moreover, since the modern minicar, with its compactness and economy of operation, make it a suitable town as well as a general-purpose vehicle, it was suggested that minicar design should be made still more generally flexible by such elaborations as larger entrance doors for town and taxi use, and the adoption of two-pedal transmission to facilitate control in traffic.

There was, moreover, at this time a revival of the idea of the small electrically-propelled town carriage which was influenced not only by the necessity of a handy city runabout, but also by the growing need to reduce air pollution in cities by exhaust fumes. Prototype designs appeared such as the Westinghouse Markette, the Tube Investments car, the Carter Coaster, and the Japanese Kansai and Chubu cars. These were generally two-seat models powered by multiples of 6 or 12 volt lead-acid batteries, except the latter which had an alkaline battery, and capable of a run of 50 miles before needing recharging. Design was concentrated on the reduction of weight and the development of new forms of storage batteries such as the alkaline, silver-zinc, sodium-sulphur types as well as the methanol, hydrogen or hydrazine fuel cell, which might have twice to several times the specific capacity of the standard lead-acid type. This development, however, is still in the initial development stage and its commercial viability depends almost solely on the successful development of the large-capacity, low-weight and small-size battery as a power source.

The Ford Comuta electric car was one of the first experimental prototypes to be produced by a large car firm. The producers expected the electric car to be commercially feasible within the next ten years, primarily as a city centre delivery van and suburban shopping car. The 2–3 seat Comuta design had an enclosed body and was only 6 ft. 8 in. long to facilitate parking. The lead-acid battery energised an electric motor which gave the vehicle a top speed of 40 m.p.h. and a range of 40 miles at 25 m.p.h.

Both three- and four-wheel versions of the ultra-light car appeared during this period in considerable variety, although the tendency was now towards the latter form with more elaborate equipment and somewhat larger and more powerful engines. A few examples of the still larger minicar form of three-wheeler with four-cylinder engines continued in production with styled body forms. Apart from the simpler forms of three-wheeler, which had the advantage of lower price, the production of the heavier and more elaborate three-wheeler during this period was somewhat illogical, since it cost as much to produce as its four-wheeled counterpart, and had only the slight advantage of a lower road tax.

The more elaborate four-wheel versions of the 500 c.c. ultra-light car of this period were truly complete cars in miniature. In spite of small single- and twin-cylinder engines and necessarily compact bodies, they were nevertheless capable of relatively high cruising speeds with four-passenger accommodation, economy and reliability of operation and provided acceptable passenger comfort. As well as being convenient for town use, they were equally capable of reliable long-distance travel. In addition, they possessed many of the features of the larger car in such features as car heating, indedependent suspension, adequate hydraulic brakes, and all-round vision.

The yet larger and more elaborate 750 c.c. minicar extended still further the efficient performance of the smaller ultra-light cars with higher cruising speeds and somewhat larger bodies providing additional space and passenger comfort, while still retaining a high degree of economy of operation. German and Japanese manufacturers in particular made important technical advances with this category of small car.

MOTORISED RUNABOUTS

Variants of the simplest four-wheeled motorised runabout consisted of three forms: a stripped model for racing known as a 'go-kart', the city runabout and the invalid carriage. Basically, they all consisted of a simple frame chassis, usually of triangular shape with a small-capacity two-stroke engine driving the rear wheel or wheels by means of a chain, and being equipped with seating and body accommodation according to the type of vehicle.

The simplest form of motorised passenger-carrying vehicle which became known as the go-kart, was introduced in 1959 as the ultimate in economical motor racing which provided, however faintly, some of the thrills of the real racing circuits and events. Its essential simplicity, skeleton construction and minimal equipment characterised the concept in general. The engine, usually a highly-tuned two-stroke air-cooled unit, was mounted in the rear of the frame chassis and drove the rear axle direct through a chain or through an intermediary gearbox in the larger sizes. A direct-acting steering mechanism controlled the front wheels. Driver accommodation was confined to the essentials of a seat and footrests, which gave the driver a crouching attitude. The single-gear vehicles required to be pushed for starting, while some of the larger models were fitted with gearboxes and kick-starters. Operation was at continuous full throttle. Two classes of racing were established: Class 1 with engines of 100 c.c. capacity with direct gear, and Class 2 with engines of 200 c.c. capacity with a gearbox. The engines generally used were of Villiers make; a single unit powered Class 1 vehicles, and two coupled units powered Class 2 vehicles. An elaborate American design of go-kart had a longer wheel base to permit a reclining position for the driver, and shallow built-up sides.

The city runabout was generally a three-wheeled vehicle with more flexibility of control for city driving and an enclosed body to provide suitable weather protection. In this period, quite a number of designs of this kind went into small production as a partial solution of traffic congestion in cities. The smallest examples of this form of transport were the German Breutsch Mopetta and the English Peel Trident designs. The Peel Trident was a three-wheeled two-seat saloon, the body of which hinged forward to give entry. A 49 c.c. D.K.W. air-cooled two-stroke engine developing 4 h.p. at 6500 r.p.m. with a compression ratio of 8·2 to 1 drove the rear wheel through a three-speed gearbox, without a reverse gear. The Breutsch Mopetta had a 49 c.c. engine and was of similar specification, but was available with either a saloon or open body. A larger example of the city runabout was the Scootacar (Plate 31) three-wheel design which had a steel platform chassis and an enclosed body entered by a single wide door which provided seating accommodation for two persons in tandem. A Villiers 197 c.c. two-stroke engine drove the single rear wheel through a four-speed gearbox; a Siba dynamotor provided a full electrical system including starting. This vehicle had a top speed of 50 m.p.h. and a petrol consumption of 80 m.p.g. Hydraulic brakes worked on the two front wheels. The steering was by handlebar control column.

The motorised invalid carriage has been used occasionally for many years, one of the first examples being the bath-chair form fitted with a 1 h.p. Autowheel unit, originally intended for bicycle propulsion, which was used as a quick improvisation for the incapacitated of the First World War. After 1945, the invalid carriage evolved from an open machine with the bare necessary equipment to a well-developed enclosed car with full electrical equipment and flexibly designed controls which could be modified to suit handicapped persons and also assist them in entering and leaving it. This development included the addition of two seats to the specification with the psychological benefits that companionship gives, thus getting away from the former idea that the invalid carriage must be a single seater. An elaborate modern design of this kind was the Harper Mk. VI invalid car which had a styled coupé body of glass fibre plastic laminate. A 197 c.c. Villiers two-stroke air-cooled engine, fitted with a Siba Dynastart unit, drove one of the two rear wheels through a four-speed gearbox and chain. The single front wheel was tiller steered; three steering leverages were available to suit the strength of the invalid driver. The Greaves invalid carriage was another example. Some manufacturers of ultra-light cars provided a flexibility of design to accommodate these small yet capable vehicles to the individual requirements of incapacitated persons. Moreover, these modern designs had the virtue of reliability which is of first importance to this class of users.

ULTRA-LIGHT CARS

Designs of the ultra-light form of simple car, of both the three- and four-wheeled kinds, had gained a certain amount of popularity as a means of economical motoring for up to two persons since 1945 and several of these designs continued in production in improved appearance and with slightly larger engines. In addition, progressive designs from newcomers, such as the Japanese and Russians, entered this market with a variety of models so that this later period offered a wide choice.

Three-Wheeled Designs

Among the original designs which were supplied in improved form were the three-wheeler Bond 250G model, which could be fitted with either a 250 c.c. Villiers single-cylinder engine developing 11 h.p. at 4500 r.p.m., or a 250 c.c. Villiers two-cylinder engine developing 14·6 h.p. at 5500 r.p.m. These models had improved styled saloon bodies, and could also be supplied in open tourer and estate car versions. The single-cylinder four-stroke engine of the B.M.W. Isetta Plus had its capacity increased to 295 c.c. and its power output to 13 h.p. at 5000 r.p.m. This engine could be fitted with a Smith Selectroshift magnetic clutch, thus investing the car with two-pedal control. The Heinkel design was manufactured in England as the Trojan 200, whose 198 c.c. single-cylinder four-stroke engine developed 10 h.p. at 5500 r.p.m. The Messerschmitt KR 201 cabin scooter still used the 191 c.c. Sachs single-cylinder two-stroke engine, but with an 8 to 1 compression ratio at which it developed 12 h.p. at 5250 r.p.m. Reverse gear was provided by the unusual practice of running the engine in the opposite direction of rotation. This design of ultra-light car was later produced as a four-wheeled version. The 346 c.c. A.C. Petite, the 174 c.c. Heinkel Cabin Cruiser, the 197 c.c. Gordon, and the 322 c.c. Anzani Powerdrive were designs which were also continued in improved form. New designs of this category included the Breutsch two-seat car with a 191 c.c. engine or three-seat car with a 247 c.c. engine, Progress Tourette with a 197 c.c. Villiers engine, and the Pashley Pelican with a 600 c.c. J.A.P. four-stroke engine. The considerably larger Reliant and Bond 875 designs powered respectively with a 748 c.c. front-mounted four-cylinder water-cooled engine and a rear-mounted 875 c.c. Hillman Imp engine appeared with styled saloon bodies to seat four passengers.

Four-Wheeled Designs

This period was notable for an advanced specification for the more powerful category of ultra-light cars which was adopted by all the countries concerned in the manufacture of the four-wheeled kind of vehicle. Space being of primary importance, compact design was an essential and this resulted in the adoption of the general formula of combined engine and gearbox unit located either in front or rear of the car and driving the pair of wheels to which it was adjacent; the engines were usually of the two-cylinder kind and air-cooled, thus avoided the complication and space required for a water-cooling system. This general arrangement permitted the maximum space for passengers and luggage within the miniature saloon bodies. The advanced general equipment included in these designs such as heating systems, adequate hydraulic brakes, elaborate electrical systems, all-round vision and efficient suspension and road-holding characteristics gave these small vehicles a progressive character which had inherited none of the features of their crude cyclecar forebears.

Among the first and most typical of the two-cylinder category of ultra-light cars were the Fiat 500 and 500 D models (Plate 31). The 499·5 c.c. (67·4 mm. by 70 mm.) twin-cylinder air-cooled vertical engine (Plate 37) of the latter model developed 17 h.p. at 4400 r.p.m. The engine of the commodious station-wagon version was disposed horizontally which lowered the centre of gravity and added to available space. The two air-cooled cylinders were shrouded and cooled by a turbo fan mounted on the electric generator shaft. An efficient air cleaner and a centrifugal oil cleaner were fitted, and hot air from the cooling system heated the interior of the car and demisted the windscreen. This car was capable of a speed of 60 m.p.h. and a fuel consumption of 60 m.p.g. In spite of the short wheel base of 6 ft., the car was capable of carrying two persons together with reasonable luggage. A considerably improved version of the hitherto severely utilitarian Citroën 2 c.v. design appeared in the Bijou model which had a styled glass fibre two-seat coupé with a rear seat for children. An enlarged flat-twin air-cooled engine of 425 c.c. capacity (66 mm. by 62 mm.) developed 12 h.p. at 4000 r.p.m. with a compression ratio of 7 to 1. Constant velocity joints were fitted to the front wheel drive half-shafts, and the elaborate interconnected coil-spring suspension system as used with the earlier 375 c.c. capacity model was retained.

The Toyo Koygo Mazda R.360 design was a two-seat coupé fitted with a 356 c.c. capacity (60 mm. by 63 mm.) vee-twin cylinder air-cooled four-stroke engine, which was located neatly in rear of the chassis and drove the rear wheels through articulated half-shafts. With a compression ratio of 8 to 1, the power output was 12 h.p. at 4000 r.p.m. Alternative transmissions were offered: a conventional four-speed gearbox with synchromesh on the upper three ratios, or a three-element, two-phase torque convertor in conjunction with a two-speed and reverse gearbox which dispensed with the clutch pedal. A freewheel between convertor output shaft and the gearbox input simplified gear changes and improved fuel consumption. All wheels were independently sprung on trailing arms controlled by rubber-in-torsion springs together with double-acting dampers.

An example of a proprietary engine unit in this category was the efficient German Horex 18 design of 392 c.c. capacity (61·5 mm. by 66 mm.) which was capable of developing 18 to 28 h.p., depending on the degree of tune. This twin-cylinder air-cooled parallel-cylinder engine had such features as a single-overhead camshaft driven by a chain, with valves at an included angle of 80 degrees, and a Hirth serrated-joint built-up crankshaft. Ball and roller big-end and journal bearings were used, and a dynamotor unit with which was incorporated a radial fan ducted to supply cooling air to the shrouded cylinders was mounted on the crankshaft.

Four-Cylinder Engines

As has been seen, the power unit for the ultra-light car was either of the single- or two-cylinder varieties, which were generally adequate for this small kind of car. Some highly-developed examples of small cars fitted with four-cylinder power units were produced by the remarkably progressive Japanese firms which initially broke into the motorcycle world market with rapid commercial and racing success.

This previous experience with advanced highly-tuned multi-cylinder small-capacity motorcycle engines later served to produce two Honda four-cylinder air-cooled units known as the 360 and 500 models for small car propulsion. The Honda 360 model (48 mm. by 49 mm.) and the 500 model (52 mm. by 59 mm.) (Plate 31) develop respectively 33 h.p. at 9000 r.p.m. and 47 h.p. at 8500 r.p.m. The built-up crankshaft was supported in roller bearings, and the twin-camshafts were supported on three needle bearings and driven by a double roller chain. These alternative high-output units were incorporated in a styled light sports body. The engine unit was constructed largely from aluminium alloys with wet cylinder liners, and was installed at the front end of the chassis and inclined at an angle of 45 degrees to reduce bonnet height. The drive was taken through a normal single plate clutch and a five-speed gearbox and cardan shaft to the differential gear, the casing of which was attached to the chassis. At each side of the differential casing there was a two-piece casing, inside which was a chain and sprocket drive to each rear wheel. These oil-bath chain cases also served as trailing arms for the rear suspension, and were supported by combined coil spring and damper units.

The Toyo Koygo Company produced the lively Mazda Carol four-door saloon weighing 11½ cwt. which could be fitted with a four-cylinder water-cooled engine of either 358 c.c. capacity (46 mm. by 54 mm.) or a 586 c.c. capacity (54 mm. by 64 mm.) engine mounted transversely at the rear in unit with the 4-speed and reverse transmission to the rear wheels. The torque converter transmission provided for the simpler R.360 twin-cylinder coupé already mentioned was not available for these more sophisticated models.

Two-Stroke Engines

The simple two-stroke engine of one or two cylinders continued to serve these small ultra-light cars although, as has been seen, the four-stroke engine was favoured for the larger examples. Improved design techniques as well as larger cylinder capacities and higher engine speeds provided these units with increased performance.

An example of this improvement was the Goggomobil TS 400 model whose rear-mounted 392 c.c. capacity (67 mm. by 56 mm.) twin-cylinder air-cooled two-stroke engine developed 20 h.p. at 5000 r.p.m., and gave the car a speed of 60 m.p.h. This was one of the most successful cars of its category, and the neat sports coupé body with which this model was equipped added still further to its quality. An added feature of particular interest was the electrically-controlled preselector gearbox and the double plate clutch working in oil. Another example of a complex transmission being fitted to an ultra-light car was the Victoria Spatz design, which used a 245 c.c. single-cylinder two-stroke engine in conjunction with a Getrag five-speed wedge-ball engagement preselector type of gearbox. The German Maico design was equipped

126

Plate 25

Gutbrod engine: 1951

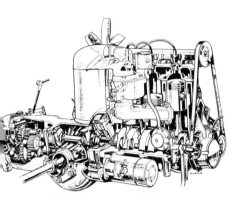

D.K.W. engine: 1953

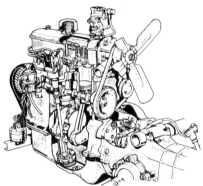

Renault engine: 1954

Fiat engine: 1956

Plate 26

Volkswagen: 1954

Ford Prefect: 1955

Plate 27

Porsche engine: 1955

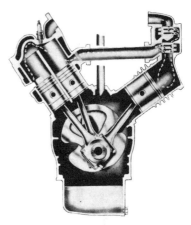

Ford Consul engine: 1955

Trojan engine: 1955

Lancia engine: 1954

Plate 28

H.R.G.: 1956

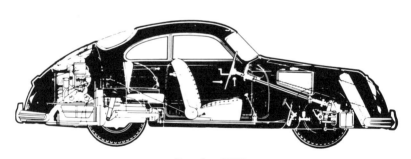

Porsche: 1956

Plate 29

Reliant minicar chassis: 1955

B.M.W. Isetta minicar chassis: 1956

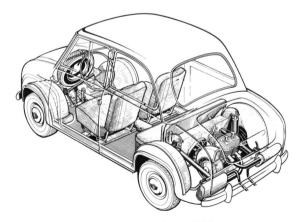

Goggomobil minicar: 1956

Plate 30

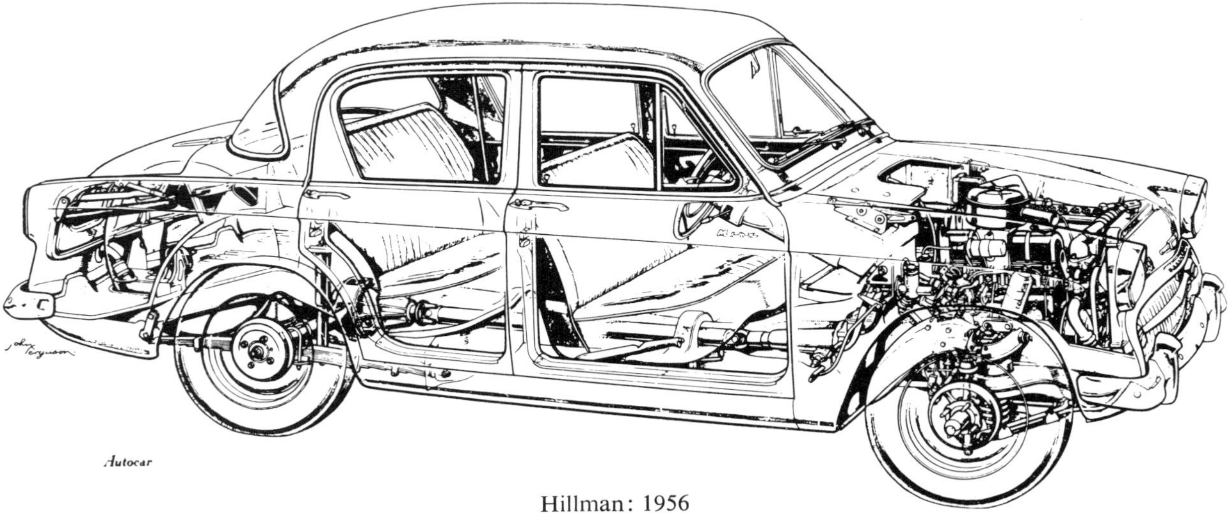

Hillman: 1956

Autocar

Plate 31

Scootacar: 1958

Fiat 500: 1961

Honda 500: 1962

Plate 32

Citroën 2 c.v.: 1957

Fiat 600D: 1961

N.S.U. Prinz: 1962

with a Heinkel 425 c.c. twin-cylinder two-stroke engine mounted behind the rear axle and driving through a four-speed gearbox. The smaller Zundapp Janus fitted with a 248 c.c. two-stroke engine had rear-facing back seats; this latter feature was considered bad psychologically since the inability of the rear passengers to see ahead tended to generate apprehension (Fig. 24).

New examples of this category of ultra-light car included the Italian-designed Vespa 400 model which was manufactured in France. The 394 c.c. capacity (63 mm. by 63·5 mm.) in-line two-stroke engine developed 14 h.p. at 4350 r.p.m.; it was mounted in rear of the four-wheeled coupé car with cylinders inclined 30 degrees. To improve crankcase volumetric efficiency the induction tract was formed on the joint face of the crankcase, and the crank webs were made to act as rotary valves to provide more effective inlet port timing and permit the incoming petrol-oil mixture to spray directly on to the big ends to improve lubrication. This provision permitted a low ratio of oil to petrol of only 1 in 50.

The simple Subaru designs of small two-stroke ultra-light cars were introduced in Japan as a result of taxation grading being made in favour of the small car in order to provide motoring for the lower-paid workers. There was one basic model of Subaru fitted with alternative sizes of vertical-twin two-stroke rear-mounted engines of 360 c.c. and 450 c.c. capacities respectively. The smaller capacity car had the advantage that in Japan it is easier to obtain a driving licence for cars under 360 c.c. capacity. The Mitsubishi Minica design had a 359 c.c. capacity two-stroke engine. The D.K.W. twin-cylinder 400 c.c. design was a reversion to simpler models produced by this firm in the 1930's.

MINICARS: to 750 c.c.

The largest category of small cars, which thirty years before were typically represented by such designs as the 748 c.c. Austin Seven developing 17 h.p. at 4000 r.p.m., and the 855 c.c. Citroën, now consisted of such equivalents as the 746 c.c. D.A.F. developing 30 h.p. at 4000 r.p.m. with equal reliability and longer life in spite of almost double the specific output and greater complexity of design. With only one notable exception, all the engines of this category were of the four-stroke variety and mostly of the four-cylinder kind, although there were still a proportion of two-cylinder engines. All manufacturers of light motor cars, including newcomers such as those in Japan and Russia, contributed a wide variety of designs having diverse detail characteristics and a variety of cylinder dispositions including in-line, vee and horizontally-opposed. As specific outputs increased, so did body size and accommodation become compactly larger in proportion. It may be noted that this was now a general tendency with all categories of light car design, so that those of the largest category, namely, between 1300 c.c. and 1600 c.c. had by now tended to become enlarged to the extent that they must be deemed to be passing from the light car to the medium car class.

Certain firms which had a long experience with the development and wide production of efficient motorcycles, such as N.S.U. and B.M.W., had a sound technical basis for producing compact two-cylinder air-cooled power units capable of developing high specific outputs which served as eminently suitable and reliable engines for this class of small car.

Two-Cylinder Engines

One of the more interesting and original of this class of small fully-developed saloon cars which, despite the comparative simplicity of its engine and compactness of its body, was capable of advanced performance, was the N.S.U. Prinz model (Plate 32) the engine unit of which exemplified advanced techniques. The 598 c.c. capacity (76 mm. by 66 mm.) parallel twin-cylinder air-cooled engine developed 30 h.p. at 5500 r.p.m. with a compression ratio of 7·5 to 1 (Plate 37). A four-speed and reverse gearbox with synchromesh on all forward speeds was arranged in unit construction with the crankcase; the engine unit was moreover mounted transversely across the rear of the chassis and drove the rear wheels through articulated half shafts. The angled overhead valves were actuated by an overhead camshaft which was driven from a half-time wheel by means of a pair of eccentric straps set at 180 degrees to one another. A Siba Dynastart generator was mounted on one extension of the crankshaft and a radial fan was carried on the other extension, and the cooling air generated by the latter was ducted to the shrouded cylinders. Hot air from the cylinders and pressurised by the fan supplied warm air for interior heating of the body. The Austrian Steyr-Puch 500 model which was based on the Fiat 500 design and built under licence, but had a horizontally-opposed air-cooled rear-mounted engine of 493 c.c. capacity (70 mm. by 64 mm.) which developed 16 h.p. at 4600 r.p.m. The Honda N.600 developed 45 h.p. at 7000 r.p.m.

The B.M.W. concern of Munich also had long experience with the production of highly-efficient motorcycles and from this experience was evolved a fully-developed small saloon car known as the 700LS model. The engine of this car was of the two-cylinder air-cooled horizontally-opposed kind, as were the majority of designs of this class, the preference no doubt being dictated by the compactness and good balance characteristics which this form of cylinder disposition offered. The 697 c.c. capacity (78 mm. by 73 mm.) engine units developed 32 h.p. at 5000 r.p.m., which gave the somewhat heavy saloon, which weighed dry some 13 cwt., the remarkably high mean maximum speed of 76 m.p.h. The four-speed and reverse gearbox, with synchromesh on all forward ratios, was in unit construction with the engine and drove the rear wheels; the Lloyd 600 and the Goliath 700 designs had these similar characteristics. The Japanese Toyota Publica UP10 was an example of the front-mounted engine driving the rear axle through a propeller shaft. Another advanced and novel design having a horizontally-opposed engine was the D.A.F. 600 Model with a 590 c.c. capacity (76 mm. by 65 mm.) developing 22 h.p. at 4000 r.p.m., mounted in front and driving the rear wheels through a cardan shaft, an automatic centrifugal clutch and a system of belts and variable pulleys which automatically adjusted the gear ratio to the speed and load. This unusual automatic transmission system is described in Chapter 13, page 157. The life of a pair of these transmission belts was said to be the same for a set of tyres, namely, 25,000 miles. The DAFfodil model had a larger engine of 746 c.c. capacity (85·5 mm. by 65 mm.), which provided a better performance with the 30 h.p. it developed at 4000 r.p.m.

Some of this class of small car using a horizontally-opposed twin-cylinder engine adopted a front-mounted position for driving the front wheels. An important example of this arrangement was the Citroën AMI 6 design, whose basic forerunner was the unorthodox and essentially utilitarian Citroën 2 c.v. model (Plate 32). The AMI 6 model was a fully orthodox and developed design using a 602 c.c. capacity (74 mm. by 70 mm.) horizontally-opposed air-cooled engine, front-mounted and driving the front wheels in the manner of the earlier model, and developing 22 h.p. at 5000 r.p.m. This model also had the independent-suspension system incorporating interacting coil springs between front and rear. The Glass T600 model was another example of this kind, having a horizontally-opposed air-cooled engine mounted in front and driving the front wheels. The 586 c.c. capacity (72 mm. by 72 mm.) engine with a compression ratio of 6·8 to 1 developed 25 h.p.

Four-Cylinder Engines

There were a certain number of more elaborate designs in this category of small cars which established their claim to be complete cars in miniature by the adoption of four-cylinder engines, although these were still within the capacity limit of 750 c.c. The four-cylinder engine in this category compared with the two-cylinder engine was not only smoother running but was also, because of smaller pistons together with short strokes, capable of remarkably high engine speeds with resulting higher specific outputs and performance.

The well-established Fiat 600 model with a rear-mounted four-cylinder water-cooled engine of 633 c.c. capacity (60 mm. by 56 mm.) developing 28 h.p. at 4600 r.p.m., and provided with a well equipped four-seat saloon body, was produced in great numbers from the vast Turin factory and adopted widely for both home and foreign use. The later Fiat 600D (Plate 32) model had several detail improvements incorporated through its long period of production, besides the larger engine of 767 c.c. capacity (62 mm. by 63·5 mm.) which developed 32 h.p. at 4800 r.p.m. These progressive detail improvements included such items as: interior courtesy light, improved suspension, larger radiator, improved car interior heating, fold-down seats to increase luggage space, light and direction-indicator switch mounted on steering column, padded instrument panel, larger capacity battery, improved windscreen wipers, redesigned steering gear, new clutch plates with rubber dampers, combined ignition and starter switch, parcel shelf under instrument panel, and fully-reclining front seats. This list of detail improvements added over a period of ten years of large production illustrates how a basic model could be consistently improved.

A newcomer to this class of small car which was not based on an antecedent design, except in the use of the earlier 4 c.v. engine, was the Renault 4L model produced by one of the largest and oldest established manufacturers (Plate 34). This was basically a utility design, which did not depart drastically, as had the Citroën 2 c.v. model, from acceptable saloon-station waggon lines.

The transmission layout was orthodox, with a front-mounted engine of 747 c.c. capacity (54·5 mm. by 80 mm.) driving the front wheels through a three-speed synchromesh gearbox. This engine developed 26 h.p. at 4500 r.p.m., which gave the car a top speed of 54 m.p.h., it was, however, soon replaced by a larger, more up-to-date engine of 845 c.c. capacity (58 mm. by 80 mm.) which developed 28 h.p. at 4700 r.p.m. With considerably improved torque characteristics, although with only 4 h.p. increase, the mean maximum speed was increased to 70 m.p.h. The engine cooling system was sealed.

The Reliant Rebel (Plate 34) was, by contrast, the production of a small manufacturer who had hitherto concentrated on a three-wheeled car of the more elaborate sort fitted with a 598 c.c. capacity (56 mm. by 61 mm.) four-cylinder water-cooled engine. The four-wheeled Rebel model had the same basic aluminium engine with improved cylinder-head characteristics, which increased the power from 21 to 27 h.p. at 5250 r.p.m. The front-mounted engine drove the live rear axle through a four-speed gearbox and propeller shaft. Examples of this class of small four-cylinder engined car having an unusually high specific power output were the Japanese Mitsubishi Colt of 594 c.c. capacity rear engine design, and the Madja Carol N.600 of 586 c.c. capacity. The high specific output of some 80 b.h.p. per litre capacity and the high maximum crankshaft speed attainable for normal operation of up to 9000 r.p.m. illustrates the notable progress that Japanese automobile engineers had achieved over so short a time during this period.

The Russian Zaporozhets four-cylinder air-cooled vee-engine of 746 c.c· capacity (66 mm. by 55 ·5 mm.) installed in the Cossack light car was an interesting miniature example of this cylinder arrangement whose design was related to the climatic conditions in which it had to operate. Earlier prototypes had a flat four-cylinder arrangement, but the vee arrangement was eventually considered more suitable for Russian weather and road conditions. For instance, shorter induction passages reduced cold starting and other carburation problems, and the vee formation was more easily protected from mud and dust when travelling over unmetalled roads, which would adversely affect cooling of the flat type, particularly of its valve gear. The low compression ratio of only 6 ·6 to 1 confined the output to 20 h.p. at 4000 r.p.m., which was intended to ensure a high degree of reliability and infrequent overhauls. The overhead valves were operated by push rods and rockers from a central camshaft. Cooling was effected by an axial fan which drew air through the space between the cylinders, which were fitted with baffles to direct the air efficiently. Two interesting features of this design were a counter-weighted secondary shaft geared one-to-one in the opposite direction of rotation to the crankshaft to damp out-of-balance forces inherent in the 90 degree cylinder formation, and a centrifugal oil filter built into the crankshaft pulley. Apart from the advantages mentioned, the vee formation for small multi-cylinder engines intended for small cars had the additional one of a short stiff crankcase and overall compactness inherent in this arrangement.

An example of a small proprietary four-cylinder water-cooled engine of high specific output by a specialist engine manufacturer was the Coventry

Climax which had a cylinder block of aluminium with dry pressed-in steel liners. The overhead camshaft, operating valves set at 20 degrees from the vertical, was driven by a single roller chain. The unit four-speed and reverse gearbox was supplied with splined shaft extensions for articulated half-shaft drive to either front or rear wheels.

Two-Stroke Engines

Small cars having engines of capacities between 500 c.c. and 750 c.c. were in general equipped with four-stroke engines, and only a few examples had two-stroke engines which were used more generally for the smaller classes of these small cars since their inherent simplicity accorded logically with the simpler vehicles. The largest examples of two-stroke engines with capacities larger than 750 c.c. capacity used for light cars were of the three-cylinder kind, as described in the next chapter.

The D.K.W. 600 was perhaps the most important example of this class of light car fitted with a two-cylinder two-stroke engine of 660 c.c. capacity which developed 30 h.p. at 4200 r.p.m. This small model, based on the long specialised experience of this firm with two-stroke engined motorcycles and small cars, followed their usual layout of a front-mounted engine driving the front wheels. This model had a comparatively large and commodious body which was apparently too large for the power provided by the small engine, and was thus an example of poor power-weight ratio for this kind of small car. The German Trabant, which could be fitted with an automatic clutch, was of similar characteristics with a two-cylinder two-stroke in-line air-cooled engine which drove the front wheels through a synchromesh four-speed gearbox. This model was also apparently too heavily bodied for the power available and required too frequent use of the gear lever. The Polish Syrena was almost the same as the Trabant but with a larger 744 c.c. capacity engine; a top speed of 65 m.p.h. was claimed for it, so presumably the larger engine provided the better power-weight ratio which the D.K.W. 600 and the Trabant lacked. The D.K.W. 600 and the Trabant perhaps illustrate a tendency to expect more from these small class of cars than was rationally possible, a fault avoided by such mature designs as, for instance, the compact Fiat 500D and Fiat 600D, the N.S.U. Prinz and the B.M.W. 700 designs, which provided four-seat bodies of compact yet adequate size with both acceptable performance and economy of operation.

131

Light Cars: from 1956

Although the general design requirements of the passenger car, whether of the light or medium class, do not materially change, general technological progress in this prolific mid-century period as well as changing social conditions, had a continuous detail influence on design which produced the modern motor car. The major detail developments resulting from these contemporary influences may be here summarised.

One general result of the high performance, reliability and efficient operation to which both the light and medium size cars had by now attained was to demonstrate by comparative production figures that the large luxury car was gradually becoming to be considered unnecessary, except for special occasions. The new minicar had established itself internationally as a competent four-passenger vehicle, and the largest sizes of light car had in performance and body accommodation begun to equal the medium 2-2½ litre car of a decade before, so that it was now capable of most of the duties that had heretofore been performed by the largest cars, and at substantially lower initial and operating costs.

This general competency of the light car had come about through significant general and detail improvements. To begin with, cars were now designed with an international rather than a national outlook which made them generally competitive in places where standards of living were progressing and thus fostering potential car ownership. As well as investing overall design with a robust reliability that resulted from a study of world operating conditions, modern cars were also made more commercially viable. Rear or front-mounted engines and particularly transverse-mounted engines provided up to 80 per cent of the car length for passenger and luggage accommodation in the smaller cars. Such departures from the long established orthodox car layout as originated by Levassor and Maybach were, however, not generally adopted in the larger car designs, presumably as their more commodious bodies did not need such careful conservation of space at the expense of comfort and appearance. It is yet to be seen in future designs whether this trend towards mechanical compactness and space conservation will be eventually adopted for larger cars.

Engine specific outputs were increased by improved combustion head design permitting higher compression ratios, and square or oversquare dimensions permitting higher engine speeds with yet permissible piston speeds. In this and the preceding chapter, the bores and strokes and compression ratios of individual engine designs are quoted to illustrate this trend in design. To deal with the higher crankshaft speeds and power outputs larger, stiffer yet lighter hollow cast-iron crankshafts were introduced. Tentative use was made in production of fuel-injection systems and transistor-ignition systems, but the comparative high cost of such systems produced in small initial quantities gave no firm promise that they would replace the still efficient and cheap existing systems at least in the near future.

The provision and use of overdrive units and automatic transmissions giving two-pedal control, were increasing even for use with a few of the smallest cars. The present excellence of baulk-type synchromesh gearboxes, in conjunction with the diaphragm-type clutch which required only light pedal pressures, however, tended to make automatic transmissions particularly on the smaller cars, something of a luxury. The increase in performance, road congestion and related road accidents increased the importance of efficient road holding and safe control. The race-proved disc brake on either the front or all four wheels was increasingly included in production car specifications. Improved tyres of both radial and transverse cord construction with a variety of scientifically designed tread patterns to contribute to better road holding in all weather conditions were becoming generally available, and with the increase of road speeds up to and beyond 100 m.p.h., the phenomenon of aquaplaning in wet weather was studied. Good road holding as well as passenger riding comfort were contributed to by independent four-wheel suspension, although some examples of the unsprung live rear axle still survived on a few of the larger cars. The provision of balanced steel spring, air or hydro-elastic suspension systems to reduce pitch and bounce by some designers heralded a future general trend.

Car bodies, generally of the four-five seat saloon type, were now artistically styled as well as efficiently engineered with low frontal area and profile of good aerodynamic shape, with all-round vision windows and lights and large doors. Precise ergonomic design of seats and passenger posture provided improved travelling comfort, reduced fatigue and minimised accident injury. Air pollution in cities and towns from engine exhaust gases was also becoming imperative of solution, and caused the formulation of legal directives for the design and installation of devices for preventing or consuming these gases.

LIGHT CARS: to 1000 c.c.

There were still in the smallest class of light cars of up to 1000 c.c. capacity a considerable number of models which continued in the orthodox layout of a front-mounted engine driving through a single-plate dry clutch, a synchromesh gearbox and an open articulated propeller shaft to an unsprung live axle. This long-established formula had been in wide general production for many years and, although new and advanced engine locations and transmission drives were now appearing in increasing variety, this original formula still had for a while an extended production life, usually with improvement in details and with slightly larger and more powerful engines.

These continued production models included such designs as the Austin A.35 and the Morris 1000, both of which were now fitted with the BM.C. Type A four-cylinder water-cooled engine of 948 c.c. capacity (63 mm. by 76·2 mm.) which developed 34 h.p. at 4750 r.p.m.; this represented an increase of 10 per cent compared with the output of the 803 c.c. capacity of the Austin A.30 model. This B.M.C. Type A engine design of 948 c.c. capacity was also used with higher stages of tune to provide the power unit of livelier models of the B.M.C. range of touring, sports, competition and even racing cars. Among these were the later version of the Morris 1000 and the new Austin

A.40 which, with an S.U. HS2 carburettor, had an output of 40 h.p. at 5000 r.p.m. The Austin Healey Sprite and the M.G. Midget models were both fitted with the Type A engine having twin carburettors; with a compression ratio of 9 to 1 an output of 50 h.p. at 5500 r.p.m. was developed. These two models were fitted with sports two-seat open bodies and were capable of speeds up to 85 m.p.h. Still larger outputs were obtained from this basic design by additional modifications, particularly in cylinder-head design but still retaining overhead push-rod valve rocker gear, to produce an engine suitable for Formula 2 racing. With the cylinder bores increased to give a total capacity of 1095 c.c., the ultimate power output achieved with this design was 95 h.p. at crankshaft speeds of up to 8500 r.p.m. with a compression ratio of 11 to 1. This progressive increase of power output with the same basic engine design illustrates the tuning techniques now available and being employed, and the ability of a sound standard design to produce substantially increased performance with unimpaired reliability in operation.

The Ford Anglia 105E and 109E models were examples of progressive development of a long-established design. The 997 c.c. capacity (81 mm. by 48·4 mm.) engine was remarkable for the marked oversquare engine dimensions with a stroke to bore ratio of 0·6 to 1 and a crank throw dimension of slightly less than 1 inch. The output developed was 39 h.p. at 5000 r.p.m. with the low piston speed of only 1582 feet per minute by virtue of the designed short stroke, which permitted high cruising speeds without distress, combined with smooth running, which was also contributed to by the light hollowed-out short-throw crankshaft of cast-iron construction with its low out-of-balance mass and the large diameter journal bearing surfaces. A novel feature of this new Anglia model was the reverse-angle rear window which gave the body increased passenger headroom as well as a new and attractive profile. The 105E push-rod engine was also developed for Formula 2 racing, with a capacity enlarged to 1100 c.c., and modified cylinder head and carburation. Substantially higher outputs were obtained with the five-bearing Ford Classic 116E cylinder block reduced to a capacity of 997 c.c.; fitted with an overhead camshaft and two twin-barrel carburettors, an output of 124 h.p. at 9000 r.p.m. was obtained.

Other examples of this orthodox layout included the Triumph Herald with an engine of 948 c.c. capacity (63 mm. by 76 mm.) which developed 39 h.p. at 4500 r.p.m. Examples of European and Asiatic origin included the Glas S-1004 of 992 c.c. capacity (72 mm. by 61 mm.) which developed 42 h.p. at 4800 r.p.m., and had an overhead camshaft driven by a steel-reinforced cogged flexible belt and a five-bearing crankshaft; the Opel Kadet of 993 c.c. capacity; the Japanese Datsun 1000 with a 988 c.c. engine, which was built on Austin lines; the Mitsubishi Colt 1000 with a 977 c.c. capacity (72 mm. by 60 mm.) which developed 51 h.p. at 5000 r.p.m.; and the Daihatsu 800 of 797 c.c. capacity (62 mm. by 66 mm.) which developed 41 h.p. at 5000 r.p.m.

Advanced designs, however, were now replacing the former orthodox layout. These had either front or rear-mounted engine-transmission units driving the adjacent pair of wheels which had been introduced in the 1950's and were now being widely adopted in production in the smaller sizes of light car because of the advantage of their inherent compactness. Models which had been in production during the past decade were now made in improved and more powerful versions. Among the front-driven designs was the Panhard PL 17 Tiger with its basically simple yet potent 848 c.c. capacity (85 mm. by 75 mm.) flat-twin air-cooled engine which, in the standard version developed 50 h.p. at 5800 r.p.m., and in the later Tiger version developed 60 h.p. at 6300 r.p.m., which latter output gave the car a maximum speed of 93 m.p.h. This sole product of the Model 17 from one of the earliest motor car manufacturers was a notable example of refined design of a basically simple layout. The German Lloyd Arabella model had a water-cooled flat-four cylinder engine of 897 c.c. capacity (69 mm. by 60 mm.) which developed 38 h.p. at 4800 r.p.m. The Japanese Subaru design had a front-mounted 1 litre horizontally-opposed four-cylinder water-cooled engine which developed 55 h.p.

The rear-mounted engine driving the rear wheels appeared to be more favoured by designers for this small category of light car. The Fiat 600D model (Plate 32) was another example of a current model developed from an earlier lower powered one. The Fiat 850 was a further development of this typical Italian theme, with an 843 c.c. capacity (65 mm. by 63·5 mm.) engine which, with a compression ratio of 8·8 to 1, developed 37 h.p. at 5100 r.p.m. and gave the car a maximum speed of 75 m.p.h. The four-seat saloon body was of more orthodox profile than that of the 600D model, with front and rear ends slightly extended to provide more room. The Renault R8 design with a 956 c.c. capacity (65 mm. by 72 mm.) four-cylinder water-cooled engine succeeded the successful Dauphine model. The R8 engine in standard tune developed 48 h.p. at 5200 r.p.m., which gave the car a maximum speed of 80 m.p.h. An automatic transmission comprising an electro-magnetic control system and magnetic power coupling, used in conjunction with a normal three-speed all-synchromesh gearbox, with push-button control, could be fitted as an alternative to the normal four-speed and reverse gearbox. Another French design of this general type was the Simca 1000 (Plate 33) whose 944 c.c. capacity (68 mm. by 65 mm.) five-bearing engine developed 50 h.p. at 5000 r.p.m., which gave the car a maximum speed of 80 m.p.h. and the ability to cruise continuously at 70 m.p.h. A centrifugal oil filter mounted on the crankshaft permitted the oil in the engine sump to be used for 6,000 miles before a change was necessary. The Simca-Ferodo automatic transmission unit was provided as an alternative to the standard hydraulically-operated clutch and fully-synchronised four-speed and reverse gearbox. The automatic transmission unit provided two-pedal driving and incorporated a sealed three-element hydraulic torque converter and a three-ratio all synchronised gearbox. The Czech Skoda 1000 MB model had an engine of 998 c.c. capacity (68 mm. by 68 mm.) which developed 46 h.p. at 4650 r.p.m. (Plate 38). The installation of this Skoda engine unit in the rear of the chassis was made more compact by the cylinder block being tilted 30 degrees from the vertical, thus reducing height. The 875 c.c. (68 mm. by 60·4 mm.) engine of the

Hillman Imp, which developed 39 h.p. at 5000 r.p.m., also had this feature of the cylinder block being tilted at 45 degrees. The advanced features of this design were a die-cast all-aluminium engine with steel liners, a compression ratio of 10 to 1, high crankshaft speeds up to 7000 r.p.m., and a chain-driven overhead camshaft. This all-aluminium construction reduced the weight of the engine unit to only 170 lb. Another model of this design, known as the Singer Chamois, with detail improvements in body and fittings and developing 42 h.p., was also provided.

A notable example of this small category which was of both very advanced design and performance was the Honda S800. The engine was a four-cylinder light-alloy water-cooled unit installed at an angle of 45 degrees. It was of 791 c.c. capacity (60 mm. by 70 mm.) and developed 70 b.h.p. at 8000 r.p.m. The valves were operated by chain-driven twin-overhead camshafts. Not the least interesting feature of this design was its break from advanced practice by the adoption of a long stroke which, at 8000 r.p.m., gave a mean piston speed of 3750 f.p.m. The 3-bearing built-up crankshaft of the pressed-in type was carried on roller bearings and was designed and balanced to act as a flywheel, and a very light and small diameter flywheel only was necessary. Carburation was by four Keikin carburettors which were unique in combining the constant-vacuum principle of the S.U. design with an emulsion tube main jet of the Zenith principle. Compression ratio was 9·2 to 1.

The Russian Zaporozhets air-cooled vee four-cylinder was produced in a later version of 877 c.c. capacity (75 mm. by 54·5 mm.) which developed 27 h.p. at 4000 r.p.m.

Transverse Engines: to 1000 c.c.

Some early precedents exist for the transversely-mounted engine such as the Christie racer built in the U.S.A. for the 1906 Vanderbilt Cup race, and the prototype Franklin air-cooled engine of 1904, as well as one or two other designs which appeared in this country before 1914. This unusual arrangement was not fully exploited, however, until the novel design of Alec Issigonis which went into full production in 1959 as the British Motor Corporation's Austin Seven Mini (Plate 35) and the Morris Mini models. The essential compactness of this transverse engine mounting, together with front-wheel drive, permitted the maximum passenger and luggage space to be available in a manner hitherto unattainable. Only 18 inches of the car's length were taken up by clutch, gears, differential, transmission and, in later models, automatic two-pedal transmission unit. An important addition to the specification was the novel Hydrolastic system of balanced suspension which automatically compensated longitudinally and laterally for uneven road conditions, which materially improved riding comfort. This Issigonis formula was an immediate major international success, as had been the Ford Model T of 1909 and the Austin Seven of 1922; moreover, a design trend was established by it and other major companies such as N.S.U., Peugeot, and Honda began to design and produce cars with transversely-mounted engines, positioned either in front or in rear of the chassis.

The 848 c.c. capacity (63 mm. by 68·3 mm.) engine of these B.M.C. Mini models was a development of the well-tried Type A engine which had been in full production during the past decade. In the crankcase of this basic engine there was neatly incorporated a four-speed and reverse gear and differential assembly, from which the front wheels were driven through articulated half shafts equipped with constant-velocity joints. With a compression ratio of 8·3 to 1, 34 h.p. was developed at 5500 r.p.m. A thermostatically-controlled and pressurised cooling system was assisted by an impeller and fan. With a final drive ratio of 3·765 to 1, a maximum speed of 70 m.p.h. and a cruising fuel consumption of 50 m.p.g. were obtained. The engine sump formed an oil bath for both engine and gear assembly. The B.M.C. Riley Elf and the Wolseley Hornet models were produced to this same specification, but with more body space and more elaborate fittings and retaining the respective Riley and Wolseley traditional radiator shapes.

The Cooper-Mini sports version of this B.M.C. design had a capacity increased to 998 c.c. (66 mm. by 68·3 mm.); with a compression ratio of 9 to 1 and two S.U. type H.S.2 carburettors, this enlarged engine developed 55 h.p. at 5800 r.p.m. A maximum speed of 80 m.p.h. was obtained with this model, and disc brakes on the front wheels were fitted as standard. The notable reliability of the Cooper-Mini under sustained operation in arduous rally conditions was shown by its consistent success in such events as the Monte Carlo Rally, the East African Safari and the R.A.C. Rally. This basic Mini design was also used for an open platform type of utility vehicle known as the Mini Moke.

The novel Spencer Moulton Hydrolastic balanced suspension system was added to production Mini models in 1966. With this system, all four wheels independently supported the chassis through individual sealed shock absorber units of rubber which were filled with an anti-rust and anti-freeze fluid; the pair of units on each side were interconnected through balancing valves providing automatic compensation for uneven road conditions, both forward and laterally. This system was basically simple with no wearing parts, no glands to leak and requiring no maintenance.

Following the trend of the N.S.U. Prinz 4 model with its two-cylinder air-cooled vertical engine set transversely across the rear of the chassis and driving the rear wheels, as described in the previous chapter, a larger version of this arrangement was produced in the N.S.U. 1000. This design broke new ground with this trend of transverse positioning the engine unit by the adoption of air-cooling induced by fan blades incorporated with the flywheel, for its four-cylinder in-line 996 c.c. capacity (69 mm. by 66·9 mm.) which developed 43 h.p. at 5000 r.p.m. The valves of this engine were operated by an overhead camshaft. The drive was taken through the four-speed and reverse gearbox in unit with the crankcase and articulated half shafts to the rear wheels.

LIGHT CARS: to 1300 c.c.

The established models of light cars of medium size to 1300 c.c. capacity which were still in production on orthodox lines with a front-mounted engine driving a rear live axle through a gearbox and open propeller shaft, consisted of improved versions of earlier models and also of some new models. Larger examples of designs based on the new trends of chassis layout and engine arrangement already described also appeared.

A selection of the models based on orthodox lines in this category include the following. The 1098 c.c. (64·6 mm. by 83·7 mm.) Austin A.40; the 1147 c.c. (69·3 mm. by 76 mm.) Triumph Herald and 12/50; the 1057 c.c. (74·6 mm. by 60·9 mm.) Vauxhall Viva; the 1172 c.c. (63·5 mm. by 92·5 mm.) Morgan Four-Four; the 1290 c.c. (75 mm. by 73 mm.) Peugeot 203; the 1221 c.c. (72 mm. by 75 mm.) Fiat 1100D; the 1290 c.c. (74 mm. by 75 mm.) Simca Aronde; and the 1221 c.c. (72 mm. by 75 mm.) Skoda Octavia. An advanced model based on the orthodox layout was the Fiat 124. The four-cylinder water-cooled engine of 1197 c.c. capacity (73 mm. by 71·5 mm.) with a compression ratio of 8·8 to 1 developed 65 h.p. The crankshaft was carried in five bearings. A horizontal twin-choke carburettor supplied the mixture. A full-flow replaceable cartridge type oil filter was fitted, and crankcase gases were ducted to the intake manifold and burned in the combustion chambers. There was independent suspension and disc brakes on all four wheels. With a five-seat saloon body, which had all-round vision windows, the maximum speed was 87 m.p.h. The established Alfa Romeo Guiletta, which was an example of the more expensive sports car in this category using orthodox layout, was succeeded by the Guilia 1300 model of 1290 c.c. (74 mm. by 75 mm.) which developed 78 h.p. at 6000 r.p.m. The crankshaft of this engine was supported in five main bearings, and the valves were operated by twin overhead camshafts. The dry weight of this car with full four-seat saloon body of efficient aerodynamic form weighed only 19 cwt., thus providing a favourable power-weight ratio.

Designs of cars of this category having more original and advanced engine forms included the Lancia Appia III of 1091 c.c. capacity (68 mm. by 75 mm.) and the Lancia Fulvia of 1216 c.c. (76 mm. by 67 mm.), both of which models were constructed in the characteristic Lancia compact narrow-angle vee arrangement of cylinders permitting a short crankshaft and compact engine. Another compact engine design was the Ford Taunus 12M of 1183 c.c. capacity (80 mm. by 59 mm.) which had its cylinders in 60 degrees vee formation and used an unusually short stroke in the manner which had already been established in the Ford 105E and 109E engine designs. Another advanced Ford design was the Escort model which was equipped with either a 1098 c.c. (81 mm. by 53·3 mm.) engine which developed 53 h.p. at 5500 r.p.m., or a 1298 c.c. (81 mm. by 63 mm.) engine which developed 63 h.p. at 5300 r.p.m. These engines had a compression ratio of 9 to 1, overhead pushrod-operated valves, cross-flow cylinder heads, combustion chamber pistons, and five-bearing crankshafts.

A front-wheel drive design in this category was the Triumph 1300 which had some original features. The four-cylinder water-cooled engine unit of 1296 c.c. (73·7 mm. by 76 mm.), with a compression ratio of 8·5 to 1, developed 61 h.p. at 5200 r.p.m., which gave the car with a four/five seat saloon body a maximum speed of 85 m.p.h. Separate lubrication systems were used for engine and transmission, the latter being sealed and needing no replenishment or change. The engine centre of gravity was located over the front wheels; the flywheel was placed at the front end of the crankshaft to assist this weight distribution and also to make possible easy access to the clutch assembly at the rear end of the crankshaft; this latter arrangement permitted the clutch to be renewed in 15 minutes without dismantling either engine or transmission. The steering column had a dished steering wheel and was made to telescope under impact from the driver in the event of a collision.

The rear-driven Renault R8 design was produced as the Caravelle model with a 1108 c.c. capacity (70 mm. by 72 mm.) four-cylinder water-cooled engine which developed 49 h.p. at 5100 r.p.m. The Renault Gordini version of this design was made available with the power output increased to 95 h.p. at 6500 r.p.m. This increase was effected by the use of a cross-flow cylinder head with hemispherical combustion chambers, raising the compression ratio from 8·5 to 10·5 to 1, and the use of a twin-choke Solex carburettor. Lockheed disc brakes assisted by a Bendix vacuum servo unit were provided to meet the maximum speed of 106 m.p.h.

The notable rear-drive air-cooled Volkswagen of 1192 c.c. capacity (77 mm. by 64 mm.) continued in full production for world markets in basically similar external form and with detail improvements. These improvements included a general strengthening of engine components to meet the higher loads resulting from an increase of power output from 30 to 34 h.p. at 3600 r.p.m. with the same engine dimensions and an increase of compression ratio from 6·6 to 7 to 1. Engine redesign changes involved a new crankshaft with larger webs and journals, a stiffer die-cast crankcase of magnesium alloy, and improved air-cooling of the cylinders. Although the familiar outline of the standard saloon body remained virtually unchanged, a two-seat sports version with a Karmann-Ghia body was made available. In 1965, a Volkswagen automatic clutch was available as an alternative; this clutch was sensitised by the gear lever and operated through a vacuum servo unit. The Volkswagen design was also made available as a 'Microbus' utility vehicle. In 1966, the Volkswagen 1300 model was produced with generally the same specification as the smaller engined model and with a similar engine enlarged to 1285 c.c. capacity (77 mm. by 69 mm.) which had an output of 50 h.p. at 4600 r.p.m.

Tranverse Engines: to 1300 c.c.

The novel and successful application in production of the transverse engine location which the British Motor Corporation had achieved with an 848 c.c. capacity engine unit in their Mini models, was later adopted by this concern for larger models and also by some other manufacturers for certain of their advanced models.

The B.M.C. designs using transverse engines were the Morris 1100, the Austin 1100 and the M.G. Midget models. The engine unit in all cases was the enlarged Type A of 1098 c.c. capacity (64·5 mm. by 83·7 mm.) which had a maximum output of 48 h.p. at 5100 r.p.m. The clutch was hydraulically operated by a pendant pedal; the four-speed and reverse gearbox and differential unit was incorporated with the crankcase, and both engine and transmission were lubricated from the engine sump by the engine-driven pressure pump. The final drive to the front wheels was through articulated half shafts and constant-velocity joints. An alternative automatic transmission system was also available which provided two-pedal driving with a combination of fully-manual as well as fully-automatic control over all four gears. This system is described on page 157. A Pininfarina-styled four to five-seat saloon body provided large passenger and luggage accommodation, thanks to the body space saved by the transverse mounting of the engine unit. Earlier models had a suspension system employing solid rubber cone springs, but riding comfort and road holding were materially improved by the adoption as standard of the Spencer Moulton Hydrolastic balanced independent hydraulic suspension system already mentioned in connection with the later B.M.C. Mini models, and described on page 160.

Larger engine capacity models of the B.M.C. Mini series were produced to place these smaller models in the high-performance sports and competition categories. These included such models as the Speedwell Riley Elf fitted with an enlarged engine of 1150 c.c. capacity (67 mm. by 81·3 mm.) which was tuned to deliver 90 h.p. at 7400 r.p.m. by means of a special camshaft, two 1·5 inch S.U. carburettors, and a four-branch exhaust pipe. This car had a flexible top gear performance of from 20 to 110 m.p.h. The rest of the car was generally standard. The Cooper-tuned range of Mini models included engine capacities of 970 c.c., 1071 c.c. and 1275 c.c. At the comparatively moderate maximum crankshaft speed of 5750 r.p.m. and with a compression ratio of 9 to 1, the 1071 c.c. capacity model developed 68 h.p., which was capable of being sustained with complete reliability over long and arduous trials and rallies at speeds up to 90 m.p.h. The Cooper-Mini 1275S model with an engine capacity of 1275 c.c. (71 mm. by 81 mm.) could be safely tuned to give still higher performance; with a compression ratio raised to 11 to 1 for competition work and to 12 to 1 for racing, power outputs of 100 to 105 h.p. were obtained which made possible a maximum speed of 110 m.p.h.

The old-established French firm of Peugeot adopted the transverse engine arrangement for their 204 model (Plate 40), placing the engine and transmission unit in rear and inclining the cylinder block 20 degrees forward to conserve headroom. The four-cylinder water-cooled engine of 1130 c.c. capacity (75 mm. by 64 mm.) with a compression ratio of 8·8 to 1 developed 58 h.p. at 5800 r.p.m. The crankshaft was carried in five main bearings, the valves were operated by an overhead camshaft, the wet cylinder liners were easily removable from the pressure die-cast cylinder block, and the radiator fan was of the automatic electro-magnetic disconnectable type. The diaphragm clutch was hydraulically controlled. The ZF automatic transmission unit, consisting of a torque converter flywheel, a multi-plate clutch-operated epicyclic-gear train and an automatic control box, was fitted as standard.

The braking system, consisting of front disc brakes and rear drum brakes, was servo assisted.

A larger version of the four-cylinder air-cooled 996 c.c. capacity N.S.U. Prinz 1000L known as the Type 110 model was produced with a similar transversely-mounted rear engine of 1085 c.c. capacity (72 mm. by 66·6 mm.) which, with a compression ratio of 8 to 1, developed 53 h.p. at 5000 r.p.m. This larger example of a four-cylinder air-cooled engine, together with the increased output obtained with the N.S.U. Prinz 1000 TT model with a compression ratio of 9 to 1 and using the same 1085 c.c. capacity engine of 55 h.p. at 5800 r.p.m., indicated a trend towards the use of higher powered air-cooled engines for this larger class of light car.

The Honda 1300 model was fitted with a 1289 c.c. (74 mm. by 75·5 mm.) capacity air cooled, transverse, front-wheel drive engine which developed the high output of 96 h.p. at 7200 r.p.m.

LIGHT CARS: to 1600 c.c.

In this largest category of light cars of up to 1600 c.c. capacity, it is to be noted that the majority of designs produced during this period, even those of late origin, were confined generally to the orthodox engine and chassis layout of a front-mounted engine and gearbox unit driving through an open propeller shaft to the rear wheels; the main difference from the orthodox now being in the adoption of four-wheel independent suspension, thus necessitating half shafts driving the rear wheels instead of the former generally employed unsprung live axle. With the notable exception of the air-cooled rear-engined Volkswagen and Porsche designs, the differences which these up-to-date larger cars incorporated were largely those of detail design rather than major changes of layout. Perhaps the explanation of this conservative trend was that, whereas the designers of the smaller light cars were influenced to adopt either the front or rear-mounted engine and transmission units, either in longitudinal or transverse disposition because of the additional body space provided by such compact power units, the largest examples of light car with their now quite commodious bodies were not so pressed for adequate passenger and luggage space and so could be continued in production with the well-tried classic layout.

Some of the chief detail improvements incorporated in these orthodox light car designs of up to 1600 c.c. capacity included such features as: a specific output of 50 to 60 h.p. per litre engine capacity at up to 6000 r.p.m.; five-bearing crankshafts for the four-cylinder engines which were generally used; twin-choke carburettors or, in one or two cases, pressure-injection fuel systems; improved oil filtration provided by centrifugal-type filters extending oil changes to 6000 miles: diaphragm-type clutches and baulk-ring type all-synchromesh four- and even five-speed gearboxes, or automatic transmission systems giving two-pedal control which could be over-ridden to provide manual control; disc brakes on front wheels or all four wheels; and inclined cylinder blocks to conserve headroom.

141

Since the main features and design details of this category of orthodox light cars were generally similar, it will perhaps merely be necessary to list a selection of contemporary models to illustrate the variety which was available, as follows: Austin A.55 1489 c.c. (73 mm. by 89 mm.); Borgward Isabella T.S. 1493 c.c. (74 mm. by 85·5 mm.); B.M.W. 1491 c.c. (82 mm. by 71 mm.); Fiat 1500L 1481 c.c. (77 mm. by 79·5 mm.); Ford Cortina 1498 c.c. (81 mm. by 73 mm.); Hillman Minx 1592 c.c. (77 mm. by 79·5 mm.); M.G. Magnette 1489 c.c. (73 mm. by 89 mm.); Peugeot 403 1468 c.c. (80 mm. by 73 mm.); Renault 16 1470 c.c. (76 mm. by 81 mm.); Riley 1489 c.c. (73 mm. by 89 mm.); Simca 1500 1475 c.c. (75 mm. by 83 mm.); Singer Gazelle 1494 c.c. (79 mm. by 76 mm.); Sunbeam Alpine 1592 c.c. (81·5 mm. by 76·2 mm.); Vauxhall Victor 1508 c.c. (79·4 mm. by 76·2 mm.); and Volvo 122S 1582 c.c. (79·4 mm. by 80 mm.). The Alfa Romeo Guilia Super was a larger version of the smaller Guilia model already mentioned and had an engine of 1570 c.c. (78 mm. by 82 mm.); and the Ford Taunus and the Saab 96 designs were each fitted with a Ford vee-four-cylinder short-stroke engine of 1498 c.c. capacity (90 mm. by 59 mm.).

The palm for progressive originality in this otherwise conservative category of the largest light cars must go to the genius of Ferdinand Porsche for the related but distinct Volkswagen and Porsche air-cooled, horizontal-opposed four-cylinder, rear-engine designs which have both had great commercial and competition success in their respective spheres of use. The Volkswagen 1500 was a still larger version of the standard specification and retained the same characteristic body profile; the horizontally-opposed four-cylinder engine of 1493 c.c. capacity (83 mm. by 69 mm.), with a compression ratio of 7·5 to 1, developed 58 h.p. at 4200 r.p.m. which gave this model a maximum speed of 78 m.p.h. The still larger Volkswagen 1600TL model (Plate 36) with an engine of 1584 c.c. capacity (86 mm. by 69 mm.) and an output of 54 h.p. at 4000 r.p.m. had a major change in body design which was of the styled fastback saloon form for the standard model and of station waggon form which was named the Variant model.

The initial series 356 Porsche push-rod production models, evolved soon after 1945 from the basic Volkswagen design and initially including a large proportion of Volkswagen components, pioneered the subsequent series of Porsche high-performance models for sports touring, competition work and racing with air-cooled, horizontally-opposed, rear-mounted engines having four cylinders for production models, and four, six, eight and twelve cylinders for high-speed competition work and racing. The original series 356 and the later series 912 push-rod production models increased in capacity from the initial 1086 c.c. to the 1582 c.c. (82 mm. by 74 mm.), of which the Super 75 and the Super 90 models which developed respectively 75 h.p. at 5000 r.p.m. and 90 h.p. at 5500 r.p.m., were representative examples. These models could maintain a cruising speed of 100 m.p.h.

While the development of the Type 356 push-rod engine was in progress in its transition from the original Volkswagen design to the Type 912 Super 75 and 90 models of 1582 c.c. capacity as already described, experiments were

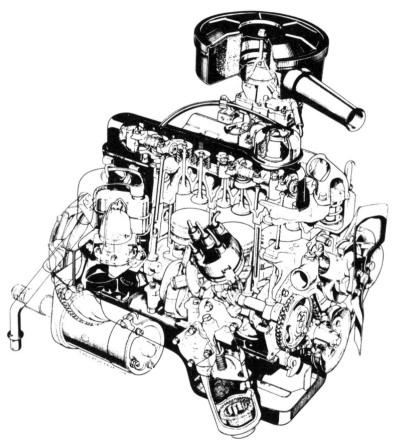

Fig. 25   Ford Cortina engine: 1966

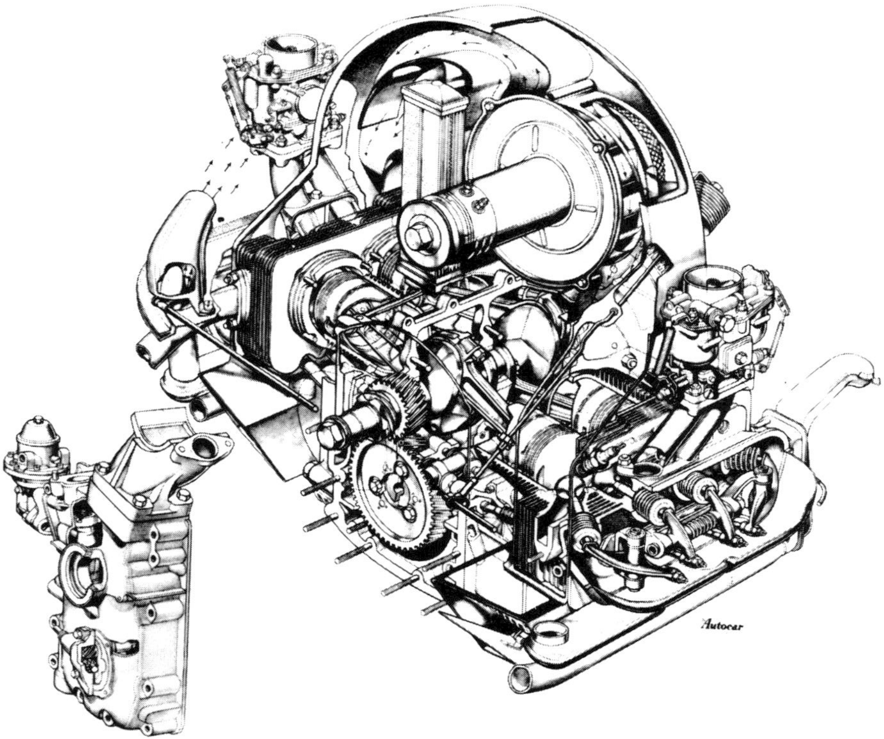

Fig. 26   Porsche Super 90 engine : 1960

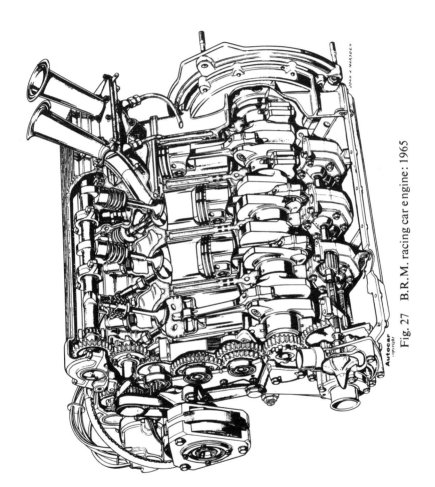

JOHN A MARSDEN

Autocar
copyright

Fig. 27   B.R.M. racing car engine: 1965

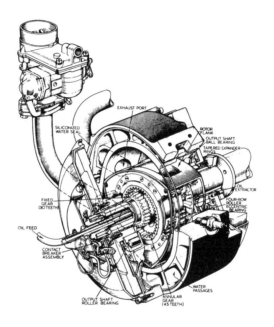

EXHAUST PORT

SILICONIZED
WATER SEAL

ROTOR
FLANK
OUTPUT SHAFT
BALL BEARING
TAPERED EXPANDER
RINGS

OIL
EXTRACTOR

FIXED
GEAR
(30 TEETH)

FOUR-ROW
ROLLER
ECCENTRIC
BEARING

OIL FEED

CONTACT
BREAKER
ASSEMBLY

WATER
PASSAGES

OUTPUT SHAFT
ROLLER BEARING

ANNULAR
GEAR
(45 TEETH)

Fig. 28   Wankel rotary engine: 1959

also in progress in connection with engine designs of substantially higher outputs for competition and racing. It was apparent that the limitations of the Type 356 push-rod design, with relatively high weights for the valve gear reciprocating masses, could not provide this still higher output. Accordingly, a new engine design was evolved known as the Type 550, which retained the air-cooled, horizontally-opposed, four-cylinder layout. This new design included such features as a strengthened magnesium-alloy crankcase having an increased dimension between cylinder centres; a Hirth-type serrated-joint built-up ball-and-roller crankshaft, which permitted the use of stiffened one-piece connecting rods with roller-bearing big ends; twin-overhead cam-shafts supported in a unit light-alloy cylinder head for each pair of cylinders, and driven by a cross-shaft from a bevel-and-shaft drive from the crankshaft; and unlined light-alloy cylinder bores which were chromium plated and dimpled to assist oil retention. The provision of these and other advanced features in the Type 550 design allowed increased valve acceleration and lift permitting improved breathing, higher crankshaft speeds, and improved cylinder cooling. A typical model based upon these design characteristics was the Porsche 1500 RSK of 1498 c.c. capacity (85 mm. by 66 mm.) which, with a compression ratio of 9·8 to 1, developed 148 h.p. at 8000 r.p.m., which gave this model a maximum speed of 130 m.p.h. As already indicated, a variety of other models of similar characteristics but of larger cylinder capacities and having greater numbers of cylinders were built with remarkable success.

Among the most technically advanced cars of the late 1960's was the Lotus sports car. The backbone of the chassis (Plate 40) consisted of an immensely strong and torsionally stiff deep-sectioned box girder of welded steel, provided with forks at each end to carry the independent coil spring and wishbone suspension. The streamlined, two-seater body was built of fibre-glass. Having low weight and little body drag, the performance was exceptionally high for a car powered by an engine of only 1558 c.c. capacity. It was fitted with a four-cylinder water-cooled engine of 82·6 mm. bore and 72·8 mm. stroke. Maximum power developed was 115 b.h.p. at 6000 r.p.m. with a compression ratio of 9·5 to 1. Capable of a maximum speed of 122 m.p.h., accelerating from rest to 100 m.p.h. in 21 seconds, recording a fuel consumption of only 28 m.p.g. and possessing excellent road-holding and cornering ability, the Lotus Elan emphasised the considerable technical benefits to be gained from long experience in modern road racing.

THREE-CYLINDER TWO-STROKE ENGINES

The more elaborate three-cylinder form of ported two-stroke engine introduced by the German D.K.W. firm after 1945 as a development of their earlier two-cylinder models, was continued in capacities ranging from 400 c.c. to 1175 c.c. in Germany, Sweden, Japan and England. The advantages of this essentially simple yet efficient form of power unit consisted in its simple construction, with the concomitant advantages of reliability, economy in constructional costs, absence of mechanical noise, and smooth torque which latter virtue was accentuated in the three-cylinder form. Moreover, this simplicity did not preclude a considerable degree of super tuning from being achieved by means of efficient port timing and high compression ratios. That high specific outputs so obtained could be used with unimpaired reliability was demonstrated by the sustained high performances of these modern two-stroke engined cars in prolonged and arduous trails and rallies.

The disadvantage of the two-stroke engine, nevertheless, continued to be uneven slow running and, compared with equivalent four-stroke engines, higher specific fuel consumption. In addition, although the fuel-oil mixture ratio had by now been reduced to 40 and even 50 parts of petrol to one of oil, the practice of adding even a small proportion of oil to the fuel produced a dirty exhaust. As a consequence, proposed new anti-air pollution laws made the future of two-stroke engined cars in some degree doubtful. The introduction in 1966 of advanced four-stroke engined models by two of the leading two-stroke manufacturers, Auto Union and Saab, gave point to this trend.

The D.K.W.-Auto Union range of three-cylinder engined models deriving from the D.K.W. Sonderklass model were of basically the same general design, with a three-cylinder water-cooled engine mounted in front and driving the front wheels through a four-speed gearbox and articulated half-shafts. The gearbox incorporated a free-wheel device, the use of which could improve fuel economy, a matter of some importance with the two-stroke engine. Ignition was by means of a separate ignition coil for each cylinder, working in conjunction with a special distributor, to reduce the spark-frequency loading that would be imposed on a single coil, particularly at high engine speeds. An automatic oil-additive dispenser was introduced to avoid the somewhat tedious procedure of achieving this by make-shift methods.

The D.K.W. Three-Six model had an engine of 896 c.c. capacity (71 mm. by 76 mm.) which developed 38 h.p. at 4200 r.p.m. The Auto Union concern later took over the D.K.W. interests and began producing models to the same general arrangement. The Auto Union 1000 had an engine of 980 c.c. capacity (74 mm. by 76 mm.) which developed 45 h.p. at 4500 r.p.m. with a compression ratio of 7·25 to 1; a tuned sports version with a compression ratio of 8 to 1 developed 55 h.p. at 4500 r.p.m. The smaller Auto Union Junior of 741 c.c. (68 mm. by 68 mm.) with a compression ratio of 8 to 1 developed 34 h.p. at 4300 r.p.m. Inboard front wheel brake drums adjacent to the differential housing were a feature of this model. Although these power outputs were higher than equivalent standard four-stroke engines, the fuel consumption of between 38 to 40 miles per gallon at 50 m.p.h. was higher. The later model of this type produced by the Auto Union concern was the D.K.W. F 102 model of 889 c.c. (74·5 mm. by 68 mm.) which, with a compression ratio of 7·25 to 1, developed 40 h.p. at 4300 r.p.m. The F 102 models had certain advanced features, including a separate oil injector which ensured that the engine only consumed oil in the proportion of approximately one per cent of fuel; the supply was regulated according to engine load and speed and the device maintained a constant flow of clean oil to mix with the fuel in the carburettor. These engines were capable of running for 60,000 miles before a major overhaul was necessary. The Auto Union 1000 SP model had a 980 c.c. capacity (74 mm. by 76 mm.) which, with a compression ratio of 8·0 to 1, developed 55 h.p. at 4500 r.p.m. This model had a commodiously styled and well-equipped saloon body.

Another German example of this class of two-stroke engined light car was the Wartburg 1000 which was made by the old-established firm of Eisenarch. This model had an unusually capacious saloon body for the 991 c.c. capacity (73·5 mm. by 78 mm.) three-cylinder two-stroke engine which developed 50 h.p. at 4200 r.p.m. The later Wartburg Knight had a body of improved styling.

The Swedish Saab concern followed their initial two-cylinder 92 model with their three-cylinder 93 model of 748 c.c. capacity (66 mm. by 72·9 mm.) which developed 38 h.p. at 5000 r.p.m. The slightly larger 96 model had an 841 c.c. capacity engine (70 mm. by 72·9 mm.) and developed 38 h.p. at 4250 r.p.m. These Saab cars (Plate 36) were of excellent manufacture with efficient aerodynamic saloon bodies, qualities which were consonant with a firm having long aircraft manufacturing experience. Substantially higher outputs were obtained with tuned Saab engines which could be used with sure reliability in long-distance trials. The results of such arduous testing were embodied in the Saab Sports model whose 841 c.c. capacity engine, with a compression ratio of 10 to 1, developed 55 h.p. at 5000 r.p.m.

The Japanese Suzuki Fronte 800 of 785 c.c. capacity and the Mitsubishi Colt 800 of 843 c.c. capacity designs both had three-cylinder two-stroke engines driving the front wheels. A particularly small example of this kind was the 356 c.c. capacity (52 mm. by 56 mm.) Suzuki which developed 25 h.p. at 5000 r.p.m. The three-cylinder air-cooled Excelsior design of 492 c.c. capacity (58 mm. by 62 mm.) was initially intended as a motor-cycle engine, but was applied successfully to certain English ultra-light cars, such as the Berkeley.

Accessories and Ancillaries: from 1956

The component parts, accessories and ancillaries that together make up the modern motor car as it has materialised after the turn of the half century were of increasingly advanced and ingenious detail design that strove always for the technical refinement and capability that would ensure improved performance, passenger comfort and customer acceptance in a highly competitive world market. This progress produced increasingly complex features as the refinements now provided in motor car design became more sophisticated.

While certain of the basic features of what had become accepted over the past half century as standard practice, many detail modifications and new conceptions were now continually added to the overall make-up of the motor car, particularly in the smaller sizes. This standard image was thus significantly modified and improved by such general details as styled bodies embodying scientifically correct seating form and posture, with more compact engine and transmission arrangements providing greater conservation of available body space; while advanced qualities of performance, control, road safety and riding comfort were contributed to by such detail aspects as higher specific engine outputs, improved carburation and ignition systems, two-pedal automatic transmissions, balanced interconnected suspension systems, improved tyre design giving better road holding in a variety of weather conditions, and improved braking systems giving still better road safety.

The following paragraphs describe briefly the chief aspects of this detail progress which has contributed fundamentally to the overall completeness and quality of the modern light car outlined in the previous two chapters.

ENGINE UNITS

Apart from the continual improvements made in materials and the refinements of engine design generally, two major aspects have contributed to the modern high-efficiency motor car engine, and the light car engine in particular, with its capability of developing high specific power outputs resulting from substantially increased brake mean effective pressures and crankshaft speeds, with a high degree of reliability and long life between overhauls. These two aspects were the adoption of short strokes to permit higher crankshaft speeds with still acceptable piston speeds, and refinements in combustion chamber design to provide efficient volumetric efficiency, charge turbulence and combustion together with high compression ratios of up to 10 to 1 with standard production units. The generally-accepted four-cylinder in-line arrangement was varied by examples of the horizontally-opposed and vee arrangements of cylinders for reasons of better dynamic balance and compactness. Compactness was also achieved with some in-line designs by inclining cylinder blocks from the vertical.

The square engine with approximately equal bore and stroke was now the rule rather than the exception, as shown by the various cylinder dimensions quoted in the previous two chapters, while the future trend was towards oversquare engine dimensions in which the stroke was substantially shorter than the bore. A notable example of this latter trend in fundamental design was to be seen in the Ford 105E and 109E and Taunus engines (Fig. 25) in which the cylinder bores were much greater than the strokes. The advantages gained from this arrangement involve some penalties which have to be mitigated by careful compensating design. The larger diameter pistons of the square and particularly oversquare engines have to conduct more heat from the piston crown, and crankpin loading is increased with the reduction of the crank throw dimension. To overcome these disadvantages, crankpins were increased in diameter which, nevertheless, increased crankpin and journal rubbing speeds and necessitated more efficient lubrication. Crankshaft design was modified to provide larger-diameter crankpins and journals, as pioneered by the Ford hollow cast-iron construction; stiffer crankshafts resulted from this method, while the additional weight incurred with the larger section crankshaft was offset by dispensing with unnecessary metal inside the shaft. As well as providing greater strength and stiffness, this form of construction was also cheaper to produce than the former method of machining crankshafts from forged steel blanks. The specialised use should be noted of built-up crankshafts, such as the Hirth serrated joint type used with some Porsche engines and the pressed-in joint type used with D.K.W. and Honda engines, which permitted the use of one-piece connecting rods and roller bearings. The invention and perfection in general production of the Vandervell thin-wall bearing contributed materially to the safe use of high crankshaft speeds and loads. The thin steel strip which was the basis of this construction was coated with alloys of copper and lead with, in many cases, an overlay of about $0 \cdot 0015$ in. of lead-indium or lead-tin alloy. This thin construction permitted higher bearing loads and better heat conductivity and reduced thermal stresses. Cheap standardised production and easy replacement were among the practical advantages of the thin-wall bearing.

Sustained cylinder-head and combustion-chamber research and design aimed at high volumetric efficiency with controlled turbulence or 'swirl' of the compressed charge. This intense research resulted in permitting substantially higher compression ratios to be used, up to 10 to 1 or even higher, within a corresponding gain in power and economy without sacrificing smooth running. The advanced form of Heron combustion chamber design with the combustion space formed within the piston crown, permitted a simple and cheap form of flat cylinder head having better port shapes, with gas entry less restricted by combustion chamber walls, together with efficiently controlled turbulence. The Auto Union Audi engine fitted with Heron-type recessed combustion chamber pistons operated normally on ordinary 98 octane premium grade fuel with a compression ratio as high as $11 \cdot 2$ to 1. A disadvantage of this system was a necessarily heavier piston. Overhead camshafts were increasingly adopted in such designs as the Hillman Imp, the Porsche Type 550, the Honda 800, the Glas S.1004 and the Ford Escort. Overhead camshafts were usually driven from the crankshaft through a half-time chain; the Glas S.1004 design employed instead a cogged steel-wire reinforced flexible belt which had the advantages of low inertia and quietness of operation; and the N.S.U. Prinz

147

design employed a pair of eccentric driven straps. The high expansion rate of aluminium cylinder blocks with push-rod valve operation made attractive the use of self-adjusting hydraulic tappets to maintain correct rocker clearance.

Average specific power outputs for normally-tuned four-stroke engines having a compression ratio of about 7·5 to 1 were in the region of 45–50 h.p. per litre capacity at 4500 to 5000 r.p.m.; for super-tuned engines having a compression ration of up to 10 to 1, specific power outputs were in the region of 60–70 b.h.p. per litre capacity at 6000 to 7000 r.p.m. Average specific power output for normally tuned three-cylinder two-stroke engines having a compression ratio of about 7·5 to 1 was in the region of 45 b.h.p. per litre capacity at 4000 to 4500 r.p.m.; for super-tuned engines of this kind having a compression ratio of about 9 to 1, the specific power output was in the region of 65 b.h.p. at 5000 r.p.m. The high specific output of which these simple two-stroke engines were capable may be noted; the wide port openings demanded with super-tuned ported two-stroke engines, however, confined the high torque range to the higher engine speeds and power output below about 3000 r.p.m. was usually deficient.

Cooling of ultra-light car engines of the simple single- and twin-cylinder varieties was generally effected by blower-fed air ducted on to shrouded and finned cylinder barrels. Air cooling was also used for some of the larger engines, notably in the cases of the N.S.U. 996 c.c. and 1085 c.c. four-cylinder in-line designs and the Volkswagen and Porsche (Fig. 26) horizontally-opposed four-cylinder designs of capacities ranging from 1000 c.c. to 1600 c.c. Some of the Super range of Porsche engines successfully used light-alloy cylinder barrels with chromium-plated bores which were dimpled to assist oil retention. Water-cooled engines such as the Hillman Imp and Triumph 1300 designs had light-alloy cylinder blocks with pressed-in cast-iron liners, a practice which saved weight and improved cooling. Permanently-sealed radiator systems were adopted by Renault, and the Leyland overflow tank which collected water that would otherwise have been lost by expansion and evaporation was adopted on the Triumph 1300 model. Devices to conserve engine power required to drive a radiator cooling fan include such examples as the Kenlowe fan driven by an electric motor supplied from the main battery; the Peugeot fan which has an electro-magnetic coupling which operated only when a thermostatic switch in the water system reached 184 degrees F; the Holborn-Eaton hydraulically-coupled fan which slipped after a certain engine speed had been reached; and the Kenlomatic fan whose blades, controlled by a wax expansion capsule located in the radiator water, were set automatically to a finer pitch as engine speed increased.

In spite of the high degree of efficiency of modern light car engines in standard operational tune, the inherent design also possessed considerable capacity to accept safely substantially higher degrees of tuning which could double the standard rated output by means of the specialised methods evolved by such specialists as Abath, Alexander, Cosworth, Cooper and Gordini. This aspect of the super-tuning capability of small engines of this period with adequate reliability is illustrated by the following list of output increments achieved with various stages of tune with a N.S.U. Prinz four-stroke two-cylinder air-cooled engine (Plate 37) of 583 c.c. capacity (76 mm. by 66 mm.) having a standard output of 20 h.p. at 4600 r.p.m., which resulted in an output of 37 h.p. at 6000 r.p.m., an increase of 85 per cent.

Normal output	20 h.p.
Polished ports	22 h.p.
Increased capacity air filter	23 h.p.
More efficient silencer	24 h.p.
Turbo-air type filter	26 h.p.
Increased carburettor choke	29 h.p.
Compression ratio raised to $7 \cdot 5$ to 1 and enlarged inlet ports and valves.. ..	31 h.p.
Increased valve overlap	33 h.p.
Modified combustion chamber, enlarged valves and ports, 9 to 1 compression ratio	37 h.p.

Anti-Air-Pollution Devices

The growing pollution of the air in cities by the free release of motor car engine exhaust gases created an increasing danger to health. The State of California were the first to decree that all new cars from 1966 should be equipped with special exhaust emission control devices that would limit the pollution content in the released gases from engines up to 1600 c.c. capacity to a maximum of 410 parts of hydrocarbons per million parts of air and a maximum of $2 \cdot 3$ per cent carbon monoxide. Such control is likely eventually to be generally adopted.

These devices were to be integral components of the car. The approved forms included a catalytic converter type, and an 'afterburner' type that sucked in addition air through a venturi and used it to re-burn the exhaust gas, with an auxiliary spark plug for ignition. Another method was to promote more efficient burning of the air-fuel mixture in the engine, rather than treat the exhaust gas in the tail pipe. This was effected by injecting pure air into the exhaust ports, supplied through an auxiliary manifold by a small engine-driven compressor; the additional oxygen and the high temperature of the exhaust gases were sufficient to consume most of the unburnt hydrocarbons.

Ignition Systems

The high-tension coil-and-battery system of ignition for car engines standardised since the 1920's proved to be fully reliable in operation and cheap to manufacture, and replaced the previously generally adopted high-tension magneto when an electrical supply source became an integral part of motor car equipment. Increased engine speeds and the multiplication of cylinders, particularly in the case of two-stroke engines, made greater demand on ignition system because of the higher spark frequency involved, and the fact that the high voltage output of a conventional coil may drop as much as 50 per cent at high engine speeds. High performance oil-cooled ignition coils and even the use of multiple coils were adopted partially to meet this situation.

New and advanced transistorised ignition systems were evolved to provide a more complete answer to these more complex ignition problems which were designed to relieve the electrical duty of the contact breaker and, in some designs, to dispense with it. The high-tension voltage supplied by a transistorised system does not fall off as engine speed rises, and the wear and erosion of contact-breaker points where these are used is much less since, in the transistorised system, the current at the contact breaker is insufficient to generate sufficient heat to oxidise the points.

No mechanical contact breaker was used in the Lucas Electronic ignition system. The timing of the spark for any number of cylinders was effected by individual inductor pole pieces incorporated in the engine flywheel or other suitable rotating component. These pole pieces passed a magnetic pick-up and induced electrical impulses, which were amplified and fed to a high-voltage transformer. The individual impulses were conveyed by means of a standard distributor head to the respective spark plugs. This system could provide accurate spark generation at frequencies of up to 1000 a second at constant voltage. This system was particularly applicable to modern multi-cylinder engines—up to 16 cylinders—running at speeds up to and in excess of 10,000 r.p.m.

The Auto-Lite Transicoil system employed a standard distributor, contact breaker and spark plugs; but instead of the usual coil and condenser, a special pack enclosing a transformer with a transistorised primary circuit was employed. The use of the transistor resulted in a lower current at the contact-breaker points, and a virtually flat high-tension output curve, which permitted a life of 100,000 hours without replacements. The Bosch transistorised ignition systems were of two forms. The simpler system used the existing contact breaker to control a transistor incorporated in the cap of the ignition coil; the extremely clean cut-off characteristics of the transistor gave the maximum inductive effect in the secondary, while the controlling current for the transistor needed to be only minute thus greatly reducing the rate of erosion. In a further development of this system, the contact breaker was replaced by a pulse generator which controlled the transistor through a tripping relay. The Clinton 'Spark-Pump' used the piezo-electric effect of a crystal which, when put under mechanical pressure, can supply an electric voltage. The crystals are located in the crankcase and stressed mechanically by linkage from the crankshaft; a force of about 80 lb. generated about 20,000 volts which was relatively constant over the engine speed range. The Wipac 'Magister' ignition system employed very high-frequency spark discharges as a means of ensuring positive ignition under adverse conditions, such as fouled spark plugs. The Delco-Remy capacitor discharge ignition system employed a timed pulse from a pick-up coil which was amplified and which triggered the discharge of a capacitor into the coil which, through a normal distributor, fired the appropriate spark plug.

Spark plugs of a variety of heat characteristics were supplied for standard use, but a few advanced types were designed to overcome the more usual faults such as fouling of the points. The Golden Lodge plug was designed with a low initial sparking voltage and also low increase of voltage necessary to deal with all fouling conditions. Within the body of the plug was a high-frequency converter consisting of a capacitor which became charged when the points were fouled. This plug was stated to have a life of 20,000 miles. Surface discharge spark plugs had a centre electrode and earth through the casing as in normal types of spark plugs, but the space between the centre electrode insulator and the casing was filled with a semi-conductive material which ionised the gap and allowed the spark to take a random path to earth; the many radial discharge paths available with this arrangement made plug failure due to erosion virtually impossible. Surface discharge plugs were assuming higher importance as compression ratios increased.

Carburettors and Fuel-injection Systems

The float-feed spray carburettor devised by W. Maybach in 1893 provided the basis from which were evolved the carburettors fitted to motor car engines since that time. The wide range of flexibility, speed control and economy required by motor car engines imposed a considerable refinement and some complexity in ensuring that the fuel-air mixture remained nearly constant under all conditions of operation. These conditions involving automatic compensation were achieved in practice by two principle systems. One method used positive mechanical metering devices for both fuel and air, as employed in the S.U. and Stromberg designs, in which a piston controlled by the intake manifold depression varied the choke area over the jet and also the quantity of fuel discharged through the jet orifice by means of a tapered needle attached to the piston. The other method used in the Zenith, Solex and Weber designs, employed a choke of constant area and metered the fuel in proportion to the load and throttle opening by means of a main jet and a compensator jet of opposite characteristics, which provide a balance of the total fuel output from the two jets and so maintained the mixture constant; a third jet for slow running was also provided. The spray carburettor provided a cheap compromise with the inherent faults of not fully efficient atomisation and even distribution of the fuel mixture resulting in not fully complete and even combustion.

The metered direct-injection of liquid fuel, originally required for Diesel engine operation, was at first adapted for use in aviation and racing car engines since the finely-atomised spray of fuel delivered directly into the combustion chamber gave more complete combustion and permitted higher compression ratios to be used and thus more power and improved fuel economy. Designs of equipment for petrol injection either at low pressures (up to 100 p.s.i.) into the induction manifold or direct at high pressures (up to 3000 p.s.i.) into the combustion chamber, have since 1960 been evolved for use with production cars and tests have shown that improvement in power output and fuel economy results from their use. The extremely fine tolerances to which this equipment has to be manufactured, however, make it costly compared with the well-established production carburettor, a disadvantage which large production may eventually remove. Various fuel-injection designs specialised for light car engines are in either prototype or partial mass production; these vary in complexity from a simple fuel-injection valve incorporated in the butterfly valve to the fully-compensated direct-injection unit with its ability to meter fuel accurately in minute quantities by means of a positive high-pressure displacement pump. The relatively simple systems which deal in low-pressure delivery, and so do not require such high precision and therefore costly machining, are considerably cheaper to produce than the high-pressure direct-delivery systems which are more complex and must be made to very fine tolerances.

One of the simplest systems was the Brandwood pressure metering fuel-injection valve incorporated in a butterfly valve situated in the air-intake manifold; the valve had a hollow spindle through which fuel was fed under a pressure of from 3 to 12 p.s.i. The amount of fuel fed to the cylinders was controlled by a tapered needle valve controlled by a bellows subjected to manifold depression, which was sensitive to throttle opening, manifold depression and ambient temperature. The Simms petrol-injection system was also of the simpler port-feed type; it had a simple pumping element feeding one injector nozzle in the intake manifold and an eccentric on the half-time driven shaft which deforms a synthetic rubber ring, supplied with the fuel by an engine-driven pump, to effect fuel delivery which continued for only 10 degrees of crankshaft rotation halfway down the induction stroke. A governor sensitive to engine speed, and a capsule sensitive to manifold depression and engine temperature controlled the effective length of the pumping stroke; the amount of fuel fed to the injector nozzle was a function of engine speed, load and temperature. Other generally similar systems employing low-pressure port injection included examples developed by General Motors, Daimler Benz and Fuscaldo. The American Bosch system used a single-plunger delivery pump which supplied metered fuel to a distributor which, in turn, supplied the fuel in proper sequence to the intake orifice of each inlet valve. The amount of fuel injected was varied according to engine speed and load by a control unit. The Bendix system supplied fuel at constant pressure and metered to each induction port by electrically-operated injector valves. The Tecalemit-Jackson operated at low pressures between 1 and 75 p.s.i. on the continuous-flow principle, with separate nozzles for each cylinder injecting into the manifold branches. Speed and density requirements were met by means of an engine-driven fuel pump and a manifold-pressure-controlled bleed-off valve to vary the pressure in a fuel-ring supply main.

The Kugelfischer system, with low-pressure nozzles placed close to the inlet valves and so directed to inject through the valve openings, was fitted as standard equipment to the Peugeot 404 model. With a compression ratio increased from 7·2 to 8·5 to 1, the power output of this engine when so fitted was raised from 72 h.p. to 85 h.p. at 5500 r.p.m. with improved economy and flexibility. The Lucas low-pressure system had an injection pump and a common metering unit which served each cylinder in turn through reversed injector nozzles which sprayed against the incoming air flow to improve atomisation. The metering unit consisted of a hardened steel shuttle, the movement of which was effected by the pressure of the fuel from the electrically-driven feed pump. The effective travel of the shuttle, and therefore the amount of fuel delivered, was adjusted by means of a variable stop incorporated in a mixture-control unit. The S.U. system had the same number of plungers as engine cylinders; the plungers were operated by a variable swashplate mounted on a Z-shaft and delivered metered fuel through a rotary distributor valve. A capsule, sensitive to manifold temperature and pressure, controlled the effective stroke of the plungers by moving the Z-shaft backwards or forwards by means of an oil-pressure servo unit.

High pressure direct-injection units which deliver metered fuel at pressures up to 3000 p.s.i. directly into the combustion chamber through pintle type nozzles derive directly from Diesel engine practice; examples have been produced by Bosch, Lucas, C.A.V. and S.U. and used in racing cars and some high-performance sports cars. The Bosch system had a separate jerk-type constant-stroke plunger pump for each individual cylinder. Surrounding each plunger was a control sleeve connected to a common rack and pinion; the quantity of fuel injected by each stroke was controlled by the movement of the rack which modified the relative setting of ports and transfer grooves in the plungers and control sleeves. An aneroid capsule, sensitive to variations in air temperature and pressure in the intake manifold, was linked to the control rack; and a diaphragm was connected to the throttle venturi and also linked to the control rack which sensed the quantity of air consumed by the engine. This form of unit, by reason of its complexity and extremely high quality required in production, was several times more expensive than the simple mass-produced carburettor and in the light car field was acceptable only for special applications, such as Formula 1 racing and high-priced sports cars.

Lubrication

High-pressure lubrication by an engine-driven pump to main and big-end bearings and, at reduced pressure, to such lesser-stressed components as overhead-valve gear, camshaft bearings, gear wheels and chains and the like was standard practice in motor car engine design. Progress in lubrication technique was concentrated on oils and oil filtration.

Oil cleanliness reduces engine wear and various forms of oil filter have been devised to ensure that the oil during its circulation through the engine is kept as clean as possible. The initial wire gauze filter in the sump prevents large impurities and solid particles from being put into circulation by the pressure pump. A secondary easily-replaceable fine filter of paper or metallic mesh, of the partial-flow or full-flow type, extracts the finer dimension impurities of combustion and metallic particles which accumulate during the operation of the engine. Some engine designs such as Fiat, Vandervell and Simca have an alternative or even additional filter in the form of a small hollow flywheel mounted on the front end of the crankshaft into which the oil is fed from the pump before it proceeds to the crankshaft oil channels; solid particles and the heavier impurities in the oil are extracted by centrifugal action. The Glacier centrifugal oil filter was an example of this kind of filter which was driven by the engine oil pressure. Petrol-oil mixture in the proportion of up to 50 to 1 was used for the lubrication of two-stroke engines; some designs have also a metered force feed to the main and big-end bearings, controlled according to engine speed and load, to supplement a still smaller proportion of oil in the petrol. The D.K.W. automatic mixing device avoided the somewhat awkward procedure of mixing oil in the correct proportion when refuelling.

Considerable progress was made in the constitution of lubricating oils for use with the motor car and particularly with its highly-stressed engine. Oils were available with detergent additives which neutralised the acid and other impurities due to combustion thus avoiding excessive wear and corrosion; multi-grade oils had the property of retaining a set viscosity between high and low temperature limits, thus avoiding the former necessity of changing oils because of climate variation; molybdenum disulphide additives reduced friction still more because of the higher lubricating properties of this substance; and there was the promise of new synthetic and almost indestructible oils which would have an unlimited life in the engine oil sump. This latter quality was foreshadowed by such designs as the Simca which required an oil change only after 6,000 miles, and the sealed gearbox and transmission unit of the Triumph 1300 which was filled with oil for life and never needed changing.

Generators and Alternators

Direct-current generators having the orthodox arrangement of total enclosure, electrically-excited field, multipole armature, commutator and current-collecting brushes have been used for many years in wide production, in conjunction with a cut-out to isolate the battery from the generator when the voltage generated was insufficient to overcome the battery voltage, and a voltage regulator to control the charging current in respect of the needs of the battery. Over the past forty years, the weight of the direct-current generator for motor cars has been reduced from 30 lb. to 17 lb., and the output increased from 12 amps. to 30 amps. It would appear that the limit in this development has now been reached.

This limitation of the direct-current generator, together with its low-output capabilities at low speeds and mechanical instability at high speeds, turned attention to the possibilities of the alternator and caused its adoption for standard production. For electrical loadings of around 30 amps. upwards, the advantages of the alternator in size, weight and performance are of major importance, as shown in the Lucas alternator which, for a weight of only 9 lb. was able to supply an output of 35 amps. Besides being light and more compact, the alternator is potentially more reliable because of its robust construction, absence of generating-coil windings rotating at high speeds, and brushes collecting heavy current, together with a simpler control system. Moreover, the alternator can run at much higher speeds, up to 12,000 r.p.m., thus making for a more compact unit of smaller bulk and less weight; it can also deliver a higher output at low speeds. The alternating current supplied by the alternator is rectified into a direct current for battery charging by small semi-conductor solid-state rectifiers; voltage regulation is applied to the field circuit by a simple vibrating-contact regulator.

The electric starter has for many years been of standard design, being essentially a normal direct-current series-wound motor which incorporated a starting pinion, either of the self-engaging Bendix type or the Marelli type in which the starter pinion was engaged with the flywheel gear ring, either manually or by means of a solenoid working in conjunction with the engine ignition switch, before the starter motor was activated. The latter arrangement, being of more gentle engagement action, caused less wear on the flywheel gear ring teeth. The combined starter motor and generator, known as a dynamotor, which was used to some extent in the 1920's because of its simpler installation and quieter action, was revived in this period for use with small engines. A current example of this later, more compact form was the Siba Dynastart design.

CLUTCHES

The former forms of engine clutches, such as the leather-lined cone type, the Hele-Shaw multi-plate type and the drum type have all long since been superseded by the simple, efficient and compact dry single spring-loaded asbestos-fabric lined plate type incorporated in the flywheel of the Borg and Beck design, which gave long and reliable service. Improvements in this form included a spring-cushioned plate type which gave smoother clutch engagement, and the diaphragm spring type which dispensed with the multi-springs for clutch engagement and provided lighter clutch pedal loads of about 40 lb.

Advanced design, particularly in respect of the growing use of automatic transmission, brought about the adoption of other forms of clutches which, being automatic in operation, dispensed with the need for a clutch pedal. The fluid flywheel, which has been in production for many years, consist of a casing partly filled with oil in which the vane-equipped driven and driving members act as the impeller members of a centrifugal pump. The fluid interaction between these two members progressively transmit torque in proportion to engine speed to the point where they are both locked in positive drive. The fluid flywheel was incorporated in several types of automatic and semi-automatic transmission systems. The Renault Ferlec and the Smith designs were examples of the electro-magnetic automatic clutch, containing iron powder which was solidified electro-magnetically to transmit torque. The DAF pair of centrifugal clutches used with a variable-ratio belt drive incorporated weights which automatically caused the engagement of the clutch as engine speed increased. These forms of automatic clutches could be used either by themselves to provide simple two-pedal control, or in conjunction with fully-automatic transmission systems in which clutch engagement and gear variation to deal with varying speeds and loads when the car was in motion were controlled solely by throttle movement.

TRANSMISSIONS
Gearboxes

The early sliding-pinion type of gearbox with straight-cut teeth needed judgment and skill to operate it properly, and the later constant-mesh pinions with dog clutches made this operation only slightly less difficult, although the eventual adoption of helical teeth gears made for quieter running. The synchromesh type of gearbox in which the gears to be engaged were, on selection, first synchronised by means of miniature friction cone clutches before they actually mesh in positive engagement, considerably simplified the act of gear changing and eliminated the need for skill in this operation. Synchromesh mechanism was at first applied to top and third gears, but later designs of gearboxes were so equipped on all forward gears. With the conventional form of synchromesh arrangement in general use, there was a single pair of cones which engaged just before the main teeth of the selected gears mesh, and so synchronised the two speeds for silent engagement. The improved multi-cone or baulk-ring synchromesh system was designed to reduce operating loads on the gear lever and make gear engagement quicker and more efficient; moreover, the increased area of the multiple cones gave longer wearing life.

Automatic changing of gears which would make manual operation unnecessary and, in the ultimate, relate the gear ratio automatically to speed and torque requirements has always been desirable. The semi-automatic preselector Wilson gearbox had been in production for many years employing a fluid-flywheel in conjunction with manually preselected trains of epicyclic gears. Fully automatic units were first applied only to the larger and more expensive cars because of the added complication and cost involved with such units as the Borg-Warner and the Hydramatic designs, both of which used a fluid-flywheel torque converter in conjunction with epicyclic gear trains. Experience gained with the larger units eventually permitted simpler and more compact units suitable for use with light cars, even of the smallest kind, to be made commercially available.

A fully-automatic transmission system consists essentially of a clutch that engages automatically as engine speed increases, a gear train usually of the compact epicyclic variety whose gear ratios are selectively engaged by means of individual clutches servo activated through a control system which is sensitive to the engine speed and torque load of the transmission. The forward motion of the car is thus controlled solely by the accelerator pedal, the clutch engagement and the selection of the optimum gear ratio for any speed or load being effected automatically by the mechanism described. The following types of automatic transmission were developed specially for application to light cars.

The Smith Selectroshift system employed the electro-magnetic powder clutch. There was no clutch pedal; when the first gear was engaged, the windings received current from the dynamo and, as the throttle was opened, the dynamo output rose and the corresponding increase in magnetic flux caused the clutch to take up the drive. When the gear changes were made, the switch in the gear lever was opened, thereby disengaging the clutch. The Smith Autoselective transmission used two powder electro-magnetic clutches in conjunction with a three-speed layshaft gearbox.

The Automotive Products automatic transmission was designed to be incorporated compactly in the sump of the B.M.C. Mini transverse engine units. Manual selective control of the system was by a centrally-mounted lever which provided seven positions: reverse, neutral, and automatic, plus first, second, third and top gears for manual operation. This provision allowed the system to be used in three different ways:

1. As a fully-automatic four-speed transmission giving smooth progression from rest to maximum speed. 'Kick-down' control to a lower gear for greater acceleration, and engine braking on hills was provided.

2. Use of the selector lever giving full manual control of all four gears.

3. For leisurely driving, it was possible to engage any gear and use the smooth take-up of the torque converter for starting from rest.

The Simca Ferodo unit fitted to the Simca 1000, the ZF unit fitted to the Peugeot 404, and the Toyoglide unit fitted to the Toyota Corona automatic transmission systems all employed a fluid-flywheel torque converter in conjunction with an epicyclic gear train automatically selected by a control unit and engaged by separate clutches of the band, cone or multi-plate types. The control unit engaged the selected gear in response to the speed of the car and the torque requirements of the transmission to the driving wheels.

The D.A.F. Variomatic infinitely-variable gear gave automatic changes of gear ratio by means of a combination of centrifugal force and induction manifold vacuum to meet varying speed and torque conditions. The gear unit was driven from the engine through a centrifugal clutch and propeller shaft which, in turn, drove a cross-shaft through bevel gears. Each divided pulley mounted at each end of the cross shaft drove by means of an endless vee belt a similar divided pulley mounted on each half shaft. Controlling fly weights and bell-crank levers acting on cams moved the pulley halves endwise by centrifugal force, assisted by the depression in the induction manifold acting on pistons incorporated in the pulleys. The expanding and contracting pulley diameters varied the gear ratio as required, at the same time maintaining the belts at an even tension. The two pairs of pulleys being mutually self-adjusting, a separate differential gear unit was not required. Reverse gear was obtained by manually-operated dog clutches within the bevel gear cross-shaft casing.

Differential Gears

The simple differential gear which permits the driving wheels of a car to revolve at different speeds when rounding corners, without affecting an equal application of torque to both wheels, has been a necessary transmission component from the beginning of motoring. With its unlimited range of differential speeds in the simple form, however, there are certain conditions in which the conventional differential gear is at a disadvantage, namely, when the grip of one tyre is much less than that of the other, as can happen on slippery road surfaces. Whenever traction at one wheel is reduced, the torque which can be transmitted through that wheel is also reduced. The device known as the controlled-slip differential permits a transfer of torque to the wheel whose tyre is not slipping; this is achieved by providing resistance to rotation of the driving bevels relative to the differential housing. Essentially, a form of clutch-brake is incorporated between the side driving bevels and the differential housing; clutches are of the cone type as in the Borg-Warner

157

design, multi-plate type as in the Salisbury 'Powr-Lok', E.N.V. and Trac-Aide designs, or the wedged pawl-and-cam type as in the German ZF design. The retardation of the differential action so achieved enables a greater proportion of the driving torque to pass to the gripping wheel than to the opposite wheel which is slipping, and so assists in restoring drive stability. Limited-slip differential gears were now being generally adopted in production for the larger light cars.

Overdrive Gears

Higher gearing between engine and the driven wheels reduces crankshaft speeds and fuel consumption and lengthens engine life; a typical road test shows a 12 per cent reduction in fuel consumption resulting from a 20 per cent reduction in engine r.p.m., and engine wear should accordingly be lower by a proportionate amount. An overdrive is a gear unit additional to the gearbox which provides higher gearing than that given by the final drive crown wheel and pinion, thus providing cruising at an engine speed lower than it would be in direct top gear. While overdrive gears could be incorporated within the gearbox proper, they were usually added as a separate unit at the rear of the gearbox.

On all except the simple Murray design which was of the layshaft type with dog clutches for manual engagement, an epicyclic gear was used in the Laycock-de-Normanville design, with solenoid-operated selector valves controlling hydraulically-operated pistons actuating a cone clutch for retarding the annulus. A simplified and compact unit produced by Auto Transmissions Ltd. was designed for sandwich location between engine and gearbox. As it did not have to withstand the torque magnification of the gearbox, this unit could be used without restriction on all gears; it could, for instance, convert a normal three-speed gearbox into a six-speed unit. The Honda overdrive unit employed epicyclic gearing, the sun wheel of which was arrested for overdrive engagement by a dog clutch; a flexible diaphragm submitted to inlet manifold depression moved the dog clutch selector. The Borg-Warner unit used epicyclic gearing, the sun wheel of which was arrested by a solenoid-operated pawl mechanism for passing the drive through the planet pinions to the annulus to give overdrive. For rapid re-engagement of direct drive for acceleration, a kick-down switch was operated by the full depression of the accelerator.

Constant-Velocity Couplings

Articulated shafts transmitting torque in motor cars have for a long time depended on the simple Hardy leather or fabric coupling, or later, the needle-bearing Hardy Spicer type of basic Hooke hinged-cross joint to provide universal flexure. Since the arms of the cross are at right angles, there will be four extreme positions during each revolution when the entire angular deflection is being taken by only one half of the joint, with the cross members rocking backwards and forward between these extremes. The effect of this motion on each revolution is to vary the speed of the driving shaft in relation to that of the driven one. While independent suspension movements alone

Plate 33

N.S.U. Spider: 1965

Simca 1000: 1963

Plate 34

Renault 4L: 1963

Reliant Rebel: 1964

Plate 35

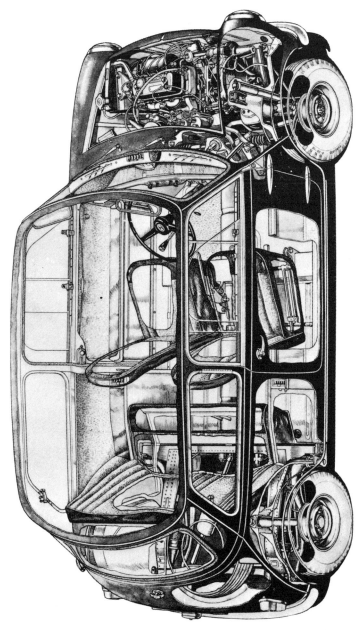

Austin Seven Mini: 1959

Plate 36

Saab: 1956

Volkswagen 1600: 1965

Honda racing car: 1964

Plate 37

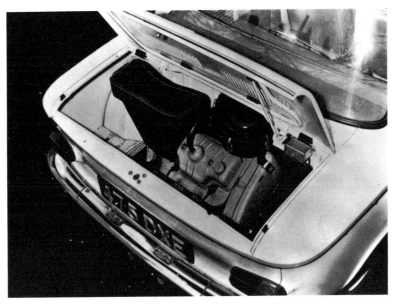

N.S.U. Prinz two-cylinder engine: 1962

Fiat 500 engine: 1966

Plate 38

Skoda 1000 MB engine: 1965

Coventry Climax racing car engine: 1965

Plate 39

Peugeot 204 transverse engine: 1965

Rover gas turbine racing car engine: 1963

Plate 40

Wankel rotary engine: 1965

Lotus Elan chassis: 1966

could be accommodated by two simple universal joints, the additional steering movements of a front-wheel drive layout cause unacceptable speed fluctuations in the drive.

To overcome this disadvantage, constant-velocity joints were used for the outboard couplings on front-wheel drives. The inboard couplings of the half shafts have only relatively small deflections from being parallel with their driving shafts, and speed fluctuations can be ironed out by means of rubber-bushed Hooke-type joints, which can twist elastically during each rotation as well as absorb torsional irregularities. The much larger deflections of the outboard couplings necessitate constant-velocity joints. These joints incorporate steel balls in curved longitudinal tracks, which not only transmit the torque but, by adjusting their position in the curved tracks during each revolution so that a plane through their centres bisects the angle formed by driving and driven shafts, provide the condition required for transmitting the drive without speed fluctuations.

Examples of the constant-velocity joint are the early Rzeppa design, from which was developed the Birfield joint, used with the B.M.C. Mini car models and with their larger derivatives the Morris 1100 and the Austin 1100.

CHASSIS

Two main forms of chassis construction have been adopted: the separate chassis frame or backbone upon which a separate body is mounted, and the stressed-skin unit body to which chassis sub-assemblies are attached. The latter method of welded construction had the advantages of cheapness in mass production and effecting a saving of weight; the main disadvantage was the difficulty of repair in case of damage. The Triumph Herald design broke away from this accepted practice and reverted to a backbone form of chassis frame and outrigger body bearers on the lines of the earlier Tatra and Skoda designs, with the body panels bolted rather than welded together which facilitated easier and cheaper repair. When the body pressings were bolted to the outriggers and to other points on the frame, the stiffness of the body shell as a whole was added to that of the separate chassis. The Herald design thus combined to a large extent the advantages of both main forms of construction.

Suspensions

Independent suspension of the front wheels and later of the rear wheels through the medium of laminated leaf springs had become standard practice on production cars since the 1930's. The coil spring which is lighter and has a wider range of effective operation than the laminated leaf spring was later generally adopted. The compact and unobtrusive torsion-bar method of spring suspension was also used. Although these arrangements were improvements on previous practice of stiff front and rear axles, there was still considerable room for improvement in achieving a balanced and compensated form of spring suspension that would even out and absorb road inequalities and improve still further passenger comfort and road holding.

The Citroën suspension system, employing long coil springs interconnected front and rear which ensured full compensation of loading by equalising the pressure supporting each of the four wheels, pioneered the application of such a system to production light cars by its application to the Citroën 2 c.v. model. The Borgward Isabella design was the first German production car to use an air-suspension system in which the usual types of springs were replaced by air vessels, the undersides of which were sealed by flexible diaphragms. Bell-shaped members fixed to the front and rear axles bore directly on these diaphragms so that the air sealed within the air vessels was compressed progressively in proportion to the load. Each pair of front and rear vessels were interconnected by a pipe through a restrictor valve. The Dunlop Pneuride air-suspension system provided suspension on air vessels which were supplied with varying air pressures to meet different loads conditions by means of an engine-driven air pump and a levelling valve. The Renault Aerostable system of air suspension fitted to the Dauphine models consisted of auxiliary sealed air-filled cushions at the rear and hollow rubber springs at the front, which supplement the normal coil-spring suspension. The air at atmospheric pressure in the rear cushions was compressed after an initial suspension movement had taken place; the hollow rubber springs at the front varied the suspension rate according to the load. The Armstrong system employed piston-type hydraulic damping units to give constant height and variable ride control.

A later and more elaborate system of hydraulic suspension, adopted by B.M.C. for certain of their production cars, including the later Mini and 1100 models, was the Spencer Moulton Hydrolastic system. With this arrangement, each wheel was supported on a sealed flexible unit containing an anti-rust and anti-freeze fluid as a damping medium. Each pair of front and rear units were interconnected to effect automatic compensation for both forward and lateral uneven road conditions, which resulted in a level controlled ride without sway or roll, and promoted good road holding and positive steering. This system had no moving parts and no glands to leak and no routine maintenance was required.

Steering Gears

The standard form of steering gear, based on the long established compensating Ackermann system, has remained standard practice since the inception of the motor car. Steering linkage arrangements have been elaborated because of chassis design becoming more complex, and control through the earlier half-bevel and pinion, worm-and-wheel, worm-and-sector and worm-and-nut forms of gears have now been superseded by improved mechanisms of higher efficiency such as the cam-and-roller, cam-and-lever, and recirculating-ball gears. The rack-and-pinion form of gear has been revived in production because of its simplicity and compactness.

The Marles design eliminated the part-sliding, part-rolling motion between the teeth of a worm and wheel by the use of an entirely rolling action; this was effected by mounting the roller on ball bearings, which ensured that friction was reduced and efficiency increased. In the Bishop gear the cam track follower was carried in the lever on needle-roller bearings; the follower thus rolled on the cam track with reduced friction. The Burman recirculating-ball form of gear had a semi-circular helical track generated on the cam, and in the nut there was an internal helical track of the same form. Assembled into the track in the nut, and running also in the track on the cam, was a continuous line of balls. These balls provided a rolling action between cam and nut when the cam was rotated, and, since the nut was fixed radially, it moved along the cam as the steering wheel was turned. This more complex recirculating-ball form of gear was initially used in larger, more expensive cars, but large-quantity production enabled the gear to be used on smaller and cheaper cars, such as the Ford Anglia. The simplest form of gear was the rack-and-pinion type which was used in the B.M.C. Mini and D.A.F. cars. A pinion rotated by the steering-wheel shaft engaged with teeth cut on a rack, mounted across the car. Transverse movements of the rack were transferred directly to a steering arm which controlled the track-rod connecting the pair of front wheels. This arrangement gave the most direct connection between steering wheel and road wheel with the least number of points at which lost motion could occur.

Power-steering servo systems which reduced the effort for steering was introduced for large vehicles. The application of such a system to light cars was unnecessary, particularly with the refinement of the modern steering gears already mentioned.

Brakes

Mechanically-operated brake systems, except for the simplest cars, were abandoned soon after 1950 and the hydraulically-operated, fully-compensated and simultaneously-acting system became established practice for production cars. This system with its equal braking effort on all four wheels contributed considerably to road safety by improving general stability and reducing tendency to skidding. The ever increasing performance of cars demanding more effective braking resulted in an increase in the area of the friction surfaces, and refinement in design provided smoother and more progressive braking action. The potentially weak aspect of the hydraulic system is the possibility of complete brake failure due to breakage of service pipes or gradual leakage of hydraulic fluid, although such failures seldom occur in practice. Complete duplicated hydraulic systems have been used on a few of the more expensive cars as a safeguard against this possibility. Well established hydraulic braking systems include such designs as Lockheed, Dunlop, Girling and Bendix.

Deceleration under braking transfers additional load to the front wheels and lessens the load on the rear wheels. To maintain a proper balance of braking efficiency, a larger proportion of the braking effort must be applied to the front wheels than to the rear. This can be arranged by the use of larger area front brake drums or fitting them with larger hydraulic cylinders, or using two leading shoe front brakes which provide a greater braking effort than other arrangements of brake shoes.

The form of brake which has been used for many years was the drum type, the brake shoes of which were lined with the friction material bearing on the inner periphery of the drum and actuated by a hydraulic cylinder. Increasingly higher road speeds of racing cars required a still more effective and efficient braking system. This was provided by the disc form of brake which was originated by F. W. Lanchester in 1902 but was not seriously studied until the 1950's. The brake disc being of uncomplicated shape and fully exposed to air flow can keep cooler than the best designs of drum brake which lessens the tendency to the phenomenon known as brake fade; moreover, water is quickly flung from the braking surface by centrifugal force. Easily renewable brake friction pads are positioned on each side of the disc and retained within a caliper unit in which is incorporated the hydraulic cylinder for pressing the pads against the disc. Intensive development under racing conditions led to the adoption of disc brakes, either for the front wheels such as in the Humber Sceptre or for all four wheels such as in the Renault R8. It is likely that they will eventually replace completely the drum form of brake in production cars. Standard designs of disc brakes were made by Girling, Dunlop which had a wedging self-servo action, Lockheed and Bendix.

Vacuum-servo units, operated by the manifold depression, have been developed which magnify the braking effort, thus needing less brake pedal effort, and provided a high degree of brake response under all conditions. Examples of such units were the Girling Powerstop, Girling Supervac, and Dunlop designs. Road safety consideration introduced the conception of the split or dual braking system employing a tandem master cylinder operating dual hydraulic circuits which control individually either front and rear pairs of brakes, or diagonal pairs of front and rear brakes. Later models of Saab cars were equipped in production with the latter system.

Tyres

The motor car tyre has progressed steadily from the early days of the high-pressure small-section beaded-edge type, which was the Achilles heel of the early tyre before it developed a moderate reliability, through the later low-pressure wired-edge type which has progressively acquired increasing reliability, durability and road holding characteristics. Tyre design made considerable progress after 1950 which rendered previous practice rapidly obsolete. Chassis and suspension improvements together with improved road surfaces and unobstructed motorways making possible sustained high touring speeds, have all influenced this rapid recent development of the motor tyre.

The conventional form of tyre construction of both the tube and tubeless varieties had plies of rayon or nylon cord fabric, laid diagonally at opposing angles to each other and at approximately 40 degrees to the tread circumference. It was, however, realised as long ago as 1913 that a radial rather than a diagonal form of construction, in which the plies are laid at 90 degrees to the tread circumference, gave improved vehicle stability but had an adverse effect on ride characteristics. The important factor in the reintroduction of the radial tyre after 1950 was the realisation that a substantial increase in tread life resulted in improved control of tread segment movement, and that it has a lower rolling resistance with resulting fuel saving. The outstanding feature of the radial tyre, however, is its improved road grip because of its rigid steel wire or nylon reinforced belt incorporated beneath the tread and its soft side walls which tend to keep the tread in firm contact with the road.

The pioneer of this new form of tyre was the Michelin firm who put into large production their very successful steel-braced X-type tyre, which earned a high reputation for long wear as well as improved road holding, especially on corners at high speeds. The Pirelli Cinturato and Dunlop SP41 radial tyres were examples of the radial textile-braced type. The majority of world tyre manufacturers also produced their individual brands of radial tyres. A wide variety of tyre tread patterns have been devised and used in production to improve road grip under all conditions of weather and road surface. Partial or total loss of adhesion at speed caused by static water lying on the road surface, known as aquaplaning, was countered by special water-rejecting tread patterns.

BODIES

Unit or 'chassisless' construction of motor car bodies was generally used, in which the stressed body shell formed a rigid base to which the main assemblies of engine and gearbox unit, and front and rear independent suspension units were attached to lugs. This body-chassis structure was designed to sustain both the static loadings of the dead weight of the car at rest and the dynamic loadings in motion resulting from varying forces of vibration, shock oscillation and torsion from road surface inequalities. This stressed body shell was stiffened by fluting or ribbing of the surfaces, and even by the three-dimensional curved surfaces resulting from streamlining and styling. This form of construction applied to saloon bodies; two-seat open bodies of the sports variety have not the inherent stiffness of the braced-box formation of the saloon and a different method of construction providing additional strengthening members was necessary.

The pressed panels which were welded, or more rarely, bolted together to form the unitary whole were generally of steel sheet for the cheaper form of car; the basic disadvantage of rust was the main drawback in the use of this material. The more expensive form of aluminium for body construction, besides not having this disability also has the advantages of high ductility and sound damping qualities; the lighter specific weight of aluminium, however, was largely offset by the necessity to use heavier gauge sheet to provide the necessary strength. Estate cars and station waggon bodies were sometimes built on older, traditional body-building methods, using wood framing and plywood panels. A breakaway from the chassisless welded form of body construction was adopted in the Triumph Herald design, which used a combination of stressed-skin body, constructed of bolted-together panels, carried on a backbone type chassis furnished with outriggers. This form of construction, which harked back to the earlier Tatra and Skoda designs, had the advantage that damaged panels could be easily and cheaply replaced.

Fibre-glass consisting of woven or matted glass fibres impregnated with

163

epoxy resin which, after polymerisation, forms a tough and resilient material impervious to corrosion, was used for light racing and sports car bodies. It was a form of construction which was not adaptable to cheap mass production. The use of plastics in injection moulding form for body fittings such as door handles, fascias, internal side panels and the like was increasing.

Leather was still used for upholstery and interior trimming for the more expensive cars, but synthetic rubber, p.v.c. and other resilient materials which can be made closely resembling leather, but without its essential qualities of appearance and wearing ability, was largely used for the cheaper range of cars. Foam rubber was used for upholstery and seats instead of the former springs and horsehair stuffing. Stainless steel, although more expensive, was beginning to be used instead of the less durable chromium-plated steel for both interior and exterior fittings.

Styling of body and form had been intensely studied by artist engineers, particularly in Italy, where engineering and art have associated rather more than elsewhere with profitable results. Specialists in this form of production included such names as Bertone, who provided bodies for the Alfa Romeo Guiletta and Guilia, Pininfarina, who provided body designs for Fiat and Lancia models, Zagato, who provided body designs for Alfa Romeo models, and Karmann-Ghia who provided a styled sports body on the Volkswagen chassis. An example of English styling was the Vanden Plas body on the Austin Princess model.

Considerable study was also now being given to the ergonomics, the synthesis of biological aspects and engineering, of car seating and passenger accommodation to enhance physical comfort and minimise driving and travel fatigue, and in the general interests of driving safety.

INHERENT SAFETY FEATURES

The increasing accident rate on the roads in many countries made imperative intensive study of causes and means of prevention, as well as mitigation as far as possible of the physical effects of such accidents to passengers. The latter study made plain the advisability of the adoption of such immediately usable safeguards as the safety belt, and the more long-term policy of designing cars with inherent safety features which would at least minimise if not entirely obviate injury.

Safety Harness

Belt harness designed to prevent the passenger being flung violently forward against the windscreen, fascia or steering wheel in the event of an accident, particularly of the head-on collision kind, were of various forms and equipped with quick-release fastenings. These belts varied from a simple waist or lap belt to the more complete waist belt and shoulder strap anchored securely to lugs attached to the body or seat structure. The more versatile designs permitted the free movement of the passenger without the restriction of a fixed belt by the addition of inertia reels which unwound at the pull of a normal motion, but locked at the sudden pull of the inertia resulting from arrested motion. The compulsory inclusion of safety harness anchor points

164

and the fitting of safety belts in new production cars was adopted in various countries. Laboratory tests and actual accidents both demonstrate the efficacy of the safety harness in preventing or reducing the extent of physical injury in road accidents.

Safety Research

A number of the larger car manufacturers now conduct extensive scientific tests of full-scale simulated road accidents for the purpose of avoiding or minimising the effects of such accidents to passengers, and to invest motor car design with as much inherent safety potential as possible. These impact and roll-over live tests have evolved some essential additional requirements to car design, such as: the passenger compartment as a whole must be sufficiently stiff to resist deformation under the influence of external impact during a collision; the front and rear structure of the body must not be too stiff, so that in the event of a collision a considerable amount of the impact energy is spent in deforming these parts of the car; the layout and furnishing of the interior of the body must be designed to deform and deflect when a body is thrown against it; and interior components should be countersunk where possible and made of resilient material or designed to be automatically collapsible under impact, such as a dished steering wheel and a telescopic steering column. The results of such accident research incorporated in production design will no doubt be gradually established by legislation and adopted by manufacturers.

Future Trends

The period of the 1960's was one of rapidly expanding technological invention and development in all spheres on an international basis, and the consequent cross-insemination of ideas and techniques affected and benefited many engineering activities, not least that of automobile engineering. This increase of technological knowledge during this period, together with growing wealth and standard of living creating wider market potential, at least in the Western world, made possible enterprising lines of speculation and experiment, which could eventually be transformed and developed into practical design and commercial production.

The direct result of this vigorous technological activity influenced not only current production thinking and prompted future lines of progress, but also brought about certain significant revolutionary technical break-throughs, which although theoretically feasible were not as yet practically possible. The chief of these activities were as follows: the intensive development of the racing car which aimed always at the possible limits of stress, endurance and reliability vigorously continued the contribution which motor racing had consistently made from the earliest days to the development of the production motor car, and assisted materially in the development of current production models having remarkably high specific outputs and unfailing reliability, together with a potential reserve for still further development; the successful development of a new forms of power units, in particular the gas turbine and the rotary internal-combustion engine, both of which by 1960 had been developed to commercial standards of manufacture and use, which were more compact, lighter and potentially capable of higher specific outputs than existing established reciprocating forms; the successful application of the small high-speed Diesel engine with its important advantage of low specific fuel consumption for light car propulsion; and the adaptation of specialised new techniques for the particular needs of the light car, such as alternators, transistorised-ignition systems, cheap forms of fuel-injection systems, servo and duplicated braking systems, and the like.

The growing need for the reduction of air pollution and traffic noise revived consideration of the electrically-propelled town carriage. Vehicles of this kind had been produced and used with success during the early years of the twentieth century but had disappeared as a result of the growing competition of the petrol-engined motor car; moreover, they had the disadvantage of having to carry large and heavy lead-acid batteries which gave only short endurance and required daily charging. The move towards lessening air pollution and noise in cities in the traffic-congested 1960's revived the possibility of electric town carriages equipped with the lighter and more efficient forms of storage accumulators as a source of electric power. This subject is discussed in Chapter II.

These and other significant research activities provided fertile sources of progress which will influence light cars of the future.

RACING CAR ENGINES

From the earliest days of the development of the motor car advanced designs of cars, and particularly engines to power them, have been consistently produced for the specific purpose of racing. This practice necessitated a continual striving after the utmost potentialities attainable within the period in question with sustained ingenuity and audacity which maintained design progress constantly at the highest endeavour and achievement. This intensive striving after the ultimate not only provided a continuous panorama of spectacular sport but, more importantly, produced a continuous and detailed technical and operational progress which provided a fertile source of inspiration and guidance for the more prosaic task of commercial motor car production. Contemporary racing car practice, evolved and tested under the arduous and sustained operational conditions of racing both on the track and the road, has always foreshadowed and then materially fashioned the production cars of tomorrow. Earlier precedents in the under 1500 c.c. capacity are to be seen in such examples as the 750 c.c. Austin of 1935 with an output of 80 h.p. at the then phenomenal crankshaft speed of 12,000 r.p.m.; and the remarkably advanced designs for their period of the supercharged Delage 8-cylinder in-line engine of 1927, which developed 170 h.p. at 8000 r.p.m., and the two-stage supercharged Mercedes Type W163 vee eight-cylinder engine which developed 254 h.p. at 8000 r.p.m. Such progressive early designs foreshadowed the complex and potent 1500 c.c. Formula 1 racing car engines of 1961–64, which themselves foreshadowed and contributed to the ever developing production cars of the future. The progress fostered by such advanced early designs is seen in modern production designs capable of normally-aspirated power outputs of 100 h.p. per litre capacity at crankshaft speeds of 8000 r.p.m.

The design, production and operational lessons learned from this rigorous form of development and testing also continually benefited motor car engineering generally in producing still further improved materials of all kinds, and design techniques relating to cylinder head shape, cam form, carburation, ignition, bearing metals and lubrication in respect of engine design; and improved brakes, suspension, tyres and streamlining of body forms in respect of chassis design. Such valuable information applied rationally to future production design materially assisted in the continual improvement of production models for the ordinary user, resulting in safer and faster motoring with unfailing reliability.

The smallest category of racing cars produced after 1945, known as the 500 c.c. category, did not however contribute materially to this activity, since it was rather of a makeshift economical nature which adopted already well developed racing motor cycle engines for their power units, such as the single-cylinder Norton and J.A.P. and the vertical twin-cylinder Triumph designs which had been developed to produce some 55 h.p. at speeds up to 7500 r.p.m. The transmission system of these simple racing cars also followed motor cycle practice, having the drive taken to the rear axle through a gearbox and primary and secondary chains. Examples of these cars were produced by Cooper, Kieft, and J.B.S.

In the Formula 2 category with a limiting category of 1000 c.c. capacity, some standard engines were used in supertuned form with specially developed cylinder heads having push-rod overhead valve or single or even twin-overhead camshafts. The B.M.C. Type A engine of 1095 c.c. capacity (67·6 mm. by 76·2 mm.) with a compression ratio of 12 to 1, developed 95 h.p. at 7500 r.p.m., with a special cylinder head but retaining overhead push-rod valve operation. Smaller examples of this high-powered class of racing engines included the 750 c.c. capacity (62 mm. by 62 mm.) four-cylinder Osca which with twin overhead camshafts and a compression ratio of 9 to 1, developed 70 h.p. at 7500 r.p.m. The Ford 100E engine of 1098 c.c. capacity (Fig. 25) equipped with an Elva overhead inlet valve cylinder head could be tuned to produce 80 h.p. A more elaborate conversion of a standard production unit was the Cosworth SCA 65 model, which was based on a five-bearing Ford Classic 116E cylinder block made to be mounted at an angle of 30 degrees from the vertical. The original capacity was reduced to 997 c.c. to conform to Formula 2 regulations, which gave the engine a bore of 81 mm. and a stroke of 48·4 mm. The special cylinder head incorporated a single overhead camshaft driven from the crankshaft by a half-time gear train. The maximum power developed by this detailed conversion was 122 h.p. at 9000 r.p.m.

Some Formula 2 one-litre racing car engines were specifically designed as such and included designs by B.R.M., Coventry-Climax and Honda. The B.R.M. design (Fig. 27) did derive to some extent from the Formula 1 engine of 1500 c.c. by adopting the cylinder head of the latter which had known flow characteristics and was in actual production. This 998 c.c. capacity (71·8 mm. by 61·6 mm.) engine had a five-bearing crankshaft and overhead twin camshafts driven by gear train; with a compression ratio of 12·5 to 1, the engine developed 120 h.p. at 9750 r.p.m. for a total dry weight of 184 lb. Fuel was injected into the inlet tracts by a Lucas fuel-injection distributor unit, and the Lucas Opus transistorised ignition system was used which was capable of maintaining spark voltages up to crankshaft speeds of 15,000 r.p.m. The engine unit was designed to be inclined at 18 degrees from the vertical. The 1097 c.c. capacity (70 mm. by 66 mm.) single overhead-camshaft Coventry-Climax engine originated as an industrial unit designed to develop 36 h.p. at 3600 r.p.m. Through various stages of tuning, such as a 15 per cent increase in valve lift and the effective valve opening increased by 9 per cent, improved induction passage flow, and a compression ratio increased to 9·8 to 1, the engine was transformed into a sports-racing engine unit developing 83 h.p. at 6800 r.p.m. The 1 litre Honda Formula 2 engine was of generally similar type to the B.R.M. design, with twin-overhead camshafts, torsion-bar sprung valves and port-type fuel injection of Honda design.

In 1961, the Formula 1 engine capacity ordained by the Federation Internationale de l'Automobile was limited to 1500 c.c. This policy produced a number of very advanced engine designs having up to 16 cylinders which were characterised by their variety, ingenuity, complexity and compactness of design, and extremely high normally-aspirated specific outputs as high as 250 h.p. at 12,000 r.p.m. Significant characteristics common to these designs were multiplicity of small cylinders having oversquare dimensions and very high crankshaft r.p.m., as well as advanced details such as fuel-injection and transistorised-ignition systems. These new smaller units demonstrated a sustained reliability and average speeds in International racing events as good as and, in some cases, superior to the earlier 3-litre units.

A notable forerunner of this advanced series of 1500 c.c. capacity racing engines was the original B.R.M. design of 1947 which had a maximum super-charged output of 525 h.p. at 10,500 r.p.m. The complex design of this B.R.M. unit had 16 cylinders in vee formation at an angle of 135 degrees. The valves in each combustion space were operated by twin-overhead cam-shafts, and mixture was supplied by a two-stage centrifugal supercharger which provided a manifold pressure of 40 p.s.i. Although this design did not attain to a full reliability, it demonstrated the performance to which a 1500 cc. capacity engine could be developed.

Among the simpler four-cylinder high-output units of this class were the Coventry Climax FPF design of 1460 c.c. capacity (81 mm. by 71 mm.) which, with a compression ratio of 10 to 1, developed 142 h.p. at 7250 r.p.m. This engine was of substantially the same design as the smaller 1097 c.c. unit already described, with twin-overhead camshafts and five-bearing crankshaft. The Maserati-designed O.S.C.A. of 1500 c.c. capacity (78 mm. by 78 mm.) which developed 125 h.p. at 6300 r.p.m. was of generally similar design. The M.G. Ex. 181 was basically a B.M.C. Series B four-cylinder production engine of 1489 c.c. capacity (73 mm. by 89 mm.) equipped with a twin-overhead camshaft cylinder head and a vane type supercharger, which developed 300 h.p. at 7300 r.p.m. This was an example of a specially-prepared unit intended for international record runs; it attained a speed over a mile of nearly 204 mp.h.

Increased outputs and crankshaft speeds were demanded by increasing progress that was outside the scope of the simpler four-cylinder units, and multi-cylinder, higher speed units of varied arrangements and more complex design were produced in horizontally-opposed and vee forms. An early example of this period (1958) of a 75 degree vee-six cylinder engine was the Ferrari Dino 246 design of 1490 c.c. capacity (70 mm. by 64·5 mm.) which, with a compression ratio of 9·5 to 1, developed 190 h.p. at 9000 r.p.m. This design followed the general layout of the earlier Lancia V-8 cylinder design, the builders of which have had many years of experience in the design and manufacture of vee-type engines. The Ferrari range of six-cylinder racing engines included a later design with the two cylinder blocks set at 120 degrees; this arrangement provided a flat unit which lessened frontal area. The Ferrari type 158/BA vee-eight cylinder engine of 1500 c.c. capacity (67 mm. by 53 mm.) with cylinder blocks set at an angle of 90 degrees was designed to run at speeds of up to 11,000 r.p.m. A Bosch jerk-type solid-fuel injector and two twin-contact-breaker and four separate induction coils supplying the two plugs in each cylinder were used. The Coventry-Climax II vee-eight cylinder design was derived from the earlier Mark I engine of similar layout, with a stroke shortened from 2·36 in. to 2·03 in. to permit the engine speed to

169

increase from 8600 to 9300 r.p.m., at which 194 h.p. was developed. The B.R.M. 90 degree vee-eight cylinder design of 1498 c.c. capacity (68·5 mm. by 50·8 mm.) with a compression ratio of 10·5 to 1 and Lucas fuel injection developed 188 h.p. at 10,500 r.p.m. Examples of the still more complex twelve-cylinder unit in vee cylinder formation was the 60 degree Maserati Type 8, the cylinder dimensions (52·2 mm. by 52 mm.) gave a square rather than an oversquare engine in the interests of adopting a smaller bore to keep down the overall width of the engine, rather than a short stroke to keep piston speeds to a minimum. The smaller cylinders with their lower piston inertia permitted a safe engine speed of up to 13,000 r.p.m., at which 170 h.p. was developed. Another interesting feature of this unit was that it was designed as an engine-transmission unit, with gearbox and differential unit incorporated in the engine crankcase and with the drive being taken by a gear wheel incorporated in the centre of the crankshaft, thereby simplifying the torsional characteristics of the crankshaft and avoiding undue torsional vibrations, each half having the same characteristics as a four-throw unit. The Honda 60 degree vee-twelve-cylinder design (Plate 36) (58 mm. by 47 mm.) was notable for its 230 b.h.p. developed at the high crankshaft speed of 11,000 r.p.m., a characteristically high performance which this Japanese firm had developed with marked success for all their large range of motorcycle and motor car engines, and the fact that it was positioned transversely in rear of the car. The drive to the rear wheels was taken from a gear wheel centrally positioned on the crankshaft.

Of the horizontally-opposed racing engine designs, the air-cooled Porsche examples were the most notable. Both four- and eight-cylinder versions of racing engine were produced. The four-cylinder unit developed 180 h.p. The considerably more complex eight-cylinder design with its added problem of cooling by air such a compact and complex multi-cylinder arrangement, had a capacity of 1498 c.c. capacity (66 mm. by 54·6 mm.) and, with a compression ratio of 10 to 1, developed 185 h.p. at 9200 r.p.m. Twin distributors and four coils supplied ignition to two spark plugs in each cylinder, and mixture was supplied by four twin-choke Weber carburettors. Twin overhead camshafts, driven by a series of horizontal and vertical shafts and matching gears, operated the two valves in each cylinder. The water-cooled flat 16-cylinder Coventry Climax unit (Plate 39) of 1495 c.c. capacity (54·1 mm. by 40·6 mm.), by virtue of its large number of small cylinders, short stroke and the good inherent balance characteristics provided by the horizontally-opposed arrangement of the cylinders, developed some 240 h.p. at engine speeds up to 12,000 r.p.m. Twin-overhead camshafts were driven through gear trains, and the main drive was taken from a centrally-positioned gear wheel incorporated in the crankshaft. Two Lucas fuel-injection distributors and a Lucas transistorised ignition system were used.

An example of an air-cooled 8-cylinder in-line design was produced in 1962 by Ferrari in conjunction with the Italian motor-cycle firm of Gilera, who had had considerable experience in the design and production of high-speed, multi-cylinder racing motor-cycle engines. This Ferrari-Gilera unit of 1500 c.c.

capacity developed 215 h.p. at 11,000 r.p.m., and was set transversely across the rear of the chassis. Twin-overhead camshafts operating desmodromic valves and four double choke Weber carburettors were used; the main drive was taken from the centre of the crankshaft. The drive to the rear wheels was transmitted through a six-speed gearbox and a self-locking differential unit.

SMALL HIGH-SPEED DIESEL ENGINES

The compression-ignition engine operating on the Diesel principle has a compression ratio of between 14 to 18 to 1 which generates sufficient heat in compressing the pure air charge in the cylinder to ignite the metered atomised fuel injected at a pressure of up to 3000 p.s.i. at the top of the compression stroke of the piston by means of an injector plunger pump. The considerably higher compression pressures at which a Diesel engine operates, together with the efficient combustion of the atomised fuel spray as delivered by the solid-fuel injector pump, results in a specific fuel consumption of about 0·35 lb./sq. in. compared with a specific fuel consumption of about 0·5 lb./sq. in. for the petrol engine.

This 20 per cent reduction in specific fuel consumption provided by the Diesel engine has for many years brought about the production of high-speed Diesel units specialised for the propulsion of heavy road transport where fuel economy is of the first importance. This long commercial development eventually influenced the design and production of smaller Diesel units with higher crankshaft speeds for use in smaller road vehicles, such as taxi cabs and even smaller passenger cars. These smaller units are usually based on a well-tried petrol engine production design suitably modified to accommodate such additional items as the fuel injector pump unit and injectors located in the cylinder head, and strengthened to operate satisfactorily at the higher stresses imposed by the Diesel operating pressures.

The Perkins Four-99 design of 1600 c.c. capacity four-cylinder unit developed 43 h.p. at 4000 r.p.m. and was intended as a replacement engine unit for certain Vauxhall and Ford models. A design of cylinder head incorporating a combustion cell suited to small size cylinders was used. Fuel was injected by a Bosch pump through pintle-type nozzles into each combustion cell. The B.M.C. Diesel engine of 1489 c.c. capacity (73 mm. by 89 mm.) which developed 40 h.p. at 4000 r.p.m., was developed from the standard Series B petrol engine. Many standard parts of the original engine were used, but a stronger crankshaft of enlarged proportions and a torsional crankshaft damper was added. Fuel injection was provided by a C.A.V. distributor-type pump. The extra weight of this Diesel unit was some 50 lb. more than for the petrol engine. An example of a small Diesel engine unit specially developed for use with light cars was the Coventry Climax design of 750 c.c. capacity. A version of the 848 c.c. capacity B.M.C. Mini engine was produced to operate as a compression-ignition power unit which developed 16 h.p.

GAS TURBINES

The successful design and development in England and Germany during the late 1930's of the gas turbine aero engine led to rapid and successful development and practical use of this novel form of internal combustion engine to the extent that, within two decades, it had virtually replaced the reciprocating internal-combustion engine as an aero engine, and had become the standard power unit for both military and civil aircraft. This development was applied to a variety of other uses from small portable industrial units to the largest sizes for ships, hovercraft, locomotive and industrial applications. The adaption of the gas turbine for motor-car propulsion was first made in experimental form by the Rover Company, who produced the world's first car of this type in the shape of their 1950 model, which was a standard Rover touring car adapted to take gas turbine power. The 1956 Rover T3 model was designed specifically as a gas turbine car, which had a two-shaft free-power turbine developing 110 h.p. at 52,000 compressor r.p.m.; this T3 and a later T4 model were used intensively for research and development work, and culminated in the proposal to enter a Rover gas turbine car in the 1963 Le Mans race as a practical test of its performance and reliability in competition with orthodox cars.

For this purpose, a Rover 2S/150 gas turbine (Plate 39) developed from the T3 and T4 units was installed in a B.R.M. chassis; this two-shaft unit developed 150 h.p. at 40,000 r.p.m. and, without a heat-exchanger, was a neat and compact unit weighing only 120 lb. The turbine drove the rear axle of the car without change-speed gears or clutch through an overall speed reduction of 21·3 to 1. This car was unofficially placed eighth in this Le Mans race, having covered a total in the twenty-four hours of 2,583 miles at an average speed of 107·84 m.p.h. with entire reliability. Without a heat exchanger, however, a fuel consumption of only 7 m.p.g. was obtained, thus emphasising the low-thermal efficiency of the gas turbine without the additional bulk and weight of a heat exchanger for the recovery of a proportion of the waste heat from the exhaust efflux, and the limitation imposed by presently available materials which prevented a substantially higher combustion temperature being used. A later run in the 1965 Le Mans race with a car when fitted with a heat exchanger, achieved a considerably improved fuel consumption of 13 m.p.g. In spite of this remarkable demonstration of the potential of the gas turbine car, there are still fundamental problems to be overcome before this form of power unit will be able to challenge the established reciprocating engine in commercial production. These problems are: part load running conditions over a wide speed range which are normal to car engine operation, do not suit gas turbine characteristics; more expensive materials and finer production tolerances required by the gas turbine make production costs higher; and acceptable fuel consumption economy demands a heavy, bulky and expensive heat exchanger and, additionally, the need for an automatically-variable ratio gearbox which will add to cost and complexity.

Perhaps at least some of these disadvantages will be overcome by future progress in materials and techniques generally which will make the gas turbine car more suitable for commercial production. This possibility is supported by the considerable research effort already made in this direction by such firms as Austin, Ford, Chrysler, General Motors and Renault, all of whom have produced individual prototypes. Even if successfully perfected for powering motor cars in general, however, it is still be be seen how applicable this form of unit will be to light cars, not only in competition with the established reciprocating internal-combustion engine, but also with the more feasible rotary engine described under the following heading.

ROTARY ENGINES

A novel form of rotary engine unit that held considerably more promise than the gas turbine as a light car power unit suitable for commercial production was the rotary combustion engine conceived by Dr. Felix Wankel in 1954 and adopted by N.S.U. for research and development and eventual commercial manufacture, not only by the parent company but also under wide manufacturing licences by many of the chief engine manufacturing companies through the world. Although there are still technical problems to be solved as may be expected with a comparatively new fundamental design, the rotary-combustion engine has already achieved standards of reliability, economy and performance which are within the limits achieved by conventional reciprocating engines.

The production form of the Wankel rotary combustion engine (Fig. 28 and Plate 41) which was eventually evolved consisted essentially of a three-lobe rotor mounted freely on roller bearings which run on an eccentric bearing surface formed integrally with a main shaft carried on ball and roller bearings. The shape of the chamber in which the rotor works is a two-lobe epitrochoid, a geometrical figure which is generated by a point on a circle which rolls on the outside of a fixed circle; its developed figure is like a figure eight with a broad waist. As the rotor moves round the chamber, its three apexes maintain continuous contact with the wall, so forming three chambers of continuously varying volume, in each of which occur the four-stroke cycle of operation consisting of induction, compression, expansion and exhaust. Single inlet and exhaust ports located in the stationary chamber are opened and closed by the rotation of the rotor apexes at correct timing intervals. The interior of the rotor is oil cooled and its apexes in contact with the casing surface are lubricated by an addition of oil in the petrol of one part to 200 parts of fuel. In one end of the rotor bore is an internally-toothed gear which meshes in the ratio of 2 to 3 with a fixed spur gear whose function is to act as a re-action member. Thus, for each revolution of the main shaft, the rotor also turns forward one flank on its own eccentric axis; three revolutions of the main shaft bring the rotor back to its original position when each flank in turn will have received a power impulse.

Intensive development of this form of rotary combustion engine by N.S.U. produced in 1963 a compact unit weighing only 128 lb. and having a lobe displacement of 500 c.c. capacity which developed 64 h.p. at 5000 r.p.m. By virtue of the 2 to 3 reaction gearing, the effective total capacity of this unit is 1000 c.c. The engine was mounted in the rear of an N.S.U. chassis and drove the rear wheels through a four-speed gearbox. This first production model of a Wankel-engined light car had a maximum speed of over 90 m.p.h. (Plate 33). A twin-rotor unit was developed from this prototype production.

The successful development of the NSU-Wankel rotary combustion engine in various forms and for a variety of purposes, both large and small, brought about the wide adoption of manufacturing licences in Germany, France, England, U.S.A., and Japan. In particular, the Japanese firm Toyo Kogyo, have specialised in twin-rotor units for car propulsion.

The Selwood orbital engine in prototype form was a 12-cylinder rotary engine of 700 c.c. capacity (1·75 in. by 1·5 in.) designed to run at speeds up to 10,000 r.p.m. The engine body was roughly spherical which incorporated six evenly spaced curved cylinders, within each of which was a pair of opposed pistons secured together by a trunnion block having a gudgeon pin by which the pair of pistons was hinged to an arm of a spider. This six-armed spider was supported on a double-row ball race on a journal which was secured to a fixed central shaft. The spider on the journal was tilted 10 degrees in relation to the fixed shaft. The whole engine mass rotated about this shaft and an output shaft was fixed to one end of the rotating casing. Because of the angularity of the spider on the fixed shaft, there was relative movement between pistons and cylinder bores as the engine body rotated. Actual reciprocating motion of the pistons having been dispensed with, inertia loads were reduced in consequence. Piston-controlled inlet and exhaust ports formed in the curved cylinders enabled this engine to work on the two-stroke cycle. Although this design had some advantages such as reduced inertia loads, it had the inherent disadvantages of poor mechanical efficiency and low torque resulting from excessive axial thrust characteristic of wobble-plate forms.

The working chamber shape of the Renault Rambler rotary-combustion engine was different from the Wankel design, being derived from an epicycloid with an exterior envelope. Admission of the combustible charge and the exhausting of the burnt gases was through five pairs of normal inlet and exhaust poppet valves radially disposed around a central casing or envelope, the various four-stroke cycles take place in each cylinder lobe, which had a separate sparking plug. The four lobed rotor rotates eccentrically around a central shaft. The number of working cylinder chambers can be varied but, being of four-stroke operation, these must be uneven in number; the rotor lobes were fewer by one than the chambers. Epicyclic gears were required to maintain the rotor in correct relationship to the envelope stator; these gears also served to drive the cam ring for valve operation. The stator envelope was was water cooled, and oil cooling was used for the rotor. Sealing strips were positioned at the peak of each working chamber in the stator envelope, and there were twin spring loaded peripheral sealing rings on each face of the rotor.

ROTARY VALVE ENGINES

The adoption of the rotary valve in place of the poppet valve or the sleeve valve has been attempted at various times during the development of the motorcar, particularly during 1912 to 1914, when a variety of rotary-valve engines were put into commercial production by such manufacturers as Itala, Peugeot, Piccard-Pictet. The inadequate materials of that time, however, together with the established reliability of the poppet valve prevented the successful development of the rotary valve in production. In the 1930's, however, when improved materials and techniques were becoming available, two advanced designs in particular made their appearance which promised the possibility of successful development. The Aspin rotary valve was of conical hollow form, liquid cooled internally, which revolved at half engine speed in a coned cylinder head. A port formed in the valve cone coincided alternately with inlet and exhaust ports formed in the cylinder head, permitting a normal four-stroke cycle of operation. The Cross rotary valve was of tubular form with ports which coincided with a port in the cylinder head. Particular attention was paid by careful and complex design to provide automatic compensation for thermal expansion to retain efficient sealing. Rotary flat-disc valves were successfully developed and used to achieve optimum inlet timing for two-stroke engines. Because, however, of the established use of the poppet valve and the advent of new engine forms of considerable promise, such as the Wankel rotary engine and possibly the gas turbine, it is unlikely that the rotary valve will be adopted in any large production.

The late 1960's witnessed the introduction of the small high-performance car incorporating many of the advanced technical features used in the contemporary racing cars. The most significant feature of these cars was their lightness and low build. Acceleration and road-holding were greatly improved and their lightness resulted in economy of operation. Many of them were built with lightweight fibre-glass bodies and fitted with reclining-type bucket seats, disc brakes and independent suspension. Engines were provided with twin overhead camshafts and a high compression ratio to take full advantage of the improved fuels available. The general concept of these cars resulted in their cost being high in relation to that of the popular mass-produced car, which had an inferior road performance but was economical in operation and maintenance.

Increased taxation and legislation, with a vast increase in the number of cars on the congested British roads, led to the great majority of cars being powered by conventional engines not exceeding $1\frac{1}{2}$ litres in capacity. Traffic conditions and the problem of parking in big cities had resulted in the increasing adoption of the more compact car for both business and pleasure travel. These small cars may be regarded as the descendants of the light cars first introduced early in this century.

Bibliography

BEAUMONT, W. WORBY	*Motor Vehicles and Motors* (vol. 1)	1900
	(vol. 2)	1906
CAUNTER, C. F.	*The Two-Cycle Engine*	1932
DAVIS, S. C. H.	*Cars, Cars, Cars, Cars*	1967
GARGANO, G. N. (Editor)	*The Complete Encyclopaedia of Motorcars:* 1885–1968	1968
HENDERSON, R. G.	*The History of A.C. Cars Ltd.*	1952
HOUGH, R. & FROSTICK, M.	*A History of the World's High Performance Cars*	1967
KNIGHT, J. H.	*Light Motorcars and Voiturettes*	1902
KARSLAKE, KENT	*Racing Voiturettes*	1950
Low, Dr. A. M.	*Two-Stroke Engines.* Temple Press Ltd.	1915
MARKMANN, C. L. & SHERWIN, M.	*The Book of Sports Cars*	1960
Messrs. Iliffe & Sons Ltd.	*The Light Car*	1913–1917
Messrs. Temple Press Ltd.	*The Lightcar and Cyclecvr* (vol. 1) (afterwards *The Light Car* from 1918)	1912
Messrs. Temple Press Ltd.	*The Cyclecar Manual* (1st edition)	1913
Messrs. Temple Press Ltd.	*The Lightcar Manual* (1st edition)	1913
Messrs. Temple Press Ltd.	*Light Cars and Cyclecars of 1913*	1913
	Light Cars and Cyclecars of 1914	1914
	Light Cars and Cyclecars of 1915	1915
PAGE, V. W.	*Motorcycles, Sidecars and Cyclecars* (U.S.A.) Chapter VII, pp. 452–494	1914
'Phoenix'	*The Motor Cyclist's Handbook*	
	(3rd edition, pp. 265–283)	1913
(C. S. Lake)	(4th edition, pp. 286–307)	1914
SAUNIER, L. BAUDRY DE	*L'Automobile Théorique et Pratique* (vol. 1)	1899
	(vol. 2)	1900
STEIN, R.	*The Automobile Book*	1964
STEIN, R.	*The Great Cars*	1967

Acknowledgments

PLATES

Plate 2.	Riley motor tricar: 1903	The British Motor Corporation Ltd.
Plate 6.	Vauxhall voiturette: 1905	Vauxhall Motors Ltd.
	Austin voiturette: 1909	The Austin Motor Co. Ltd.
	Sizaire-Naudin voiturette: 1910	The Editor of *The Autocar*.
Plate 7.	Morgan cyclecar: 1910	H. F. S. Morgan.
	Autocarrier cyclecar: 1913	A.C. Cars Ltd.
	Scott cyclecar: 1916	The Editor of *The Autocar*.
Plate 8.	Bedelia cyclecar: 1912	H. R. Godfrey.
	G.N. cyclecar: 1911	H. R. Godfrey.
	G.W.K. cyclecar: 1914	The Editor of *The Autocar*.
Plate 9.	Autocarrier engine: 1910	The Editor of *The Autocar*.
	J.A.P. engine: 1914	,, ,,
	G.W.K. engine: 1913	,, ,,
	Jowett engine: 1916	,, ,,
Plate 10.	Jowett: 1906	Jowett Cars Ltd.
	Humberette cyclecar: 1914	The Editor of *The Autocar*.
	Perry: 1914	,, ,,
Plate 11.	Morris Oxford: 1914	Morris Motors Ltd.
	Austin: 1922	The Austin Motor Co. Ltd.
Plate 12.	Saxon: 1914	The Editor of *The Autocar*
	Bugatti: 1914	,, ,,
	A.C.: 1914	A.C. Cars Ltd.
Plate 13.	White and Poppe engine: 1912	Morris Motors Ltd.
	Bugatti engine: 1914	The Editor of *The Autocar*.
	Stellite engine: 1914	Morris Motors Ltd.
	Wanderer engine: 1914	The Editor of *The Autocar*.
Plate 14.	G.N. cyclecar: 1920	H. R. Godfrey.
	Rover cyclecar: 1922	The Rover Co. Ltd.
	Morgan cyclecar: 1923	H. F. Morgan.
Plate 15.	Morris Cowley: 1923	Messrs. Morris Motors Ltd.
Plate 16.	Bugatti engine: 1928	The Editor of *The Light Car*.
Plate 17.	Ford: 1937	The Ford Motor Co. Ltd.
	Fiat: 1937	The Editor of *The Light Car*.
Plate 18.	Citroën: 1934	The Editor of *The Light Car*.
	M.G. Midget: 1937	,, ,,
	Vauxhall: 1938	Vauxhall Motors Ltd.
Plate 19.	Wolseley Hornet engine: 1930	The Editor of *The Light Car*.
	Morris engine: 1935	Morris Motors Ltd.
	Citroën engine: 1938	The Editor of *The Automobile Engine*

179

Acknowledgments—continued

Plate 20.	Messerschmitt minicar: 1956	The Editor of *The Light Car.*
Plate 21.	Villiers engine: 1954	A.C. Cars Ltd.
	Anzani engine: 1956	The British Anzani Engine Co. Ltd.
	Goliath engine: 1956	The Editor of *The Automobile Engineer*
Plate 22.	Citroën minicar: 1954	Société Anon. A. Citroën.
	D.K.W.: 1955	The Editor of *The Light Car.*
	Dyna-Panhard: 1956	Soc. Anon. Panhard & Levassor.
Plate 23.	Renault: 1954	The Editor of *The Light Car.*
	Morris minor: 1952	The Editor of *The Autocar*
	Fiat: 1957	,, ,,
Plate 24.	Renault light car: 1956	The Editor of *The Autocar.*
Plate 25.	Gutbrod engine: 1951	The Editor of *The Light Car.*
	D.K.W. engine: 1953	,, ,,
	Renault engine: 1954	Renault Ltd.
	Fiat engine: 1956	Fiat Ltd.
Plate 26.	Volkswagen: 1954	Volkswagenwerk, G.m.b.H.
	Ford: 1955	The Ford Motor Co. Ltd.
Plate 27.	Porsche engine: 1955	Dr. Ing. F. Porsche.
	Ford engine: 1955	The Ford Motor Co. Ltd.
	Trojan engine: 1955	Trojan Ltd.
	Lancia engine: 1954	The Editor of *The Automobile Engine*
Plate 28.	H.R.G.: 1956	H. R. Godfrey.
	Porsche: 1956	A.F.N. Ltd.
Plate 29.	Reliant minicar: 1955	The Reliant Eng. Co. Ltd.
	B.M.W. Isetta minicar: 1956	A.F.N. Ltd.
Plate 30.	Hillman: 1956	The Editor of *The Autocar.*
Plates 31–40.		The Editor of *The Autocar.*

FIGURES

Figs. 1–2	The Editor of *The Autocar.*
Fig. 3	H. R. Godfrey.
Figs. 4–27	The Editor of *The Autocar.*

Index

A.B.C. Cyclecar, 66
A.C. cyclecar, 14, 15, 16, 35, 39, 40, 53, 62
A.C. light car, 39, 53, 55, 59
A.C. 'Petite' minicar, 104, 124
Accles, J. C., 4
Ackermann steering, 2, 5, 10, 20, 21, 22, 23, 36, 43, 160
A.C.U. Cyclecar and Light car definition, 34, 55
Adams cyclecar, 45
Adamson cyclecar, 38
Adler cyclecar, 43, 92
Adler light car, 56
Advance tricar, 14
Air pollution, 149
Ajax cyclecar, 42
Ajax light car, 54
Alcyon voiturette, 28
Alfa-Romeo 'Giulietta' light car, 115, 138, 164
Alfa-Romeo 'Guilia' car, 138, 142, 164
Alfa-Romeo light car, 81, 97
Allard 'Clipper' minicar, 105
Alldays and Onions cyclecar, 43, 44
Alldays and Onions light car, 53
Alldays and Onions tricar, 12
Alldays and Onions voiturette, 21, 24, 28
Alpha engine, 47
Alvis Firefly light car, 96
Alvis light car, 80, 97
A.M.A.C. carburettor, 16
Amal carburettor, 86
American Bosch fuel injection system, 152
Amilcar light car, 77, 78, 81
André shock absorber, 88
Anglian speed-gear, 16
Ansaldo light car, 81
Antoine voiturette, 19, 22, 24
Anzani engine, 63, 66, 85, 104, 105, 119, 124
Apollo car, 54

Argyll, engine, 82
Argyll voiturette, 24, 26, 28
Ariel cyclecar, 67
Ariel motor tricycle, 10
Ariel tricar, 12
Aries light car, 29, 56
Armstrong air suspension, 160
Armstrong-Siddeley light car, 67, 81, 97
Armstrong-Triplex speed-gear, 38
Aspin rotary valve, 175
Aster engine, 18, 22
Aston-Martin light car, 97
Astra minicar, 103, 105
Atom minicar, 105
Austin A30 light car, 112
Austin A35 light car, 112, 133
Austin A40 light car, 113, 134, 138
Austin A50 light car, 114
Austin Big Seven light car, 91
Austin Eight light car, 91
Austin, Herbert, 5, 24, 72, 78
Austin light car, 53, 55, 91
Austin racing car, 91, 167
Austin Seven light car, 60, 74, 75, 79, 86, 89, 90, 91, 101, 105, 127, 136
Austin Ten light car, 92
Austin Twelve light car, 96
Austin Twelve-Six light car, 97
Austin Healey Sprite car, 134
Austin Seven Mini car, 136, 137, 159, 160
Austin 1100 car, 139, 159, 160, 161
Austin A55 car, 142
Austin voiturette, 27
Austro-Daimler light car, 77, 81
Autocrat light car, 53
Auto-Lite Transcoil ignition system, 150
Aut2mette cyclecar, 61
Automobilette cyclecar, 36
Auto-Transmissions overdrive, 158
Autovac petrol feed, 79, 86
Auto-Union 1000SP car, 144
Auto-Union Junior car, 144

181

Auto-Union Audi engine, 147
Averies light car, 54
Aviette cyclecar, 43
Automotive Products automatic
  transmission, 156
Auto Transmissions, overdrive units,
  158

Barnes tricar, 14
Bat tricar, 12
Bayard light car, 51
Bean car, 53
Bedelia cyclecar, 35, 36, 38, 61, 65, 66
Beeston quadricycle, 10
Beeston voiturette, 21
Belsize-Bradshaw cyclecar, 67
Belsize light car, 55
Bendix starter, 86, 155
Bendix fuel-injection system, 152
Bendix brakes, 100, 119, 139, 161, 162
Benjamin cyclecar, 68
Benz, Carl, 2, 6
Benz 'Comfortable' car, 3
Benz 'Velo' car, 3
Berkeley minicar, 105, 145
Berliet light car, 56, 81
Berling magneto, 57
Bertone body, 164
Bianchi light car, 56, 81, 96
Binks carburettor, 31, 58, 86
Birfield constant-velocity joint, 159
Bishop steering gear, 161
Blackburne, engine, 63, 65, 66
Blériot cyclecar, 65
Blumfield engine, 46
B.M.C. Type A engine, 133, 137, 139,
  156, 168
B.M.C. Type B engine, 169, 171
B.M.C. Minimoke car, 137
B.M.C. Diesel engine, 171
B.M.W. 700LS car, 92, 128, 131
B.M.W. engine, 127
B.M.W. 1491 car, 142
B.M.W. Isetta minicar, 108, 124
Bollée-Coventry 'Motette', 4
Bollée-Darracq car, 5

Bollée, Léon, tricar, 3, 5, 36
Bond minicar, 103, 124
Bond 875 car, 124
Borg and Beck clutch, 99, 155
Borg-Warner automatic transmission,
  156, 157
Borg-Warner limited-slip differential
  gear, 158
Borg-Warner overdrive gear, 158
Borgward Isabella car, 142, 160
Bosch electric-lighting set, 59, 87
Bosch magneto, 31, 42, 44, 50, 52, 57,
  85
Bosch transistorised ignition system,
  150
Bosch, Robert, 16
Bosch solid-injection fuel system, 108
  152, 153, 169, 171
Bouton, Georges, 8
Bourbeau, R., 35, 36
Bradbury tricar, 12
Bradford light car, 102
Bradshaw, Granville, 66
Branwood fuel-injection system, 152
Brasier light car, 56
Brennabor engine starter, 58
Brennabor light car, 56
Briscoe car, 56
British Motor Corporation, 136
Brolt electric engine starter, 58
Brolt electric-lighting set, 59
Brouhot voiturette, 19, 24
Brown and Barlow carburettor, 16
Bruetsch minicar, 104, 106, 124
Bruetsch Mopetta car, 123
B.R.M. engine, 168, 169, 170
B.S.A. cyclecar, 61, 62, 63, 66, 93
B.S.A. Light-Six light car, 97
B.T.H. electric-lighting set, 87
B.T.H. magneto, 57, 85, 99
Buchet engine, 54
Buchet light car, 54
Buckingham cyclecar, 37
Buckingham engine, 46
Bugatti, Ettore, 50, 56
Bugatti light car, 50, 56, 78, 89, 98

Bugatti Type 13 light car, 56, 95
Bugatti Type 23 light car, 81
Bugatti Type 37 light car, 81, 97
Bugatti Type 40 light car, 81, 97
Bugatti Type 43 light car, 98
Buick voiturette, 26
Burt McCollum engine, 82, 116

Cadillac voiturette, 26
Calcott light car, 55, 80
Calthorpe light car, 53
Calthorpe voiturette, 29, 80
Capac carburettor, 86
C.A.R. light car, 82
Carden cyclecar, 61, 68
Carden, J. V., 42, 68
Carnation light car, 56
Carter Coaster car, 121
Castle-Three cyclecar, 71
C.A.V. electric-lighting set, 45, 59
C.A.V. magneto, 57
C.A.V. fuel-injection system, 153
Century engine, 83
Century tricar, 38
Chaise light car, 90
Chalmers voiturette, 26
Chambers voiturette, 24, 26
Champion minicar, 106
Chapuis-Dornier engine, 85
Charron cyclecar, 43
Charron light car, 54, 56
Charron voiturette, 28
Chase tricar, 12
Chater-Lea speed-gear, 15, 16
Chater-Lea cyclecar, 44
Chater-Lea light car, 55
Christie transverse engine, 136
Chrysler voiturette, 26
Chubu car, 121
C.I.D. cyclecar, 38, 47
Citroën, André, 72, 79
Citroën light car, 72, 75, 76, 78, 80, 127
Citroën Twelve light car, 97
Citroën 2 c.v. and AMI 6 ultra-light
  car, 107, 118, 125, 129, 160
Citroën Bijou car, 125

Clarke motor tricycle, 10
Claudel carburettor, 31, 44, 58
Claveau cyclecar, 68
Clément Bayard light car, 54, 56
Clément voiturette, 22
Clerk engine, 47, 84
Clinton 'Spark-Pump' ignition system,
  150
Cluley light car, 80
Clyde tricar, 12
Clyno light car, 75, 76, 80
Coatalen, L., 76
Colibri cyclecar, 15
Constantinesco cyclecar, 69
Cooper 500 car, 167
Cooper-B.M.C. Mini Car, 137, 140
Cooper-Stewart speedometer, 33
Cosworth engine, 168
Corbin light-alloy piston, 42
Corona cyclecar, 70
Corre-la Licorne light car, 54
Corre-la Licorne voiturette, 28, 29
Côte engine, 68
Côte voiturette, 28
Coventry-Climax engine, 41, 47, 85,
  93, 168, 169
Coventry-Climax FPF engine, 169
Coventry-Climax V-8 engine, 169
Coventry-Climax 16-cylinder engine,
  170
Coventry-Climax Diesel engine, 171
Coventry-Premier cyclecar, 66, 70
Coventry-Simplex engine, 27
Coventry-Victor cyclecar, 70, 71
Coventry-Victor engine, 66
Cowey speedometer, 33
Cox-Atmos carburettor, 86
Cozette blower, 98
Crescent cyclecar, 41
Crestmobile voiturette, 23
Crompton cyclecar, 43
Cross rotary valve, 175
Crossley light car, 94, 97
Crouch cyclecar, 44, 66
Cumbria cyclecar, 38, 53
Cummikar light car, 51

Cycaren engine, 47
Cyklonette tricar, 13, 40

D.A.F. 600 Car, 127, 128, 161
DAFodil car, 128
D.A.F. Variomatic transmission, 155, 157
Daihatsu car, 134
Daimler engine, 1, 3, 8
Daimler fluid flywheel, 97
Daimler, Gottlieb, 1, 6
Daimler, Paul, 23, 81
Daimler, P.D. voiturette, 23
Dalman engine, 46
Darracq, A., 5
Darracq voiturette, 28
Datsun light car, 106
Datsun minicar, 90, 134
Day engine, 47
Day-Leeds light car, 53
Decauville voiturette, 19, 21, 24
Déchamps motor tricycle, 10, 21
Déchamps voiturette, 21
De Dion-Bouton axle, 10, 63, 83, 94, 99, 118
De Dion-Bouton carburettor, 19
De Dion-Bouton engine, 8, 9, 16, 18, 20, 25, 29, 30
De Dion-Bouton ignition system, 6
De Dion-Bouton light car, 46, 54, 80
De Dion-Bouton motor tricycle, 9, 10
De Dion-Bouton voiturette, 19, 20, 21, 24, 46
de Dion, Count Albert, 8
Deemster engine starter, 58
Deemster light car, 53
Deguingand engine, 84
Degory carburettor, 86
Delage light car, 56
Delage 8-cylinder engine, 81, 89, 98, 167
Delage voiturette, 28, 29
Delco-Remy ignition system, 150
Dew cyclecar, 43
Disc brake, 162
Dixi light car, 75
Dixi voiturette, 26

Dixie magneto, 57
D.K.W. cyclecar, 70, 83, 84, 90, 98, 106, 108
D.K.W. engine, 64, 84, 85, 119, 123, 143, 147, 154
D.K.W. Meisterklasse light car, 116
D.K.W. Sonderklasse light car, 108, 116, 117, 144
D.K.W. Three-Six car, 144
D.K.W. F102 car, 144
D.K.W. 400 c.c. car, 127
D.K.W. 600 car, 131
Dobler Inter minicar, 104
Dodge voiturette, 26
Donnet light car, 81
Dorman engine, 46, 47
Douglas cyclecar, 43, 45, 67, 70
Ducellier electric-lighting set, 87
D-Ultra cyclecar, 42, 51
Dunkley car, 6
Dunlop, J. B., 7
Dunlop Pneuride air suspension, 160
Dunlop brakes, 161, 162
Dunlop SP41 radial tyre, 163
Duo cyclecar, 38
Duryea voiturette, 4, 26
Dyna-Panhard ultra-light car, 107
D'Yrsan cyclecar, 71

Eagle tricar, 38
Eagle car, 57
E.E.C.C. minicar, 103
E.I.C. magneto, 31, 57
Eisemann magneto, 31, 44, 57
Eisenacher light car, 117
Elburn-Ruby voiturette, 27
Elmore voiturette, 26
Enfield-Allday engine, 82
Enfield cyclecar, 43, 45
Enfield light car, 53, 82
Enfield motor tricycle, 10
E.N.V. limited-slip differential gear, 158
Eole voiturette, 24
E.R.A. light car, 97
Eric cyclecar, 40
Euston cyclecar, 61

Excelsior cyclecar, 68
Excelsior engine, 103, 105, 145

Fafnir engine, 15, 18
Fafnir tricar, 14
Fairthorpe minicar, 105
Falcon cyclecar, 38
Fallolite burner, 59
Fedden engine, 116
Ferrari Dino 246 engine, 169
Ferrari Type 158/BA engine, 169
Ferrari-Gilera 8-cylinder engine, 170
F. & G. engine starter, 58
Fiat Balilla light car, 92
Fiat 124 car, 138
Fiat 500 ultra-light car, 76, 90, 111
Fiat 500C ultra-light car, 111
Fiat 500D car, 125, 131
Fiat 503 light car, 80
Fiat 509 light car, 76
Fiat 600 ultra-light car, 111
Fiat 600D car, 129, 131, 135
Fiat 850 car, 135
Fiat 1100D car, 113, 138, 164
Fiat 1500L car, 97, 142
Fichtel and Sachs engine, 104, 105
Fivet engine, 53
F.N. engine starter, 58
F.N. light car, 56, 81
F.N. tricar, 12
F.N. voiturette, 24
Ford Anglia and Prefect light car, 111,
    112, 134, 138, 161
Ford Classic car, 134
Ford Comuta car, 121
Ford Consul light car, 113, 114
Ford Cortina car, 142
Ford Eight and Ten light car, 91, 92
Ford engine, 63, 71,
Ford Escort car, 138, 147
Ford, Henry, 2, 73
Ford Model-T car, 26, 73, 79, 136
Ford Popular light car, 112
Ford Taunus car, 138, 142
Ford Taunus engine, 138, 142, 147
Ford 100E, 105E, 109E and 116E
    engines, 134, 138, 147, 168

Ford, quadricycle, 2
Ford voiturette, 2, 26
Fournier cyclecar, 42,
Fournier light car, 54
Françon-Chedru cyclecar, 84
Frankel and Kirchner minicar, 104
Franklin car, 26, 80
Franklin engine, 80, 136
Framo cyclecar, 69
Frazer-Nash, A, 15, 36
Frazer-Nash, light car, 80, 97
F.R.S. electric lighting set, 59
F.R.S. lamp, 58
Fulda-Mobil minicar, 105
Fuscaldo petrol-injection, 152

Gabriel shock absorber, 59, 88
Gardon motor tricycle, 10
Garrard, tricar, 12, 14
G.B. cyclecar, 69
Georges-Irat light car, 94
Getrag gearbox, 126
Gibbons cyclecar, 66
Gilyard cyclecar, 38
Girling cyclecar, 40
Girling brake, 91, 100, 119, 161, 162
Gladiator voiturette, 22
Glas T.600 car, 129
Glas S.1004 car, 134, 147
Globe cyclecar, 38
G.M. cyclecar, 68
G.N. cyclecar, 35, 36, 37, 65, 66, 80, 96
G.N. engine, 37
Gobbi carburettor, 42
Godfrey, H. R., 15, 36, 65, 95
Goggomobil minicar, 105
Goggomobil-TS400 car, 126
Goliath cyclecar, 64, 117
Goliath ultra-light car, 108, 128
Goodchild tricar, 12
Gordon car, 103, 124
Gordon cyclecar, 38
Gordon minicar, 103
Grade cyclecar, 68
Grahame-White cyclecar, 61

Grant light car, 56
Green engine, 39
Greeves car, 123
Grégoire ultra light car, 107
Grégoire voiturette, 25, 28
Grice, Wood and Keiller, Messrs., 40
G.W.K. cyclecar, 40, 41, 42
G.W.K. lightcar, 80
Gutbrod ultra-light car, 108
Gwynne light car, 77

Hampton cyclecar, 47
Hanissard cyclecar, 68
Hanomag car, 108
Hansa light car, 94
Hardy-Spicer universal joint, 99, 158
Hardy universal joint, 99, 158
Harper invalid car, 123
Hartford shock absorber, 88
Hele-Shaw clutch, 155
Heinkel engine, 117, 127
Heinkel minicar, 104, 106, 108, 117
Heinkel cabin cruiser, 124
Held, engine, 82
Henry, M., 77, 82
Hercules cyclecar, 64
Heron combustion chamber, 147
Herzmark engine starter, 58
Hillman light car, 55, 76, 80
Hillman Minx light car, 92, 113, 114, 142
Hillman Imp car, 136, 147, 148
Hirth crankshaft, 125, 147
Hispano-Suiza voiturette, 29
Hobart-Bird tricar, 12
Hobson shock absorber, 59
Holborn-Eaton fan, 148
Honda 360 and 500 cars, 126
Honda N.600 car, 128
Honda S.800 car, 136, 147
Honda 1300 car, 141
Honda V-12 cylinder engine, 170
Honda Formula 2 engine, 168
Honda overdrive gear, 158
Honold, G., 16
Hooydonk, J. Van, 11

Horex engine, 125
Horstmann engine starter, 58
Horstmann light car, 50, 77
Hotchkiss engine, 79, 85
Hotchkiss light car, 94
Hotchkiss-Morris engine, 79
Houdaille shock absorber, 59, 88
Howard tricar, 15
H.R.G. light car, 95, 114, 115
H.R.G. Singer engine, 115
Hubbard tricar, 12
Humber cyclecar, 43
Humber light car, 55, 75, 76, 162
Humber motor tricycle, 10
Humber 'Olympia Tandem' tricar, 10, 12
Humber 'Phaeton' car, 5
Humber 'Sociable' tricar, 4
Humberette cyclecar, 43, 66
Humberette voiturette, 26
Humfrey-Sandberg free-wheel, 87
Hurlin cyclecar, 38
Hydramatic automatic gear, 156

Imp cyclecar, 38
Imperia engine, 82
Invicta light car, 98
Iso-Isetta minicar, 105
Isos minicar, 117
Issogonis, Alec, 136
Itala rotary valve, 174

Jackson and Kimmys tricar, 14
Jackson cyclecar, 27, 40
Jackson engine starter, 58
Jackson voiturette, 27
J.A.P. engine, 14, 16, 36, 38, 39, 41, 43, 46, 61, 63, 66, 124, 167
J.A.R. cyclecar, 38
Jawa cyclecar, 69
J.B.S. car, 53, 167
J.M.B. cyclecar, 64
J.M. shock absorber, 59
Jones speedometer, 33
Jowett cyclecar, 15, 27, 45, 67, 102
Jowett Javelin light car, 115

Jowett light car, 94
Justicialista light car, 108

Kansai car, 121
Karmann-Ghia body, 139
Kelecom engine, 22
Kemco dynamo, 59
Keikin carburettor, 136
Kenlomatic fan, 148
Kieft car, 167
King tricar, 13
Knight engine, 27, 30, 82
Knox voiturette, 26
Kugelfischer fuel-injection system, 152

Laffite light car, 83
Lagonda light car, 53, 76
Lagonda Rapier light car, 96
Lagonda tricar, 12, 13, 14
Lamplough, F., 21
Lanchester, F. W., 162
Lanchester Eleven light car, 96, 113
Lanchester Light-Six light car, 97
Lancia Appia light car, 113, 138
Lancia Aprilia light car, 94
Lancia Augusta light car, 94
Lancia Fulvia car, 138
Lancia V-8 cylinder engine, 169
Lancia body, 83, 90, 164
Laurin and Klement, 69
Lavigne cyclecar, 51
Lawson, H. J., 5
Lawson 'Motorwheel', 5
Laycock-de Normanville overdrive
    gear, 115, 158
Lea-Francis light car, 97
Lecoy cyclecar, 66
Lenoir, E., 6
Levassor, E., 132
Lincoln cyclecar, 69
Lion-Peugeot voiturette, 28, 29
List engine, 116
Lister engine, 51
Little Princess light car, 56
Lloyd (British) ultra-light car, 108
Lloyd (German) minicar, 104, 117, 128,
    135

Lloyd-Lord cyclecar, 84
L.M. cyclecar, 38
Lockheed brake, 100, 111, 119, 161, 162
Lodge spark plug, 150
Longuemare carburettor, 11, 31
Lord cyclecar, 42
Lotus car, 143
Low, Dr A. M., 47, 83
Low engine, 83
Low generator, 59
L.S.D. cyclecar, 70
Lucas alternator, 154
Lucas electric engine starter, 58
Lucas electric-lighting set, 59, 87
Lucas Electronic ignition system, 150,
    168, 170
Lucas fuel-injection system, 152, 153,
    168, 170
Lucas engine, 57
Lucas lamp, 7, 58
Lucas magneto, 85, 99
Lurquin-Coudert tricar, 14

MacMinnies, W. G., 39
Macomber rotary engine, 57
Madza Carol car, 126, 130
M.A.F. light car, 57
M.A.G. engine, 39, 46, 63
Maico car, 126
Major cyclecar, 68
Malcolm cyclecar, 38
Mangin reflector, 59
Marelli electric-lighting set, 87
Marelli starter system, 155
Marelli magneto, 85
Marlborough engine, 82
Marlborough light car, 53, 80
Marles steering gear, 160
Marot-Gardon tricar, 10
Mars 'Carette' tricar, 13
Marshall-Arter light car, 53
Marshall voiturette, 24
Maserati light car, 97
Maserati Type 8 engine, 170
Mass voiturette, 28
Matchless engine, 63

Matchless tricar, 12
Mathis light car, 54, 75, 76, 78
Maybach carburettor, 4
Maybach, Wilhelm, 23, 132, 151
Maxwell voiturette, 26
Meadows engine, 85, 95
Medinger cyclecar, 47
Melen cyclecar, 45
Mercedes car, 23, 81, 97
Mercedes 25/40 car, 81
Mercedes Types 130 and 150 cars, 80, 97
Mercedes W163 car, 98, 167
Merral-Brown cyclecar, 70, 93
Messerschmitt minicar, 104, 124
Métallurgique voiturette, 24
Metz, cyclecar, 42
M.G. Magna light car, 97
M.G. Magnette light car, 97, 114, 142
M.G. Midget light car, 76, 91, 92, 95, 110, 114, 134, 139
M.G. Series A light car, 115
M.G. Ex. 181 engine, 169
Michelin, André and Edouard, 7
Michelin tyre, 163
Millam free-wheel, 87
Miller lamp, 58
M.I.P. engine, 47
Mitsubishi Minica car, 127
Mitsubishi Colt car, 130, 134
Mi-Val minicar, 104
M.L. magneto, 85
M.M.C. engine, 14
M.M.C. motor tricycle, 10
M.M.C. voiturette, 26
Monitor cyclecar, 62
Morgan-Adler voiturette, 28
Morgan cyclecar, 35, 38, 39, 40, 46, 60, 63, 64, 71, 93, 102
Morgan Four-Four car, 93, 102, 114, 138
Morgan Plus-Four car, 114
Morgan, H. F. S., 15, 38, 39, 60, 61
Morris Cowley prototype, 52
Morris Cowley light car, 78, 79, 86, 92
Morris Eight light car, 91, 101

Morris engine, 79
Morris Minor light car, 76, 91, 112
Morris Oxford light car, 49, 52, 53, 54, 59, 80, 114
Morris Ten-Four light car, 92
Morris Ten-Six light car, 97
Morris Twelve-Four light car, 96
Morris Mini Minor car, 136
Morris 1100 car, 133, 139, 159
Morris, William R., 52, 72, 78
Mors voiturette, 22
Mototric-Contal tricar, 14
Murray overdrive gear, 158

N.A.G. light car, 56
Napier voiturette, 28
Nardini light car, 54
New Hudson cyclecar, 70
Newton shock absorber, 88
Nomad cyclecar, 68
North-Lucas light car, 83
Norton engine, 167
N.S.U. light car, 54, 94, 95, 136
N.S.U. speed-gear, 16
N.S.U. voiturette, 28
N.S.U. engine, 127
N.S.U. Prinz car, 128, 131, 137, 147, 149
N.S.U. 1000 car, 141, 148
N.S.U. Type 110 car, 141
N.S.U.-Wankel car, 173, 174

O.H.C. light car, 78
Oil filters, 153
Oldsmobile voiturette, 23, 26
Omega cyclecar, 66, 70
Omnium cyclecar, 44
Opel light car, 56, 94
Opel Kadet car, 134
Orient voiturette, 23
O.S.C.A. car, 168, 169
O.T.A.V. cyclecar, 15
Overland voiturette, 26

Packard voiturette, 26
Panhard and Levassor, car, 82, 135

Panhard and Levassor engine, 82
Panhard and Levassor voiturette, 3, 7, 22
Panther minicar, 106
Pashley minicar, 103, 124
Peel Trident car, 123
Pennington car, 4
Perkins Four-99 Diesel engine, 171
Perry cyclecar, 44
Perry light car, 53, 59
Peugeot car, 3
Peugeot cyclecar, 43, 90
Peugeot carburettor, 50
Peugeot engine, 38
Peugeot light car, 49, 50, 72, 75, 80, 136
Peugeot 203 light car, 115, 138, 140
Peugeot 204 car, 140
Peugeot 403 car, 142
Peugeot 404 car, 152, 157
Peugeot rotary valve, 174
Peugeot voiturette, 19, 22, 25, 26, 28
Phänomobil tricar, 13, 40
Phébus-Aster motor tricycle, 10
Phelon and Moore speed-gear, 12, 16
Phelon and Moore tricar, 12
Piccard-Pictet rotary valve, 174
Pininfarina body, 140, 164
Pirelli Cinturato radial tyre, 162
Phoenix light car, 55
Phoenix 'Trimo' tricar, 11, 12
Phoenix voiturette, 28
Piccolo cyclecar, 15
Pierce 'Motorette', 23
Pierce voiturette, 26
Pilgrim cyclecar, 15
Pilot light car, 53
Pilot voiturette, 27
Pioneer cyclecar, 38
Polyrhoë carburettor, 58
Porsche, Ferdinand, 77, 81, 94, 95, 142
Porsche 356 car, 115, 141, 142
Porsche 550 car, 143, 147
Porsche 912 car, 142
Porsche 1500 RSK car, 143
Porsche 8-cylinder engine, 170
Powell and Hanmer lamp, 58

Powerdrive minicar, 104
Praga car, 92
Precision engine, 38, 39, 46, 61, 66
Premier cyclecar, 38
Premier tricar, 14
Prestwich and Company, J. A., 16
Progress minicar, 103, 124
Progress voiturette, 21
Püch light car, 54
Pyramid cyclecar, 41, 42

Quadrant tricar, 12, 14

Raleigh cyclecar, 63
Raleigh tricar, 12
Raleighette tricar, 14
Ranger cyclecar, 38
Record engine, 57
Reliant minicar, 105, 124
Reliant Rebel car, 130
Renault, Louis, 19, 20, 72
Renault light car, 75, 76, 80, 86, 142, 148
Renault 750 light car, 110, 111
Renault Monasix light car, 81, 97
Renault Twelve light car, 54, 96
Renault Dauphine car, 111, 135, 160
Renault 4L car, 129
Renault R8 car, 135, 139, 162
Renault 16 car, 142
Renault 'Aerostable' air suspension, 160
Renault Ferlec clutch, 155
Renault rotary engine, 174
Renault voiturette, 19, 20, 21, 24, 25, 26, 28
Revolette tricar, 13
Rexette tricar, 12, 13, 14, 16
Rhode light car, 77
Ricardo, H. R., 47, 77, 84, 89
Ricardo engine, 47, 84
Riley light car, 53, 77, 94, 97, 110, 114, 115, 142
Riley Nine light car, 77, 94, 97
Riley Six light car, 97
Riley Elf car, 137, 140

Riley tricar, 12, 13, 14, 16
Riley voiturette, 28
Riley wheel, 59
Robertson engine, 98
Roc speed-gear, 15
Rodley minicar, 105
Rollo cyclecar, 38
Rolls-Royce car, 79
Rontiex light car, 51
Roots and Venables 'Petrocar', 2
Roots blower, 98
Rosengart light car, 75
Rotary valve engines, 174
Rotax electric-lighting set, 87
Rotax-Leitner electric-lighting set, 59
Rover, cyclecar, 66
Rover Ten light car, 96
Rover 60 light car, 115
Rover tricar, 10, 12
Rover voiturette, 27, 30
Rover T3 and T4 gas turbine cars, 172
Rover-B.R.M. gas turbine car, 172
Rovin ultra-light car, 107
Royal Ruby cyclecar, 64, 68
Rubury-Lindsay light car, 83
Ruby engine, 71, 85, 93, 94
Rudge-Whitworth engine, 46
Rudge-Whitworth wheel, 59
Rushmore electric engine starter, 58
Rzeppa constant-velocity joint, 159

Saab 92 and 93 light cars, 108, 117,
    144, 145
Saab 96 car, 142, 162
Sabella cyclecar, 38
Sachs engine, 124
Safety harness, 164
Salisbury 'Powr-Lok' limited-slip
    differential gear, 158
Salmson light car, 77, 78, 86, 95
Salvador light car, 57
Sandford cyclecar, 64, 71, 93
Sankey wheel, 52, 59, 87
Santos-Dumont, Alberto, 9
Sascha car, 77, 81

Saxon light car, 56
S.C.A.P. light car, 81
Scarsdale tricar, 13
Scootacar runabout, 62
Schneider light car, 77
Schnuerle loop-scavenge system, 69,
    71, 106
Scintilla Vertex magneto, 99
Scripps-Booth cyclecar, 38
Scott, A. A., 68
Scott cyclecar, 68
Selwood orbital engine, 174
Senechal light car, 77, 95
Sharpe tricar, 12, 14
Siba Dynastart dynamotor, 105, 119,
    123, 128, 155
Silentbloc bush, 100
Sima-Violet cyclecar, 68
Simca Aronde light car, 113, 138
Simca 1000 car, 135, 157
Simca 1500 car, 142
Simca-Ferodo transmission, 135
Simms, F. A., 6
Simms petrol-injection system, 152
Simms tricar, 5
Simms voiturette, 26
Simms magneto, 27, 31
Singer Le Mans light car, 92
Singer light car, 53, 76, 114, 115, 142
Singer Six light car, 97
Singer tricar, 12, 14
Singer voiturette, 28
Singer Chamois car, 136
Sinpar voiturette, 28
Sirron light car, 56
Sizaire-Naudin light car, 28, 56
Sizaire-Naudin voiturette, 28
Skoda car, 92, 135, 138
Smith electric-lighting set, 59, 87
Smith, magneto, 85
Smith carburettor, 58, 86
Smith Selectroshift transmission, 124,
    155, 156
Solex carburettor, 31, 58, 86, 139, 151
Spacke engine, 38, 46
Spacke speed-gear, 38

Spencer Moulton 'Hydrolastic' suspension, 137, 140, 160
Sperberette light car, 56
Splitdorf magneto, 57
Standard light car, 53, 76, 80, 96
Standard Little Nine light car, 91
Standard Eight and Ten light cars, 92, 112
Stanhope cyclecar, 71
Star voiturette, 24, 25
Stellite light car, 53, 57
Steyr light car, 92
Steyr-Puch car, 128
Stoewer-Tatra light car, 92, 94
Stoneleigh cyclecar, 66
Stromberg carburettor, 86, 151
Studebaker voiturette, 26
Sturmey-Archer speed-gear, 38
Sturmey, Henry, 24
S.U. carburettor, 58, 86, 134, 136, 137, 140, 151
S.U. fuel-injection system, 153
Suzuki Fronte 800 car, 145
Sunbeam Alpine car, 142
Sunbeam-Talbot light car, 113
Subaru car, 127, 135
Super cyclecar, 36
Swift cyclecar, 43, 44, 66, 80
Swift light car, 53, 76
Swift motor tricycle, 10
Swift voiturette, 27
Syrena car, 131

Talbot-Darracq light car, 76
Talbot light car, 81, 92
Tamag Zepp cyclecar, 64
Tamplin cyclecar, 61
Tatra car, 77
T.B. cyclecar, 70
Tecalemit-Jackson fuel-injection system, 152
Tempo cyclecar, 69, 117
Tempo truck, 117
Thames voiturette, 27
Thomson-Bennett magneto, 57
Toyo Kaygo Mazda Carol car, 125

Toyota Corona car, 157
Toyoglide automatic transmission, 157
Toyota Publica car, 128
Trabant car, 131
Trac-Aide limited-slip differential gear, 158
Tracta light car, 81
Triplex safety glass, 100
Triumph Cycle Co. Ltd., 167
Triumph light car, 75, 92, 94
Triumph tricar, 12
Triumph Herald car, 134, 138, 159, 163
Triumph 1300 car, 138, 148, 154
Trojan light car, 47, 57, 83, 84, 86, 98
Trojan 200 car, 124
Trojan type 15 light car, 116
Trumbull car, 42
Tubeless tyre, 118
Turrell, C. McRobie, 4
Tweenie cyclecar, 41

U.H. Magneto, 57
Unicar minicar, 105

Vanden Plas bodies, 164
Vandervell bearing, 147
Vauxhall carburettor, 94
Vauxhall Ten light car, 94, 113
Vauxhall Twelve light car, 97
Vauxhall voiturette, 24, 25, 26
Vauxhall Wyvern light car, 114
Vauxhall Victor car, 142
Vauxhall Viva car, 138
Vemorel light car, 56
Vernandi light car, 81
Vernon Derby light car, 77, 95
Vespa 400 car, 127
Victor cyclecar, 38
Victoria Spatz car, 126
Viet carburettor, 16, 18
Villard cyclecar, 68, 90
Villiers engine, 62, 68, 103, 104, 105, 119, 121, 124
Vindec cyclecar, 15
Violet-Bogey cyclecar, 41, 42, 68

Index

Violet, M., 68
Vivinus-Orleans voiturette, 19
Vivinis voiturette, 22
Volkswagen light car, 90, 94, 95, 113, 114, 139, 141, 142, 148
Volkswagen 1300 car, 139
Volkswagen 1500 car, 142
Volkswagen 1600 TL car, 142
Volkswagen Variant car, 142
Volkswagen Microbus car, 139
Volvo 122S car, 142
Vox cyclecar, 47
Vulcan light car, 55

Wallace tricar, 13
Wall cyclecar, 40
Wanderer light car, 54, 57
Wankel, F., 173
Wankel rotary engine, 173
Warne cyclecar, 38
Warren-Lambert cyclecar, 44
Warrick cyclecar, 39
Wartburgh 1000 car, 145
Watford speedometer, 33
Weber carburettor, 151, 170, 171
Wellan tricar, 13
Weller, J., 14, 53
Werner voiturette, 28
Westinghouse Markette car, 121
Weston cyclecar, 47
Weymann fabric body, 99
White and Poppe carburettor, 52
White and Poppe engine, 52
Wilkinson cyclecar, 51

Williamson motorcycle, 45
Wilson-E.N.V. gearbox, 97, 156
Winter cyclecar, 38, 42, 51
Wipac 'Magister' ignition system, 150
Wizard engine, 46
Wolseley tricar, 5
Wolseley cyclecar, 19
Wolseley Hornet light car, 76, 97, 137
Wolseley light car, 67, 77, 81, 110
Wolseley 4-44 light car, 113, 114
Wolseley Sheep-Shearing Machine Company, 5
Wolseley voiturette, 24
Wolseley Wasp light car, 94
Wooler cyclecar, 70

Xtra cyclecar, 61

Ydral engine, 104
Young's Bentinck tricar, 12

Zagato bodies, 164
Zaporozhets car, 130, 136
Zebra voiturette, 27
Zenette tricar, 14
Zenith carburettor, 31, 44, 58, 86, 136, 151
Zenith-Gradua speed gear, 65
Z.F. automatic transmission, 140
Z.F. limited-slip differential gear, 158
Zoller engine, 85
Zorojovka car, 98
Zundapp car, 94, 127